GERMAN STUDIES IN THE
POST-HOLOCAUST AGE

GERMAN STUDIES IN THE
THE POLITICS OF MEMORY, IDENTITY, AND ETHNICITY
POST-HOLOCAUST AGE

EDITED BY

ADRIAN DEL CARO AND JANET WARD

UNIVERSITY PRESS OF COLORADO

Copyright © 2000 by the University Press of Colorado
International Standard Book Number 0-87081-561-x

Published by the University Press of Colorado
5589 Arapahoe Avenue, Suite 206C
Boulder, Colorado 80303

All rights reserved.
Printed in the United States of America.

The University Press of Colorado is a cooperative publishing enterprise supported, in part, by Adams State, Colorado State University, Fort Lewis College, Mesa State College, Metropolitan State College, Denver, University of Colorado, University of Northern Colorado, University of Southern Colorado, and Western State College of Colorado.

The paper used in this publication meets the minimum requirements of the American National Standard for Information Sciences—Permanence of Paper for Printed Library Materials. ANSI Z39.48-1992

Library of Congress Cataloging-in-Publication Data

German studies in the post-Holocaust age : the politics of memory, identity, and ethnicity / edited by Adrian Del Caro and Janet Ward.
    p. cm.
    Selected proceedings from a symposium held in 1995 at the University of Colorado.
    Includes bibliographical references and index.
    ISBN 0-87081-561-X (alk. paper)
    1. German literature—20th century—History and criticism—Congresses. 2. German philology—Study and teaching (Higher)—Congresses. 3. German studies—Congresses. 4. Holocaust, Jewish (1939–1945), in literature—Congresses. I. Del Caro, Adrian, 1952– II. Ward, Janet, 1963–
PT405 .G4568 2000
943.087'071—dc21

                                                                         00-048405

Design by Laura Furney
Typesetting by Daniel Pratt

Chapter 15, "Hans-Jürgen Syberberg and the State of the Ghost" by Robert Shandley, first appeared in German Quarterly 70, no. 1 (Winter 1997), on pages 1–17.

09 08 07 06 05 04 03 02 01 00   10 9 8 7 6 5 4 3 2 1

Contents

Preface	vii
Acknowledgments	xv
SECTION I: CULTURAL PHILOSOPHY AND IDEOLOGIES OF IDENTITY	1
1. Ecological Ethos and Reactionary Politics: The Political Implications of Heidegger's Philosophy of Being *Walter H. Sokel*	3
2. The Great War and the Holocaust *Robert A. Pois*	11
3. Thinking the Nietzsche Legacy Today: A Historian's Perspective *Steven E. Aschheim*	20
4. Anti-Semitism and the Judiciary in the Federal Republic of Germany *Rainer Hering*	32
5. Germans and Jews Since 1945: The Politics of Absolution, Amends, and Ambivalence *William Safran*	41
6. The Decline and Fall of the German Mandarins: Intellectuals and Post-Reunification Germany *Thomas A. Hollweck*	52
SECTION II: POST-HOLOCAUST IDENTITY DEBATES	63
7. Afro-Germans: The Invisible Visible Germans *Susann Samples*	65
8. Else Lasker-Schüler: The "Small Drama" of Subjectivity *Silvia Henke*	76
9. Some Thoughts on the Tenuous and Precarious Relationship Between Feminism and German Studies *Ruth-Ellen B. Joeres*	84
10. Germans and Jews After the Fall of the Wall: The Promises and Problems of Hybridity *Todd Herzog*	93

11. Challenging the Status Quo: Michael Wolffsohn's Views on German-Jewish-Israeli Relations 103
    Andreas Michel

SECTION III: POETRY AND IMAGES AFTER AUSCHWITZ 111

12. Paul Celan and the German of the Non-German 113
    Adrian Del Caro

13. Uncanny Holograms of the Past: Recent German Poetry and Writing After Paul Celan and Theodor Adorno 122
    Erk Grimm

14. Claiming the Victim: Tokenism, Mourning, and the Future of German Holocaust Poetry 131
    Kathrin Bower

15. Hans-Jürgen Syberberg and the State of the Ghost 140
    Robert Shandley

16. Restaging Riefenstahl: The Lure of Nazi Iconography 148
    Janet Ward

SECTION IV: SITES OF META-GERMAN MULTIPLICITY 159

17. Nazi Germany and the Holocaust in Norwegian Literature 161
    Ann Schmiesing

18. One Language—Two Literatures Again? Swiss Literature Since the Wende 169
    Martin R. Dean

19. "Not Everything Written in the German Language is German Literature": Austrian Literature—A Special Case? 176
    Karlheinz Auckenthaler

20. The Role of Literature in German Studies Programs (1945–1995): A Canadian Case Study 186
    Kari Grimstad

21. Literature as Peace Research: Re-Vision in Henrich von Kleist and Christa Wolf 195
    Jean Wilson

22. Working on German Memory: Peter Weiss and Uwe Johnson 206
    Alexander Honold

23. Anaesthetics: The Shoah in Contemporary Jewish Literature 214
    Thomas Nolden

Bibliography 222
List of Contributors 239

Preface

ADRIAN DEL CARO WITH JANET WARD

> We did not require George Steiner to inform us that the cultures of the world will never be the same again after Auschwitz, except that we do, every day, as nobody seems to have heard.
> —CHRIS JENKS[1]

I

Like it or not, teachers of German are associated with Germany/Hitler/the Holocaust; we do not like this, we even deny this, but we cannot blind ourselves to it. The issue today is: How are we teachers of German going to deal with it? Is it sufficient to counter Hitler with Goethe? Is it sufficient to counter Himmler with Beethoven? When Thomas Mann was asked to return to Germany after World War II, after he had become an American citizen in exile, he explained his reasons for not returning in a text entitled "Why I Am Not Going Back to Germany": "People should stop talking about the end of German history!" he exclaimed, for "Germany is not identical with the brief and dark historical episode that carries Hitler's name."[2] Thomas Mann was of course correct, but the "brief and dark historical episode" cannot, will not, and must not be forgotten, and every time we open the book on Germany, that grim chapter bearing the name of Hitler has to be dealt with. Our profession remains closely linked in the public imagination with German nationalism, both as a historical phenomenon and with the ongoing reality of being a German national. Is there something in the way German is studied by the other academic disciplines that might help us explain what we are about? Does one necessarily become more German, more sympathetic to Germans, the better one speaks the German language? How are we best going to improve the public misconceptions of what German studies is increasingly coming to signify in the early twenty-first century?

In fairness to our students, our profession, and ourselves, we argue that anyone involved in teaching German—be it language, literature, history, or culture—has to face up to the historical realities that have formed and continue to transform our profession. When we consider the politics of the American university, we observe that it is somewhat different to be a historian of German history, or a geographer of German urban geography, or a sociologist of German society, than it is to be a Germanist per se. For one thing, being a Germanist or professor of German has too long been equated with being a native speaker of German; students and colleagues in this country alike seem to think that "German professors" are just that—namely, German nationals who become professors of German. The following situation neatly summarizes this gulf between what we teach and research and the public's conception of us. When Adrian Del Caro, coeditor of the present volume, tells a stranger that he is a German professor, he often gets the following response: "That's funny, your name doesn't sound German." Sometimes this remark is spoken in fun, in jest, as a pun—but not often enough. Laymen (and even worse, sometimes our own colleagues in other fields), judging by name-value only, all too often assume that one is supposed to be the professor of the language associated with the ethnic heritage of one's last name. Let us agree today, and for the future as well, that being a German professor has nothing to do with being a German national. Certainly our Swiss, Austrian, Hungarian, Latvian, and Romanian colleagues, as native speakers of German, will also appreciate this.

German studies, as it is practiced in the United States in particular, has plenty of room for native speakers of German. Most of us had teachers and mentors who are native speakers, and many of our colleagues come from German-speaking central Europe; ours has been a fruitful collaboration, though frequently one-sided in favor of native speakers, and we wish for collaboration to continue. What we demand, however, is that the collaboration be fair in that it recognize the realities, idiosyncracies, and diversity of American higher education. There needs to be more teaching of general humanities-type courses by German professors; more involvement by German professors in the interdisciplinary initiatives of the humanities; more courses featuring German writers in translation; more placement of articles and books in English-language journals and publishing houses; more non-native speakers and interdisciplinary scholars evaluating nontraditional German-studies achievements, and more non-native speakers on the editorial boards of our discipline's journals. It is high time that German studies made itself more accessible, and it is totally unacceptable to retreat into the high ivory tower of high German whenever our profession falls under scrutiny.

The increasing diversity of the German professoriate in the United States, into which hundreds of non-German men and women have been admitted since the 1970s, as well as the increasing diversity of the German-studies curriculum, give clear indications that we are in fact a rapidly transforming profession. For example, students interested in, say, Nazi Germany in general, and the Holocaust in particular, do not have to rely exclusively on the history department for their information; today these students can identify professors in history, political science, geography, sociology, philosophy, art history, and yes, even German studies who are willing and prepared to teach them about Nazi Germany. And equally appealing is the fact that students interested in Lessing, Goethe, Nietzsche, Lou Andreas-Salomé, Else Lasker-Schüler, and Christa Wolf can approach professors from English, comparative literature, philosophy, women's studies, humanities, etc. for their information. Let us resolve to continue this cross-pollination; let us resolve to humanize all studies at the university by breaking down the disciplinary walls, by breaking down the stereotypes.

The decades of the 1980s and 1990s have seen remarkable and laudable interdisciplinary collaborations in higher education. University administrators, troubled by declining enrollments in most foreign-language majors and burgeoning enrollments in the various natural and social sciences, have become very concerned for the bottom line—their challenge has been to preserve the integrity of foreign-language teaching at the service level, where enrollments have traditionally held their own and there is strong campus-wide support for foreign-language requirements, while carving out a niche for more-specialized, upper-division undergraduate and graduate study in the languages, where enrollments have been miserable.[3] Professors in the languages frequently teach fewer students and this does not escape the notice of pragmatic, budget-hardened administrators. Language courses per se, those designed to teach language skills, must be capped in the teens and twenties in order to be effective (we do impart skills, after all!), and once students advance beyond the level of "language requirements," their interest in majoring in German is barely sufficient to field two or three underenrolled courses in German literature taught in German. This is a situation that evidently will not be allowed to continue as universities continue to face budgetary cutbacks.[4]

Solutions to this highly problematic situation are—thankfully!—being discussed more and more openly at recent German-studies conferences, in association reports, and in essay volumes, to which our University of Colorado–Boulder conference offers one more link in the growing chain.[5] Ironically, the very things that, for the public, are most clearly identifiable as topics of study for Germanists, namely World War II and the atrocities of the Holocaust, are already playing a key role in the strategies we must all engage in for the long-term survival of the discipline. With the marked nationwide decrease in

German-language enrollments at the university level, and with German occupying a steady but small 2.8 percent of total enrollments (and 6.12 percent of foreign language enrollments) at the K–12 level,[6] we are faced with reinventing ourselves as professors whose self-definition in the classroom has to become increasingly topics-oriented, comparative, interdisciplinary, and generalist. This reinvention of our professional selves is depicted in two main areas of curricular design for courses in translation: first, in what is traditionally considered "high" German literary culture (e.g., the Faust legend) we certainly have a dependable "cash cow" for many German programs that are now turning to the general student population; second, we are increasingly daring to apply the broad rubric of cultural studies to new courses that spring adventurously across disciplines (e.g., nature and technology, the modern metropolis, or multiculturalism in postwar Germany). In this latter grouping of cultural-studies courses, there is no denying that teaching the lowest of the "low," namely the whole sorry saga of German nationalism, is one of the most successful arenas in which to improve student enrollments; this is particularly effective in "feeder" courses that both service the general curriculum of the university and also lead to students being exposed to German studies at an earlier stage and thus hopefully opting to incorporate the German language in conjunction with other studies. We find ourselves, then, when we teach and research the Nazi Holocaust against Jewish and non-Jewish victims, bearing witness to this tragedy on the one hand, while evidently consolidating the continued existence of German studies on the other.

A detour into the personal case history of German studies at the University of Colorado at Boulder may assist here as an example of the transformational state of our field. As the fiftieth anniversary of the end of World War II approached, our institution, like many large public universities in the United States, had gone through the "fat years" of student enrollments in German in the 1960s and 1970s; those were decades when German Ph.D. and M.A. programs flourished across the country. By the early 1980s, however, the Ph.D. in Germanics was closed down at Colorado, and by the late 1980s the M.A. was suspended as well. When Adrian Del Caro was given the opportunity, as the externally hired chairperson beginning in 1992, to help rebuild a graduate program in Germanics at the University of Colorado, the decline of German graduate programs at other American universities was already well under way. Awareness of this led to the firm conviction that the traditional Germanics degree based entirely on language and literature would not serve at CU–Boulder for the renaissance of its M.A. program. With these trends and realities in mind, we at Colorado set about to design an interdisciplinary master's degree in "modern

German studies," which was launched in 1994. Both administration and colleagues were receptive to this idea, not so much because it sounded "new" but because it took fullest possible advantage of existing talent in Germanics. But taking advantage of and tapping into talent in "Germanics" cannot be a matter of identifying native speakers of German and those fluent in the language who possess the Ph.D. or the Dr. Phil. in Germanistik—the concept "Germanics" has to be opened up, expanded, and this is where "German studies" enters the picture. Likewise, the undergraduate program at Colorado needed retooling for the twenty-first century: not only have many new cultural studies and literature courses in translation been added to the curriculum, but the entire major has been made more flexible from the student's point of view. German majors at Colorado may now select a track that offers less emphasis on language and more on cultural studies; while those students who focus on the language track gain the benefit of business German courses and exams, as well as internships both local and abroad. We did not pioneer these concepts at Colorado—we learned from our peer institutions, and then merely made this transition. At the time of this writing the Germanic Studies program at Colorardo has sixty-six majors, thirty-six minors, and these numbers have risen modestly but steadily over the past five years despite a slight overall decline in entry-level enrollment. We added a concurrent B.A./M.A. program in 1997, whereby highly motivated undergraduates may earn both degrees at the same time, while enrolling in graduate seminars as undergraduates (completion of both degrees in five years). Meanwhile, our "regular" M.A. students continue to write interdisciplinary theses, choosing the "outside" committee member from a variety of disciplines (business, music, fine arts, history, political science, philosophy, comparative literature, English, geography, linguistics, etc.). Moreover, students may enter our M.A. program without the B.A. in German as long as they possess B.A.-level proficiency in German and an undergraduate degree suitable to the pursuit of graduate work in the humanities.

II

This volume offers the selected proceedings of a symposium held at the University of Colorado at Boulder in 1995. Our aim as conference organizers and as editors was to observe the anniversary of the liberation of the concentration and death camps, and the liberation of Europe and the world from unprecedented inhumanity perpetrated by Germany and its sympathizers. We simultaneously took the opportunity that this act of commemoration provided to consider some of the most important transformations in the discipline of German studies that are occurring in the light of Germany's circumstances from 1945 to 1995. We project, if only modestly, that such topics and interests will continue to be explored by our profession far into the future.

Some background information on the genesis of this conference is called for: in 1994 we set about raising the necessary funding to host an international, interdisciplinary symposium on the theme: "1945–1995: The Changing Faces of German Studies." We wanted thereby to observe the fiftieth anniversary of the liberation of Europe from Nazi tyranny, but we wanted to do this by illustrating how the discipline of German studies is evolving. Thus, our symposium was designed not only to observe a moment in time, but also to contribute to future evolutions within the discipline by providing a broadly representative sample of what transpires in the name of German studies. Our constituting theme pointedly links the collapse of Nazi brutality with the ongoing transformation of our profession. The nature of German studies is changing to become more inclusive, and we wanted to take the fiftieth anniversary of the end of World War II to observe what the German professoriate has done in recent years by representing "what is German."

In order to achieve these goals, we invited speakers both novice and well known to participate, focusing on the United States, Canada, Germany, Israel, Austria, and Switzerland. Colleagues from our own campus were also invited insofar as their work contributes to German studies. We also issued a call for papers and selected from a number of excellent proposals. In addition to Germanists, or "German professors" as we are also known, our symposium served as a forum for intellectual and cultural historians, political theorists, art historians, women's studies professors, an archivist, an English professor, comparatists, several specialists in film, and fiction writers from the United States, Austria, and Switzerland. In order to explore more openly the nature of German studies in our country in particular, we included speakers from small colleges as well as major universities, intent upon problematizing the status of our discipline by asking: what is going on today in the field of German studies? We also made a point of conducting all our symposium proceedings in English (sometimes to the discomfort of colleagues from abroad), based on our philosophy that German studies must become more accessible to those who do not speak German. As a result, large audiences for the sessions of our conference were indeed garnered from among the undergraduate and graduate student populations of the University of Colorado at Boulder. In publishing these deliberations on modern German studies in the post-Holocaust age, we hope to continue to bring us all closer to each other and to our students. We are hopeful that they will serve as a source of inspiration for students and teachers whose interest in things German leaves them always curious and concerned about the "German question."

III

A great diversity of interest, as well as an extremely high quality of discourse, are evident in these papers, all revised for publication in the present volume. The volume is divided into four main sections. The essays of Section I, "Cultural Philosophy and Ideologies of Identity" (by Walter H. Sokel, Robert A. Pois, Steven E. Aschheim, Rainer Hering, William Safran, and Thomas Hollweck), address the intersecting problematics of nationalism and anti-semitism in modern and contemporary Germany, in political as well as philosophical arenas. Section II, "Post-Holocaust Identity Debates," raises issues concerning the German "Other"; the essays of this section (by Susann Samples, Silvia Henke, Ruth-Ellen B. Joeres, Todd Herzog, and Andreas Michel) provide innovative views on the hybrid state of German cultural production as evidenced in the new subjectivities of race and feminism, both in Germany today and for Germanists in North America. The contributions of Section III, "Poetry and Images After Auschwitz" (by Adrian Del Caro, Erk Grimm, Kathrin Bower, Robert Shandley, and Janet Ward), offer a unique insight into the apparently "forbidden" areas of artistic creation after Adorno's initial anti-graven image dictum in the face of Shoah atrocities. The concerns of the volume are concluded in the essays of Section IV, "Sites of Meta-German Multiplicity" (by Ann Schmiesing, Martin R. Dean, Karlheinz Auckenthaler, Kari Grimstad, Jean Wilson, Alexander Honold, and Thomas Nolden); this section explores German literature and literary studies as international vehicles for reflection on the Holocaust and for the ongoing renewal of national identities.

NOTES

1. Chris Jenks, *Visual Culture* (New York: Routledge, 1995), 3.

2. Thomas Mann, "Warum ich nicht nach Deutschland zurückgehe," *Gesammelte Werke in zwölf Bänden,* ed. Hans Bürgin. Vol. 12 (Frankfurt a.M.: Fischer, 1960), 961.

3. German college enrollments are below 100,000 today, compared to 133,000 six years ago and 220,000 around 1970. A recent survey by the Modern Language Association, cited in the *New York Times* (October 9, 1996), reports that college enrollments in German are down by 28 percent in the period 1990–1995; other European languages (Italian, French, and particularly Russian) are also significantly down, and with strong rises in only Spanish, Chinese, and Arabic.

4. One example of this is the loss of the German department at the State University of New York's Albany campus in 1996.

5. Cf. Heidi Byrnes's report in the newsletter of the *American Assocation of Teachers of German* (32.1, 1996) on "The Future of German in American Education," based on the AATG's invited forums during 1995–1996 (at Stanford University, Anaheim, Washington University, Georgetown University, and the Chicago Modern Language Association). On ways to improve the visibility of German programs, see Robert Di Donato, "Undergraduate German Programs: Strategies for Success," and

Dieter Jedan, "Shifting Enrollment Patterns: Departmental Perspectives," both in *ADFL Bulletin* 30.1 (1998): 12–14 and 15–17, respectively. Cf. also John A. McCarthy and Katrin Schneider, eds., *The Future of "Germanistik" in the USA: Changing Our Prospects* (Nashville, TN: Vanderbilt University Press, 1996); Jörg Roche and Thomas Salumets, eds., *Germanics Under Construction* (Munich: Ludicium, 1996); John Van Cleve and A. Leslie Willson, eds., *Remarks on the Needed Reform of German Studies in the United States* (Columbia, SC: Camden House, 1993); a special issue of *The German Quarterly* 62.2 (1989) dedicated to "Germanistik as German Studies: Interdisciplinary Theories and Methods"; David P. Benseler, Walter F. W. Lohnes, and Valters Nollendorfs, eds., *Teaching German in America: Prolegomena to a History* (Madison: University of Wisconsin Press, 1988). Most recently, the topic of curriculum forum was addressed by Elizabeth B. Bernhardt and Russel A. Berman, in "From German 1 to German Studies 001: A Chronicle of Circular Reform," *Die Unterrichtspraxis* 32 (1999): 22–31. A conference on this topic was held at the University of Wisconsin–Madison in September 1996 on "Shaping Forces in American Germanics."

6. Cited in the American Council on the Teaching of Foreign Languages' 1994 summary report, "Foreign Language Enrollments in Public Secondary Schools," by Jamie B. Draper and June H. Hicks, in *ACTFL Annals* 29.3 (1995): 305, 306.

Acknowledgments

We thank the following organizations, offices, and individuals for their financial support for the conference: The German Academic Exchange Service, and in particular Dr. Heidrun Suhr and Dr. Gottfried Gügold; the former Consul General of the Federal Republic of Germany in San Francisco, Mr. Ruprecht Henatsch; the former Chancellor of the University of Colorado at Boulder, Dr. Roderic Park; as well as the former Dean of Arts and Sciences, Dr. Charles R. Middleton; the Dean of the Graduate School, Dr. Carol Lynch; and the former Associate Vice Chancellor for Faculty Affairs, Dr. Albert Ramirez—without their generous support, the symposium would not have been be possible. Support for the conference was also provided by the Council on Research and Creative Work and the Graduate Committee on the Arts and Humanities at the University of Colorado at Boulder. We are also greatly indebted to the two anonymous readers of this volume for the University Press of Colorado: their enormously insightful comments provided us as editors with a critical engagement as well as a dialogic springboard for the sense and organization of this volume's incorporation as selected proceedings of the conference. And finally, we extend our gratitude to all the conference participants and contributors of this volume, noting especially their sincere dedication to the future well-being of German studies as it reflects on its post-Holocaust past and present.

GERMAN STUDIES IN THE POST-HOLOCAUST AGE

Section I: Cultural Philosophy and Ideologies of Identity

1
Ecological Ethos and Reactionary Politics: The Political Implications of Heidegger's Philosophy of Being

WALTER H. SOKEL

Being for Heidegger is not a substance or an entity. It is a happening in a relationship. Being is the flash of insight that illuminates and overwhelms a human being or *Dasein* when it is struck by the full force of the realization that the being it encounters *is*—that it "is there" ("Da-sein"), that it exists. Therefore, Heidegger replaces the signifier "man" or "human being" by the words "da sein" ("There or Here Is Being") to indicate what is essential in human being. It is the capacity of wonder, of care for the being of beings. *Dasein* is, or should be, "the shepherd of Being." Therefore, Heidegger vehemently opposes the humanist pride that encourages humanity to treat all beings as material for human use. His continuous dwelling on *Dasein*'s humble role in caring for Being anticipates, in some essential respects, contemporary concern about the limits of human privilege in the face of a rapidly progressing threat to nature. It is akin to the ethos of ecology.

The notion of Being as a happening, an event, has temporality built into it. The revelatory encounter of the Being of beings occurs at a particular moment in time when Being *first* impresses itself upon a *Dasein*. Thus Being is a historical process, an emerging that gradually weakens to routinized perception and enduring. Eventually the *sense* of Being vanishes. Thus Heidegger's philosophy of Being privileges beginnings. "A beginning is in fact the greatest thing of all."[1] That there is Being rather than nothing hits us "in moments of rejoicing when all the things around us are transfigured and seem to be there for the first time."[2] Being occurs in poetry and in art where "each thing" presented, "a tree, a mountain, a house, the cry of a bird—loses all indifference and commonplaceness."[3] The basic content of all philosophy, of the discourse in which true thinking occurs, is "the inexhaustible richness of what on every single day is as though that day were its first."[4] Only in its beginning is the being of a being complete.

This privileging of beginnings is linked to the explosive character truth possesses for Heidegger. Truth results from the removal of the covers in which Being hides before it reveals itself. Heidegger emphasizes the privative character of the Greek word for truth, *a-letheia*, "uncoveredness." Truth is the moment of dis-covery. It is the experience of an explosive revelation. The privative prefix *a* ("un") in *aletheia* ("uncovered") signifies the revolutionary force of the event that is the emerging of Being, and this emerging is what Heidegger understands as truth. But it also indicates its temporary, indeed fleeting, nature. The truth of Being cannot shine for long. Its enemy is routine. When Being no longer appears radiantly emerging from the foil of nothingness, when Being is taken for granted, its cover-up begins. Being starts to vanish as soon as it turns habitual, self-evident, common. When the view prevails of those who routinely pass by beings without being struck by the wonder of their being, then Being begins to be covered up. This cover-up is inevitable, since the glory of a beginning cannot possibly last.

The privileging of beginnings implies a reactionary view of history. Like all reactionaries, Heidegger poses a past golden age compared to which all subsequent ages can be seen as a decline. For Heidegger this golden age was the age of the pre-Socratics. They had been the first to glimpse the meaning of Being. Because thinking began with them, the wonder of Being was first revealed to them. Since those early happy days, the history of the West has been a progressive darkening of Being, lost in conceptualizing abstraction and ultimately in utilitarian instrumentalism, reaching its nadir in the twentieth century.

However, "reactionary" implies the possibility of action that might regain the bygone state of glory. It is possible to reconnect with the beginning, and Heidegger's philosophizing is devoted to this task. The beginning is not simply gone forever. Being does not die. It merely slips out of sight for long ages in which abstract and instrumental reason displaces the original revelatory vision of the truth of beings. Being has gone into hiding, but it might conceivably be resurrected by recollection. Such recollection aims at the regaining of an attitude that will allow *Dasein* again to see Being in its truth and splendor.

Here the reactionary turns visionary, and this sheds light on the attraction Nazism held for Heidegger.[5] In his oration as the new rector of the University of Freiburg, confirmed by the Nazi authorities, Heidegger called on the German university to support the new regime. He did so with the understanding that the "German revolution," as the Nazis' coming to power was called, might and should facilitate that reconnecting with the distant beginnings of the West and place Germans "under the power of the *beginning* of our spiritual-historical being [*Dasein*] . . . All research remains bound to that beginning of philosophy.

From it, it draws the strength of its essence," and it does so "only if it remains equal to this beginning."[6] Heidegger then goes on to say that this beginning "still is." "It does not lie behind us, as something that was long ago, but stands *before* us." The beginning of the West lies now before the new Germany and her university as their destiny.

This projected attempt to return to a great beginning constitutes a remarkable parallel to the ideology of National Socialism. Nazism too looked back to a glorious beginning of Germanic being in the ancient Teutonic tribes who had defeated and conquered Rome, and it looked back nostalgically to the earliest appearance of the German nation as the center and titular superpower of medieval Europe. And that quest for the retrieval of essence, which motivates Heidegger's thinking of Being, finds a distant parallel in the Nazi obsession with restoring the purity of the essence of Aryan-Germanic being, notwithstanding the considerable difference between Heidegger's notion of essential *Dasein* as openness to Being and the Nazis' biological notion of race as the essence of a people. The Nazi cultivation of violent and eruptive change, their celebratory rituals countering and erupting into the routine of everyday life as well as their new style of politics and diplomacy that held the world in breathless expectation—all that can be seen as akin to Heidegger's notion of truth as an explosive happening.

Heidegger's thinking comes especially close to the warlike ethos of fascism where it weds the notion of the explosive nature of the truth of Being to a tragic-heroic contempt of individual self-preservation. Being in the sense of mere enduring in existence is, for Heidegger, the betrayal of Being as the happening of truth. For enduring blunts Being as the event of disclosure, as the effulgent happening of revelation. It degrades Being to mere routinized existing, to mere presence. Long-enduring presence of a being corresponds to the loss of the visionary flash in thinking and its degradation to conceptualizing and thus routinizing thought. Heidegger calls stabilization that which brings "monstrosity" (*Unwesen*) into Being and perverts its truth into deception.[7] It turns being into pseudo-being, into mere semblance from which the original effulgence and revelatory power of true Being has departed.

Though reactionary, Heidegger's thought is anticonservative. It turns against continuity and favors violent overturning. Heidegger's notion of authentic Being agrees very well with the apocalyptic and millenarian extremism of the Nazis as well as with their cult of death-defying heroism. For Heidegger, decline and death are written as the law of fate into each being. They should be accepted readily. Acceptance of one's allotted mortality is an essential part of Heidegger's ethic. In 1941, he writes: "Constancy and continuity of presence is not what is decisive in a being."[8] What is lasting rests on continued effectiveness of the power of the initial thrust of Being. "Justice" and "propriety" for a being is to recognize and accept its built-in limit, boundary, or term. Resistance to the limit, insistence on continuing forever, is a stubborness improper and disgraceful in a being.

Heidegger's opposition to Western modernity can be seen as resting on a conflict between the irreligious stance of the individual's defiant insistence that its own life be its ultimate value and the religious spirit of the individual's surrender to a being greater than itself. However, Heidegger's religious spirit is aestheticized. Unlike the Judaeo-Christian God, Being does not constitute what we could perceive as moral superiority. It does not issue the moral law. The ethical content of the notion of Being is reduced to the admittedly jubilant awareness that there is being rather than nothing. Beyond that, Being has no end and purpose except providing *Dasein* with the experience of the brilliance, splendor, and power of its manifesting itself. Such an end and purpose is a purely aesthetic one.

The political implications of this aestheticized ontology and religiosity become clear when we dwell on the last-mentioned attribute of Being's self-manifestation—power. In *Being and Time*, Heidegger had not yet ascribed power to Being. Power emerges as an attribute of Being in the early Nazi period, in *Introduction to Metaphysics* (1935), where Heidegger equates Being with *physis*, i.e., with the power that makes beings emerge into the light. This notion of *physis* anthropomorphizes and deifies Being in a way absent in Heidegger's earlier thinking. In *Being and Time*, Being was conceived of as a gerund, the "showing itself" of a phenomenon. It was a happening, an activity, a process, and a relationship between the Being of a being and the *Dasein* perceiving it. The so-called *Kehre* or "Turn," which Heidegger himself discerns in his thinking and which roughly coincides with the Nazi assumption of power, consists of the substantivizing of the verb character of Being, which Being had possessed earlier. Without ceasing to be a verb form, now Being also tends to become a noun. This change tends to personalize Being. Although *Dasein* by no means loses its responsibility as the "shepherd of Being," Being itself takes a much more active role, which makes it more of a person and resembling a divine one.

This personalization of Being is associated with power. Heidegger sees *physis* as the power that makes beings emerge into the light. *Physis* thus transforms Being into power, or, to put it more precisely, it adds power as an aspect to Being. This attribution of power to Being soon followed the Nazi assumption of power, and can indeed be associated with the cult of power virulent in the new Germany, of which the National Socialist interpreter of Nietzsche, Alfred Bäumler, was typical.

Being as *physis* imparts its power to particular beings. It gives an individual the power to show itself forcefully and to stand, as Heidegger puts it, *upright* in the light. This power is not bestowed in equal measure. There is an elitist differentiation in the degree of Being with which individuals are endowed. Only a few beings can be expected to manifest Being, in the way they show themselves to *Dasein*.

At this point, the nature of a true community, as Heidegger envisions it, should become clear. A true community shows the convergence of a few beings who can show most powerfully, in and by their being, what Being is—their convergence with a *Dasein* able to discern it in them and proclaim it. The former are the authentic nobles. The latter are the true poets. Their complementarity forms the aristocratic community as exemplified by the early Greek *polis*. Again a Greek word plays a crucial role here for Heidegger. This word is *doxa* which, as Heidegger shows,[9] originally signified regard, the regard in which a human being stands in his community. If this regard amounts to high esteem, it is the power of Being in the individual showing itself in the community's regard as "fame and glory." Heidegger is at pains to point out that glory for the early Greeks was something akin to divine grace. Glory was not "something additional which one might or might not obtain" through one's works. Rather glory was a part of one. It was one's aspect or way of appearing, one's being as given by the Being that one manifested. Even though Heidegger personalizes and, as it were, deifies Being, it yet remains inseparable from the particular beings that manifest it. When Being appears, it appears in and as particular beings. Between the glory of a being and its truth there is no difference. For the early Greeks— and it is axiomatic for Heidegger that they were right—glory "was the mode of the highest being."[10] Glory was the radiance of Being in and about an individual being. Thus we see how Heidegger's thinking accommodates the *Führer* principle.

Yet the problem of how true Being can be distinguished from mere show haunts Heidegger. It became particularly relevant in the political context of the time. How could an authentic *Führer* be distinguished from a charlatan? And was Hitler, for instance, one or the other? Here it is instructive to observe how Heidegger relies on the argument of power. False appearance or mere semblance appears as a decline in power, in the quite literal sense of an inclining away from that authentic uprightness that is true Being. False semblance is a crookedness resulting from the waning power of Being left in a being that can no longer stand upright by itself in the light that is truth or uncoveredness. We shall see how this view of the fall of Being into falseness and mere semblance applies to Heidegger's changing views of Hitler and Nazism.

What corresponds in *Dasein* to the decline, i.e., the progressive withdrawal of Being from once-powerful beings, is *Dasein*'s increasing abstractness and instrumentalism of thought that reaches its nadir in the triumph of the technological view of the world. What is then left of beings is their degradation to the status of manipulable objects, instruments of use for the human subject. The subject collectivizes itself as the will to power of the human species. It is this will to power that makes *Dasein* oblivious of Being and changes it into the cerebral beast of prey that uses intellect as its weapon in the subjugation of all beings. Science and technology become the instruments that the species' will to power uses to dispose of Being according to its hungry will and insatiable desire. Since all beings are reduced to instruments, their Being, in Heidegger's sense, has, of course, totally vanished. Secular humanism, with its twin offspring of utilitarianism and pragmatism, becomes for Heidegger the fiendish enemy of Being. Its nightmarish goal is a totally administered, exploited, and enslaved universe in which human hybris reigns supreme. The incarnation of this hellish vision of a future rapidly becoming the present was, for Heidegger, on the one hand, America, and, on the other, the Soviet Union. In 1935, he lists them together as the twin embodiments of a mortal menace closing in on Europe and threatening to strangle it in their grip. As though precisely echoing Heidegger's assessment, the Axis powers, a few years later, claimed that they had to wage total war to save the culture of Europe from the alliance of the same enemies Heidegger had pinpointed—"plutocratic" America and Soviet Communism. Thus there can be little doubt where Heidegger's sympathies lay in the Second World War.

Nazism had presented itself to Heidegger, in 1933, as the possible, and even likely salvation from a world without Being, a world in which instrumental rationalism and the technological will to mastery of the universe had crowded out *Dasein*'s capacity for wonder, reverence, and enthusiasm in the face of Being. This is how, immediately after the German defeat, Heidegger sought to account for the appeal Nazism had held for him:

> I saw in the movement that had gained power the possibility of an inner recollection and renewal of the people . . . Certainly it would have been more comfortable to stay on the sidelines, to turn up one's nose at these impossible people and sing the praises of what had been, without any regard for the historical situation the Western world found itself in.

He characterized that situation as "the universal rule of the will to power within history, now [ready to] embrace the planet." From such a fate, so Heidegger hoped, Nazism, if properly guided, might save the West. He concluded: "Is there not also guilt incurred by failing to do what is essential?"[11]

That Nazism, one of the most ruthlessly power-intoxicated movements in human history, should have appeared as a salvation from the will to power may seem strange, indeed absurd, to us. However, it may appear less bizarre if we realize that Heidegger's entire thinking revolved around the radical opposition between two opposed meanings of power. On the one hand, power as the ability to control and bend being to human purpose and individual and collective benefit; and, on the other hand, the power of Being, a power that is not ours, but comes from our readiness to let ourselves be overwhelmed by the being of something other than ourselves. This readiness allows us "to let Being be." "Letting be" has the double meaning of noninterference and of opening ourselves to the rapt wonder that there is Being rather than nothing. And it is, of course, only by virtue of a quietist abstention from interfering with things that the sense that they *are* can hold sway over us.

To be sure, Heidegger was insistent that Nazism was in need of guidance toward his own idealizing interpretation of it. "What would have happened," he writes in retrospect," and what would have been prevented if, in 1933, all capable forces had aroused themselves and joined . . . in order to gradually purify and moderate the movement . . .?" Having failed to accept this "guidance," which Heidegger was most eager to furnish, Nazism, as Heidegger saw it, fell total victim to that very same will to power that motivated and corrupted all modernity. Nazism participated and excelled in that same ruthless mobilization of resources, that total organization of existence, which had already shut off the technocratic democracies as well as Marxist Russia from Being. By succumbing to the will to power, Nazism showed that the power of true Being had deserted it. It had become a sham. After this spectacular failure of one of the most promising possibilities of rescuing the Western world from itself, Heidegger concluded, near the end of his life, that "only a god can save us." [12]

What I have attempted to show is a paradox—the paradoxical closeness of a quietist and quasi-ecological ethos of reverence for the Being of beings to a politics that made the annihilation of beings—human beings—its primary program and ghastly achievement.

NOTES

1. Martin Heidegger, *Introduction to Metaphysics*, trans. Ralph Manheim (Garden City: Anchor Books, 1961 [c. 1959]), 13.
2. Ibid., 1.
3. Ibid., 22.
4. Ibid., 82f.
5. The best treatment, in English, of the political dimension of Heidegger's philosophy is: Richard Wolin, *The Politics of Being: The Political Thought of Martin*

Heidegger (New York: Columbia University Press, 1990). My own approach to the subject differs from Wolin's in essential respects. Wolin approaches Heidegger's political philosophy from the existential decisionism of *Being and Time*, while my own approach is based on the notion of Being as beginning, as the flash of discovery. Some overlappings inevitably occur, especially with chapters 3–5 of Wolin's book. However, since I developed my argument independently of Wolin, I wish to refer to his valuable study solely by way of this general note.

6. Martin Heidegger, "The Rectorate 1933/4: Facts and Thoughts," trans. Karsten Harries, *Review of Metaphysics* 29 (1975–1976): 473.

7. Martin Heidegger, *Grundbegriffe: Freiburger Vorlesung Sommersemester 1941*, ed. Petra Jaeger (Frankfurt a.M.: Klostermann, 1981), *Gesamtausgabe II*, Abteilung Vorlesungen 1923–1944, vol. 51, 113.

8. Heidegger, *Grundbegriffe*, 114.

9. Cf. Heidegger, *Introduction to Metaphysics*, 87f.

10. Ibid., 87.

11. Heidegger, "The Rectorate 1933/4," p. 485f.

12. Ibid.

2
The Great War and the Holocaust
ROBERT A. POIS

Many Europeans greeted the Great War with an intense enthusiasm that has fascinated students of history ever since. Even if, over time, caveats have emerged concerning "the magic of the August days," the fact that so many Europeans from all walks of life were enthusiastic about the coming of war or, at the very least, were willing to positively accept it, still exercises a sort of drawing power. Of course, the offensive plans and fantasies, so useful in sustaining initial respective national enthusiasms, evaporated in the face of technological and logistical realities. With the supervention of trench warfare, emphasis could no longer be placed on "heroic" offensive warfare. Rather, for the average soldier on either side, it became a matter of stolid endurance in the face of situations and conditions previously unimaginable.

Emphasis upon endurance in the face of a grinding form of combat that, for soldiers, was probably the worst in modern times, produced its own form of self-conscious "heroism." Here, it is plain that the war quite simply "got into the souls" of at least some of those participating in it. British Second Lieutenant Edwin Campion Vaughn's journal recorded a voyage through the hell of "Third Ypres." In the end, only fifteen men were left out of the company he commanded. Yet, about to be sent home on leave, he recorded the following: "So this was the end of 'D' Company. Feeling sick and lonely I returned to my tent to write out my casualty report; but instead I sat on the floor and drank whiskey after whiskey as I gazed into a black and empty future."[1] As horrible as his graphically recorded experiences had been, Lieutenant Vaughn had become an extension of the war and, after a brief return to "blighty," he returned to service with much enthusiasm. We can also ponder the letters of the German expressionist painter Franz Marc, wherein we find the following letter of June 23, 1915: "What is this war but another, perhaps more honest, form of the previous situation that prevailed during peacetime? Instead of competition, now there is war." Another letter, dated February 22, 1916 (recorded on the second day of the Verdun offensive, which would kill Marc less than two weeks later), confided: "The war, too, is part of nature; you cannot place the war . . . entirely outside of natural phenomena. The collective behavior, which it undoubtedly represents, has its cause in nature."[2] Obviously for folk such as these there was a self-confirming aspect to the Great War. Hideous though it was, it had come to embody something natural, a heightened form of authenticity. In fact, the very brutality and hardness both generated and necessitated by it became the contents of a more authentic life. Marc mentioned seeing truly terrible things but in one of his last letters, that of March 2, 1916, he declared that "my nerves are truly untouched to my own amazement."[3] Caught up in the fury of one of the most horrific campaigns in history, this most sensitive of painters had risen to an inwardly posed challenge and toughened himself to all that was around him.

As made plain by Vaughn's spiritual confusion upon confronting his going on leave—to be fair about it, Marc declared that he was looking forward to his own—there were soldiers on both sides who seemed to have adjusted to war as being a crucial, and positively meaningful, part of their lives. In the end, though, Allied soldiers came home to countries that, while many mourned, were awash in the enthusiasm of "victory," however hollow such victory might have proved to have been. German soldiers came home in defeat to a land ravaged by the Allied starvation blockade. Soldiers of all armies had been hardened by the Great War. Home-front opinions had been hardened if not warped by propaganda. Defeat, though, made a difference, both with regard to how some chose to remember the war, and what for some was central to such remembrance.

Of course, the average German, in the face of daunting odds—the fall of the old regime, civil unrest, and the continued enforcement of the Allied blockade—tried to pick up where he or she had left off in August, 1914. Yet if in the cases of peoples everywhere a victorious war was to have provided for spiritual and social needs, many had to have found it impossible to assimilate defeat, moreover one sustained after so heroic a struggle on battle and home fronts. For them the war could not end; rather, they had to become its continued validating expression. The story of such people has been told often.

George L. Mosse has spoken of how the Great War was "trivialized" by propagandists on all sides while it was going on and afterwards as well.[4] In Germany, though, the war had brought defeat and a bitter sense of national humiliation, something which led to what Mosse has called "the brutalization of German politics," the most obvious immediate expression of which was the Free Corps.[5] In this context Mosse has made it plain that probably one of the most crucial elements leading to the rise of Nazism and the eventual Holocaust was how many in Germany chose to remember the war or, perhaps better put, give it meaning. Here the role played by trivialization was not so great. Rather one can observe an emphasis upon a certain quality that had sustained the war and in turn had come out of it—a quality that rendered defeat (if so recognized) irrelevant, while assuring that in one way or the other the war would rage on.

Here it is plain that war-engendered "rage," now sharply honed by defeat, found expression in an emphasis upon the one redeeming quality that many saw as rising above, perhaps even annulling military disaster: hardness. For many, after the debacle of the Great War, hardness had to be accepted for its own sake. We must note that even the avowed pacifist Erich Maria Remarque saw the war as nurturing a new, perhaps more authentic form of friendship, that of "comrades": "I am no longer a shuddering speck of existence, alone in the darkness;—I belong to them and they to me; we all share the same fear and the same life, we are nearer than lovers, in a simpler, a harder way; I could bury my face in them, in these voices, these words that have saved me and will stand by me."[6] To be sure, as time went on Remarque moved beyond the idea, so prevalent in his best-known work, that "hard"—in truth, somewhat misogynist—friendships forged in war were somehow more "authentic" than others. For those for whom the war raged on, however, "hardness" remained central to a positive memory of the war. After all, it was the most crucial quality that gave it meaning, a vessel carved out of stone into which one could pour one's wrath.

There can be no doubt that "trivialization" of the war had crucial roles to play both in sustaining the war effort and later in glorifying its memory. It would be however misleading to suggest that those who had come to see the Great War as the definer of some sort of new being were oblivious to its horrors. Ernst Jünger who without question saw more of the war than Remarque described them in some detail:

> . . . everywhere, spades uncovered something buried. Every secret of the grave lay open in an abomination before which the most bizarre dreams paled in comparison. Hair fell in shocks from skulls as faded leaves from autumn trees. Many dissolved into green fish flesh, which, at night, glowed through torn uniforms . . . In other cases, flesh dropped from bones as red-brown gelatine.[7]

Whether or not, as has been suggested, Jünger was concerned with "aestheticizing" mass death is uncertain.[8] What is not is that Jünger, and doubtless many others like him, recognized that this new kind of war produced deaths so hideous, and on so massive a scale, that old canons of heroism had been rendered superfluous, if not ridiculous. What replaced them was not merely an acceptance of the horrors of this new kind of war, but these became the point of departure for a new being. "A race such as ours," Jünger proudly maintained, "has never before stepped into earth's arena." The war "carved and hardened us to that which we are . . . War is not only our father, but our son; we have sustained it, and it us."[9] This new type of creature, hardened as no other before him, would indeed make combat into a true "inner experience." War, Jünger maintained, was not the "source" of this new being's important characteristics. Rather, it was an "expression" of what had to be sought out "inwardly."[10]

Germany might well have been defeated, and it is sometimes overlooked that towards the end of the war Jünger himself recognized that the war had been lost.[11] In the end, though, war as a spiritual experience, one that had hardened a new generation, had won, and Jünger rejoiced in its triumph. Indeed the emergence of a new, battle-hardened man allowed war to be pursued to a hitherto unattainable but nonetheless logical conclusion. Here we can consider the words of the Free Corps man Friedrich Wilhelm Heinz: "The pure *Landsknechte* ['Freebooters'] didn't care much why or for whom they fought. The main thing for them was that they were fighting . . . War had become their career . . . They had no desire to look for another . . . War made them happy—what more can you ask? I liked this group."[12] For some of these self-consciously hardened men, the very country for which they fought did not seem to matter all that much. Jünger sneered at those benighted souls who had little sense for concepts such as "state and nation" but knew what *Heimat* meant. "This," the avid warrior declared, "is a feeling already sensed by plants."[13]

In point of fact, fighting for "nation" or "state" seemed not to be the main point either. What was of importance for Jünger at any rate was the willingness to fight for "an idea." Courage was the "hurling of the idea against the material." At the same time, *human beings* were material "which, without knowing it, the idea consumes for its own purposes."[14] What this "idea" in fact was supposed to be is, at least from this vantage point, unclear.

Certainly, Jünger and other Free Corps–like mentalities were nationalists. But in the end what was of ultimate importance was the will to accept the fact that "with our marching out, a hundred-years war had begun." And "a new race, self-educated through the hard nurturing of war, became visible."[15] Of course, particularly for one who never lost his sensitivity to those horrors he encountered every day, "hard nurturing" could be taxing. What allowed him to sustain, indeed advance, the hardening process was an ability to forget, at least consciously, events and circumstances that could spiritually destroy "normal" beings. In a most significant statement, Jünger remarked with regard to a particularly disquieting event: "We already would have forgotten it on the morrow.

We are regular forgetting machines."[16] At one point Jünger, like Marc before him, brought timeless natural processes into play. In *Das Wäldchen 125* (*Copse 125*), he rejoiced that in this new war's battles the soldier could "now again become nothing other than a piece of nature, which subordinates him to her impenetrable laws and is [thus] used as an essence of blood, muscle, tooth and claw."[17] Except as a collection of anecdotal paeans to the emergence of the "new man," memory—certainly historical memory, in any case—was to be abandoned in favor of subordination to timeless natural truths. Nature, of course, in its timelessness, has no memory, and thus a "forgetting machine" would be a quite logical expression of it.

With reason, Nazism is considered to be the most significant of the Great War's legacies. Over the years, increased attention has been devoted to analyzing the nature of Nazism itself, and with ample justification some have come to view it as a "secular religion."[18] As such it has to be seen as having a kind of logical consistency to it, even if one is constrained to draw a sharp line between what is "logical" and what is "rational." It is plain, though, that as part and parcel of a movement to which religious, even millenarian, motives can be ascribed, there was an element that does lend credence to Hermann Rauschning's description of Nazism as a "revolution of nihilism." This was the strong emphasis placed by its leading personalities, and no doubt a host of smaller fry as well, upon the ability to live with, indeed incorporate, brutalization: in a word, hardness. And, to be sure, all in the name of an "idea." Of course, one would be correct in raising the point that the National Socialist idea, that of the triumph and advancement of the "new, Aryan man," was a bit more coherent than that of Jünger and peers. Yet, it is plain that the measures to be used in the attainment of an Aryan utopia were not merely of faciliatory significance, but rather were congruent with the end itself.

It is true that, in *Mein Kampf*, Adolf Hitler graciously allowed for pacifism once Aryan supremacy had been assured.[19] Yet, both accompanying and informing such metahistorical speculations was Hitler's devotion to the "new man." According to Rauschning, Hitler himself, a self-proclaimed messenger of this being, was terrified of him. "He is here!," Hitler declared in 1934. "I will tell you a secret. I have seen the vision of the new man—fearless and formidable. I shrank from him."[20] What the features of this new man would be were obvious. German youth was enjoined to be "as tough as leather and as hard as Krupp steel" (which, one assumes, appreciated the free advertising). Why? Well, obviously, to fight the second Great War that was well on the way. But after that it would be war without end. Thus we can consider the following passages, drawn from *Hitler's Secret Conversations*:

For the good of the German people, we must wish for a war every fifteen or twenty years . . . Wars drive people to proliferation, they teach us not to fall into the error of being content with a single child in each family. (Night of August 19th–20th, 1941)

A permanent state of war on the Eastern front will help us to form a sound race of men, and will prevent us from relapsing into the softness of a Europe thrown back upon itself. (September 25, 1941, midday)

As a general principle, I think that a peace which lasts for more than twenty-five years is harmful to a nation. Peoples, like individuals, sometimes need regenerating through a little blood-letting. (Evening of August 26, 1942) [21]

What is plain is that Hitler looked forward to a kind of dystopian millennium in which, even after racial security had been assured, war would follow upon war. But why then would war be necessary? From what Hitler said one can only conclude that the "new man" was to be defined in terms of a war-grounded hardness to be treasured for its own sake. Certainly, despite occasional bows in the direction of the beauties of the German landscape, Germany itself did not matter all that much. In a conversation recorded on January 27, 1942, we find the following: "I see things with the coldest objectivity. If the German people loses its faith, if the German people were no longer inclined to give itself body and soul in order to survive—then the German people would have nothing to do but disappear!" [22]

Hitler, the heralder of the "new man," had little use for *Heimat*-sensibilities. As is well-known, in the last days of the war the *Führer* was eager that all of Germany be laid waste in the face of conquerors from the east; a people who through military success had demonstrated its superiority.[23] What had emerged as triumphant in the Hitlerian ideology was harshness, the ultimate instructor of "laws of life."

In the course of carrying out the "final solution," there were crucial tasks that had to be carried out. With regard to some of those most immediately involved, one can detect an almost self-congratulatory emphasis upon being able to stick with them. In a letter of October 19, 1942, *SS-Obersturmführer* Karl Kretschmer, engaged in *Einsatzgruppe* activities, wrote to his family that he was bothered from time to time with "*stupid thoughts*" concerning what he had to do. Then, appreciating that the latest action was "*justified*," he declared that the phrase "*stupid thoughts*" was not correct. "*Rather it is a weakness not to be able to stand the sight of dead people; the best way of overcoming it is to do it more often. Then it becomes a habit.*" [24]

In this most unusual of combat operations, a special type of hardness certainly was called for to see matters through to a successful conclusion. Yet there is the uncanny sense that somehow one emerged with one's character improved from participating in such events and being increasingly willing to engage in more of the same; that somehow hardness, toughness, whatever, had become as much a goal as a means of attaining one. Here, one can ponder perhaps the best-known words of the incredibly inelegant Heinrich Himmler:

> Most of you know what it means when 100 corpses are lying side by side, or 500 or 1,000. To have stuck it out and at the same time—apart from exceptions caused by human weakness—to have remained decent fellows, that is what has made us hard. This is a page of glory in our history which has never been written and is never to be written.[25]

After pondering such a statement, the following question comes to mind— to become "hard" toward what purpose? Once the Jews and other natural enemies had been exterminated, what next? History would not, could not, record the deeds themselves. In fact one gets the idea that for Himmler, history really did not matter very much anyway. Jünger's "forgetting machine," the embodiment of that hardness fitting for a "new man," had become integral to the attainment of goals that, in the final analysis, would produce—hardness. A timeless product of natural laws that Himmler, Hitler, and many others saw Nazism as embodying, the quality obviously was self-justifying.

Robert Whalen has concluded his fine work, *Bitter Wounds*, by applying Sigmund Freud's distinction between mourning and melancholia to post–Great War Germany. Mourning as Freud saw it involved confronting a loss, either personal or national, directly and in due course accepting it. Melancholia was informed by an unwillingness to confront loss directly. Rather, one immersed oneself in self-recrimination and a morbid inability to let go of a loss through accepting it. Loss of self-esteem was the inevitable result and if a person so afflicted did not seek psychological help the only ways out of a melancholic state were suicide or a kind of "manic activity."[26] Germany, Whalen has told us, was in a melancholic state, and those who hitched themselves to the Nazi star avoided confronting a recent humiliating loss by plunging themselves into manic activity whose idiom was brutality. It is plain that crucial to this idiom was the image of that hardened being that emerged as a positive product of the Great War.

Whether or not leading National Socialists read Jünger or others writing in a similar mode, it is plain that his killing automaton, the hardened "forgetting machine," was a being that could have emerged only from the German Great War experience. During the Holocaust, a forgetfulness that was supposed to annul history in the name of an idea grounded in nature was extolled as part and parcel of a sanctified hardening of that elite organization that was the basis of a "new man."

Even if he was never drawn to the National Socialist ideology, Ernst Jünger's mission as affirming the reality of the defeat-defying, toughened new man was completed in Heinrich Himmler's. Verdun, the Somme, Flanders/Babi Yar, Treblinka, Auschwitz—there were obvious linkages here, and certainly one of the most crucial of these was that of the hardened warrior, characterized by rage-tinged memory and an altogether understandable reliance upon historical amnesia. This allowed Hitler, who like Jünger truly came alive in the Great War, to remark after the Stalingrad battle had ended: "Man recovers very quickly." [27]

NOTES

1. Edwin Campion Vaughn, *Some Desperate Glory: The World War I Diary of a British Officer* (New York: Henry Holt & Co., 1981), 232.

2. Franz Marc, *Letters From the War*, ed. Klaus Lankheit and Uwe Steffen, trans. Liselotte Dieckmann (New York: Peter Lang, 1992), 58, 109.

3. Ibid., 112.

4. George L. Mosse, *Fallen Soldiers: Reshaping the Memory of the World Wars* (New York: Oxford University Press, 1990), chapter 7.

5. Ibid., chapter 8. Though first published in 1952, Robert G. L. Waite's work remains the best on the subject. See Waite, *Vanguard of Nazism: The Free Corps Movement in Postwar Germany, 1918–1923* (New York, W. W. Norton, 1969). A more recent work on the subject, Nigel H. Jones's *Hitler's Heralds: The Story of the Freikorps, 1918–1923* (New York: Dorset Press, 1992), while well-written and replete with interesting photographs, adds little to what Waite has said.

6. Erich Maria Remarque, *All Quiet on the Western Front*, trans. A. W. Wheen (New York: Ballantine Books, 1984), 186.

7. Ernst Jünger, *Der Kampf als inneres Erlebnis*, in *Ernst Jünger Werke*, vol. 5, Essays 1 (Stuttgart: Ernst Klett Verlag, 1960), 24. All translations are mine, unless otherwise noted.

8. As an example of this, see Robert Weldon Whalen, *Bitter Wounds: German Victims of the Great War, 1914–1939* (Ithaca: Cornell University Press, 1984), 45.

9. Jünger, *Der Kampf als inneres Erlebnis*, 13–14.

10. Ibid., 85. For a fascinating discussion of how participation in war can serve expressive needs, see Johannes Volmert, *Ernst Jünger: "In Stahlgewittern"* (Munich: Wilhelm Fink Verlag, 1985), 21ff.

11. As an example of this, see Ernst Jünger's *Das Wäldchen 125*, in *Ernst Jünger Werke*, vol. 1, *Tagebücher I* (Stuttgart: Ernst Klett Verlag, 1960), 399.

12. Waite, *Vanguard of Nazism*, 42.

13. Jünger, *Der Kampf als inneres Erlebnis*: 87.

14. Ibid., 52 and 85.

15. Jünger, *Das Wäldchen 125*, 393 and 462.

16. Jünger, *Der Kampf als inneres Erlebnis*, 84.

17. Jünger, *Das Wäldchen 125*, 349.

18. As examples of this see Friedrich Heer, *Der Glaube des Adolf Hitler: Anatomie einer politischen Religiosität* (Munich: Bechtle, 1968); Robert Pois, *National Socialism and the Religion of Nature* (London: Croom Helm, 1986); James M. Rhodes, *The Hitler Movement: A Modern Millenarian Movement* (Stanford: Stanford University

Press, 1980); Jean-Pierre Sironneau, *Sécularisation et religions politiques* (New York: Mouton, 1982).

19. Adolf Hitler, *Mein Kampf*, trans. Ralph Manheim (Boston: Houghton Miflin, 1943), 288.

20. Hermann Rauschning, *Hitler Speaks: A Series of Political Conversations With Adolph Hitler on His Real Aims* (London: Heinemann, 1939), 243. Over the years, there has been some debate over Rauschning's reliability as a historical source. Theodor Schieder, though, has made a convincing argument that while at times Rauschning probably was not being completely literal in his setting down Hitler's words, he came as close as some and closer than most to capturing Hitler's world view and thus should be taken seriously. See Theodor Schieder, *Hermann Rauschning's "Gespräche mit Hitler" als Geschichtsquelle* (Opladen: Westdeutscher Verlag, 1972).

21. Adolf Hitler, *Hitler's Secret Conversations: 1941–1944*, ed. H. R. Trevor-Roper, trans. Norman Cameron and R. H. Stevens (New York: Farrar, Straus and Young, 1953]), 23–24, 34, 537.

22. Ibid., 210.

23. See Albert Speer, *Inside the Third Reich: Memoirs*, trans. Richard and Clara Winston (New York: Macmillan, 1970), 440.

24. Ernst Klee, Willi Dressen, and Volker Riess, eds., *"The Good Old Days": The Holocaust as Seen by Its Perpetrators and Bystanders*, trans. Deborah Burnstone (New York: The Free Press, 1991), 171. Emphasis is the editors'.

25. Benjamin Sax and Dieter Kuntz, eds., *Inside Hitler's Germany: A Documentary History of Life in the Third Reich* (Lexington: D.C. Heath & Co., 1994 [orig. 1992]), 393. These words were delivered during the course of an address to SS personnel in Posen, October, 1943. Emphasis was Himmler's.

26. Whalen, *Bitter Wounds*, 182, 189–190.

27. William Craig, *Enemy at the Gates: The Battle for Stalingrad* (Toronto/New York: Bantam Books, 1982), 322.

3
Thinking the Nietzsche Legacy Today: A Historian's Perspective
STEVEN E. ASCHHEIM

To speak of the Nietzsche legacy today immediately alerts us to the historically conditioned dimension of Nietzsche appropriations, indeed, of "Nietzscheanism" itself. The interpretations and annexations of Nietzsche today differ from those of the past and—if you believe, as I do, that his protean relevance remains strikingly alive—presumably of the future as well. It would be only partly facetious to declare that every culture, every generation, every political movement constructs the Nietzsche (or Nietzsches) it deserves! Certainly, however, the nature and remarkably varied extent of Friedrich Nietzsche's impact upon politics, culture, and our collective and individual sense of self has always functioned as a historically dynamic phenomenon simultaneously influencing, reflecting, and being reshaped by the fluid political and cultural circumstances of which it was a part.[1]

The history of the manifold, still very-much alive, Nietzsche legacy has always operated as a relatively open-ended, reciprocal, creative process, that entailed selective filtering and constant interpretive reshaping of Nietzschean thematics according to divergent perceived needs. "Great men," Ernst Bertram wrote in 1918 (with Nietzsche specifically in mind), "are inevitably our creation, just as we are theirs."[2] The twentieth-century fin-de-siècle "Nietzsche" must be located not as some kind of ultimate statement but rather as part of this ongoing history and made amenable to the kind of historical analysis applicable to all other Nietzsche annexations. Nietzsche today must be considered precisely that—without foreclosing who or what he will be tomorrow.

If we are to get a proper historical handle on today's Nietzsche, to understand the elasticity and multiple implications of the legacy, we have to remind ourselves of something that twenty years ago was blatantly obvious but which today has been (or stands in danger of being) almost forgotten. If today's Nietzsche is, above all, the "postmodernist" Nietzsche, during the 1930s and

1940s the—not entirely implausible—Fascist and Nazi Nietzsche virtually eclipsed every other version.[3] To be sure, there were always dissenting voices both within and without the Nazi camp. Nevertheless, the paradigmatic Nietzsche of the 1930s, 1940s and early 1950s was the Nietzsche who was held to be the thinker most crucially and intimately definitive of the Nazi order. The resuscitation of Nietzsche and his appropriate reconstruction into a prophet eminently suited to postwar times (as he is refitted for all other times) required that he emigrate from Germany (where, until very recently, he remained a rather tarnished figure) into more hospitable waters. The work, which began in the early 1950s and has continued since then, was accomplished mainly in France and in the United States and was the product of two quite different intellectual forces.

First, Walter Kaufmann, Nietzsche's most insistent and influential postwar expositor, translator, and popularizer, exegetically sought to rid Nietzsche of these sullied associations and to provide him with the kind of liberal-humanist face consonant with American academic values of the time. His 1950 masterwork portrayed the "Nazified" Nietzsche as an almost wholly inexplicable distortion. Kaufmann's Nietzsche was essentially a good European, a thinker who had to be grasped in terms of his emphases on creativity, culture, and critical individualism and whose contempt for nationalism, racism, and anti-Semitism could not have been more apparent.[4]

Kaufmann was, of course, a more or less systematic philosopher who insisted upon pressing Nietzsche's thought into a comprehensible and comprehensive system. Such systematization is, of course, quite anathema to those who since, in a different, less liberally certain and determinate age, have most dominantly colonized Nietzsche (and at the same time been crucially shaped by him!)—those various exponents of what, for lack of a better name, we lump under the rubrics of "postmodernism," "poststructuralism," and "deconstructionism." Unlike Kaufmann, for them (with the conspicuous exception of Jacques Derrida[5]) the issue of National Socialism by and large goes virtually unmentioned, unnoticed; the very need to even engage the putative Nietzsche-Nazi link has been virtually obliterated. In obvious ways, their Nietzsche is quite dissimilar to Kaufmann's: this Nietzsche is the radically skeptical perspectivist, the anti-totalizing prophet of heterogeneity, fragmentation, and discontinuity.[6] But both—the poststructuralists and Kaufmann[7]—fashion an ultimately epistemological[8] and rather sterilized Nietzsche, shorn of all vestiges of his vitalist *Lebensphilosophie*, his eugenic prescriptions, and Great Politics of degeneration and regeneration.[9] If anything the post–World War II Nietzsche has undergone what appears to be a radical metamorphosis. Indeed, for many younger people educated from about the 1970s on, the Nietzsche-Nazism identification seems virtually incomprehensible. No longer the embodiment of National Socialism, he now is presented as its veritable antithesis, even its curative antidote.

There is a striking conjunction between the insistence upon Nietzsche's centrality and the putative pivotal role of Auschwitz in the very genesis and disposition of postmodernism (at least as far as many of its major proponents self-consciously define it). Nietzsche, we are constantly told, "paved the way for the philosophical concept of postmodernism" itself. In this view Lyotard's increasingly authoritative definition of postmodernism as a "distrust of metanarrative" is simply drawn from a particular strain within Nietzsche's thought.[10] And for Lyotard, it is the epoch-making event of Auschwitz that, above all, reveals the bankruptcy of the grand metanarratives of the Enlightenment and their accompanying belief in progress and reason. In a post-Auschwitz world these destructive totalizing, homogenizing, and manipulating modes must give way to essentially Nietzschean forms of heterogenous, pluralistic, and ironic narratives.[11]

We shall later critically elaborate on this conjunction. First, however, it is necessary to document and analyze Nietzsche's ubiquitous role, his insinuating presence, within the various poststructuralist sensibilities. In ways that would probably have both dismayed and delighted him, Nietzsche possesses virtual canonic status within a body of thought that seeks to problematize the very notion of canon.

Of course, it would be an error to lump all these trends and thinkers together. Not all are equally enthusiastic Nietzscheans and not all use him in the same way. Indeed, at times they critique each other. (Derrida once accused Foucault of a most un-Nietzschean act, that of "confirming metaphysics in its fundamental operation," perhaps the most dire deed in the entire deconstructionist lexicon.[12]) Yet, there can be little doubt that—together with another old Nietzschean, Martin Heidegger[13]—Nietzsche and what has been called his "unremitting interrogation of Western civilization"[14] figures most pivotally in this project. Derrida has analyzed this paradigmatic centrality in terms of the distinction between Nietzschean and Augustinian biography and the paradox of the proper name or signature: "It's always the same thing, but each time it's different; each time it's a different history to which one must pay close attention. In this way one may see, that, in spite of everything, finally . . . Nietzsche attempted something which . . . was, precisely, of a 'deconstructive' type."[15]

Nietzsche's genealogical conception of history, and what is taken to be—not always convincingly in my view—its radical problematizing of origins[16]; the emphasis on the discourse of power; the radically skeptical perspectivism; the experimental quest for self-creation; the fascination with the outer reaches of human experience (the realms of madness, cruelty, violence, and pain repressed by metaphysics and reason); the transgressive ("beyond good and evil"), "Dionysian" impulses; the dissolution—or better, the problematization—of the very category of the self; the notion that truth is alternatively illusory, metaphorical, and institutional; the sense of stylistic play, heterogeneity, indeterminacy, and rupture; these Nietzschean echoes are all indissolubly part of the postmodernist project. (This Nietzsche, we should note, is not all that new. Already in 1950—in his post-Nazi phase—the German expressionist poet Gottfried Benn wrote that Nietzsche had destroyed philosophy, theology, causality, eros, truth, being, and identity. There was no transcendental, binding Archimedean point. Nietzsche had demonstrated the error of assuming that humans had an intrinsic or metaphysical content. There was, indeed, no such thing as the "person"—there were only symptoms.[17])

Unlike the 1930s and 1940s, Nietzscheanism today is not most clearly and officially represented in the life and ideologies of radical political movements but more as an infiltrative atmospheric presence informing the culture, most centrally the academy, and defining the lives of particular individuals. The case of the most famous Nietzschean of our time, Michel Foucault, is too familiar to bear repeating in detail here but it does exemplify many of the above themes—and perhaps some of the hidden commonalities between the "older" Nietzsche and its putative contemporary opposite.[18] The centrality of Nietzsche to Foucault's project is not in dispute. His analyses of the historicity (rather than fictitiousness) of the constructed self as it emerges within shifting discourses and institutional settings and his perception that power creates its subjects (rather than being exercised by them) were explicitly inspired by Nietzsche as was his own individual quest to understand "how one becomes what one is."

Increasingly it has been established to what degree, however, Foucault's work and life—for Foucault, an ultimate Nietzschean, the two were utterly intertwined—consisted not (as so many of his admirers believed) of a critique, an attempt to escape the grasp of power, but as a celebration of it. His sadomasochism was a kind of exercise of the will-to-power, a fascination with the domination of self and other. What could be more resonantly Nietzschean than his disdainful definition of the humanist, Enlightenment tradition as "everything in Western civilization that restricts the desire for power." His *Discipline and Power*, as various commentators have recently pointed out, is replete with vitalistic reveling in blood and cruelty that stands in clear contrast to the demonization of the coolly efficient institutions of modern life.[19] The internalization of surveillance is condemned, as Mark Lilla has put it, not because it subtly perpetuates power but because it seeks to displace it from body to soul.[20] In Foucault's work, then, the question of nihilism is left wide open. In the absence of any unchangeable rule or norm the positive and destructive capacities of which Nietzsche spoke coalesce as permanent possibilities.

In various feminist quarters, and to a quite astonishing extent, this postmodernist Nietzsche similarly acts as inspirational source.[21] Derrida has spectacularly demonstrated the radical heterogeneities, the reversals, the encoded complexities of his treatment of women ("Nietzsche might well be lost in the web of his text, lost much as a spider who finds he is unequal to the web he has spun") and their centrality to his project.[22] But its politicization too often elides such complexities. Here Nietzsche is simply invoked "to find ways of understanding and affirming sexual differences that do not imply social relations of domination and subordination; . . . conceptions of power and practices of criticism which are not confined to the reactive perspective of slave morality; . . . the desire . . . to find . . . forms of relations to other, to knowledge and to self which might provide bases for less oppressive social relations."[23] The mighty exegetical efforts involved in suitably transforming the Zarathustran whip and the explicitly and radically antidemocratic, antiegalitarian Nietzsche into this soft humanizing role has not been lost even amongst the most enthusiastic of these circles.[24]

Contemporary feminist Nietzscheanism may have its own particular emphases[25] but, we should remind ourselves, it is no new creation. The same interpretive imperatives and tensions between Nietzsche's apparent dismissal of women and its exegetical interpretive overcoming, his radically emancipatory and transvaluative side[26] and his emphasis on a biologistic, essentialist conception of the "identity" of women—beset its advocates (many of whom flirted openly with various forms of bio-eugenic politics) as early as the 1890s.[27] It may be salutary to remember that historically there have been feminist Nietzscheans of all stripes. For example, the futurist-vitalist Valentine de Saint Point who sought "to make lust into a work of art" and, who argued that after battle "*it is normal for the victors to turn to rape in the conquered land, so that life may be re-created*," translated the notion of the Übermensch into a new myth of the masculinized Superwoman. Give woman, she proclaimed, "a war cry and with joy she will ride again on her instinct and lead you towards undreamed of conquests . . . *Let woman rediscover her own cruelty and violence that make her turn on the beaten* . . . and mutilate them."[28] While for some de Saint Point's construction may have been less attractive, can postmodernist method claim that it is less "true to the master" than the rival feminist appropriations of her own or the present day?

This is not the place to examine some of the more obvious transparencies involved in some of the postmodernist popularizations and political annexations of

Nietzsche. Still, it is worth quoting the conclusions of one recent commentator. Nietzsche's philosophy, he writes, appropriately purged of subjective political views, implies a "pluralistic society in which egalitarianism underwrites individuality."[29] The Nietzschean collapse of any metaphysical source of authority is held to bring liberation from repressive closures in discourse and practice, undreamed of transvaluations and a newfound freedom going beyond all previously sanctioned limits.

But only a very slightly developed historical sense will remind us of the irony that the advocate of the "merciless extermination" of the weak, the degenerate, and the parasitic—a man whose thought, whether parodistically or not, could be regarded as foundational to and definitive of the Nazi order—should now be commonly heralded as a powerful advocate of tolerance and *différence*, as spokesman for the emergence and protection of the powerless Other, as prophet of relationships shorn of domination.[30] In good deconstructionist manner we cannot know what Nietzsche *really* meant when he wrote that the Jews were the "most catastrophic people of world history," guilty of nothing less than the radical falsification of "all nature, all naturalness, all reality, of the whole inner world as well as the outer."[31] Good scholarship and Nietzsche apologists can no doubt casuistically explain and contextualize such remarks. But that is just the point. The history of Nietzsche appropriation is replete with just such casuistry by all interested sides; when anti-Semites—of the most radical kind—invoked and were influenced by such passages, they did not concern themselves with the finer points of textual emendation.[32] The current liberationist Nietzsche fits into a long tradition of Nietzsche appropriation by progressives of all sorts. It demonstrates the ongoing remarkable capacity to filter out an enormous amount of many very unambiguous and extreme antidemocratic, antisocialist, antiegalitarian, elitist, even eugenic and racist convictions.

But beyond this, and despite the purging of these overtly reactionary ingredients, for many observers Nietzschean postmodernism remains an object of suspicion. Jürgen Habermas has been arguing consistently that there are at least hidden similarities, unacknowledged affinities, between the "new" and the "old" Nietzsche.[33] Various critics have pointed to suspected commonalities of irrationalism, nihilism, and the concerted "attack" upon "the Enlightenment" and "reason." One would certainly not want to overdo this. Moreover, the social and political contexts out of which they emerge are fundamentally different. Still, the (widely-accepted) Lyotardian juxtaposition between a suspect Enlightenment and a liberatory postmodernism with which we began turns out to be far from clear-cut. In this reductive treatment of the Enlightenment, Terry Eagleton incisively writes that all narratives suffer a certain spurious homogenizing: "modernity" for Lyotard would seem *nothing* but a tale of terroristic Reason and Nazism, little more than the lethal terminus of totalizing thought. This reckless travesty ignores the fact that the death camps were among other things the upshot of a barbarous irrationalism which, like some aspects of postmodernism itself, junked history, refused argumentation, aestheticized politics and staked all on the charisma of those who told the stories.[34]

Needless to say, in the history of *critical* Nietzsche-reception, these are qualities that have quintessentially been associated with the master himself. The point is *not* to argue for some kind of vaunted lineage between postmodernism and Fascism (although it is worth noting the remarkable extent to which the whole debate over postmodernism has tended to revolve around accusations and counter-accusations of possible linkages to Nazism.) What is relevant in our context is, as Richard Wolin wryly puts it, that as a result of the poststructuralist "exclusively textualist understanding of Nietzsche's influence and impact, the historico-political ramifications of his doctrines are woefully undervalued."[35] It is perhaps the determined disdain for historical context and, indeed, for historical self-contextualization, that renders these positions less open to appreciate the highly ambiguous cultural and political implications of their own (almost always "postliberal") Nietzscheanism.

For all that, I believe the postmodernist insistence upon plurality and textuality to be very beneficial and in many ways my own conception of writing the history of the Nietzsche legacy has been shaped by the perception that Nietzsche has been read (and has encouraged such reading) in vitally heterogenous ways.[36] It may even very well be that, in normative terms, this appropriation *is* richer than most others for it incorporates and thematizes Nietzschean complexity and multiplicity into its own reading. But if the postmodernist Nietzsche emphasizes self-subversion, one wonders whether it leaves room for its own self-subversion. The deconstructionist insistence upon the openness of texts to historical and future others in principle opens up the way for its practitioners to regard themselves as also only part of an ongoing history, a chapter of an unfinished Nietzsche legacy. In practice, however, like many of the other competing "Nietzscheanisms" of the past, they have, in effect, "essentialized" the philosopher, and selectively molded what they take to be the "paradigmatically" postmodern Nietzsche.[37]

But if there is one constant in the history of Nietzsche-reception it is the perception, variously and continuously reinterpreted, of "essential" and "paradigmatic" Nietzsches. The notoriously vague and shifting meanings of terms like "modern," "modernism" and "postmodern" need not detain us here. Suffice it to say that, for our purposes, these designations may themselves be regarded as landmarks of changing modes of historical self-understanding, and that Nietzsche—the man of multiple faces—has consistently been regarded as the very exemplification of these changing paradigmatic conditions and self-representations.

Many contemporary critics argue that the construction of this poststructuralist Nietzsche in fact entails not the jettisoning of metaphysics but rather the elaboration of yet another sort (we leave aside the highly problematic claim that a politics shorn of metaphysics is a necessarily improved, freer sort of politics). They make the argument that Nietzsche himself was the first to see through such claims and that his intralinguistic play "does not amount to an absence of origins and absence of foundation," a mere play of signifiers, but an overabundance of plastic forces, a surplus of force, part of the *physics* of the will to power.[38] Indeed, some have claimed that, for all Nietzsche's iconoclasm (indeed, perhaps because of it) he remains, after all, fundamentally within the classical philosophical mode, a "seeker after truth."[39] One critic has recently gone so far as to suggest a "Nietzsche who is merely rehashing familiar Kantian themes, minus the rigor of Kant's exposition."[40] For these interpreters, Nietzsche has an insistently judgmental stance. Positing the principle of rank-order as overriding, such commentators argue, presupposes a "supraperspectival" truth that postmodernists deny.[41] They remind us that the canonic postmodernist Nietzschean text—"On Truth and Lie in an Extra-Moral Sense"[42]—was only published posthumously, and that many "deconstructionist" musings appeared in the *unpublished* notes to *The Will to Power*. Indeed, *this* Nietzsche very much insists both upon the notion and the possibility of "incorrect reading." In this view, the philosopher attacked specific modes of logic and rationality, not Western thought as a whole, disavowing particular conceptions of truth, not the possibility of truth as such. Very recently, John Richardson has written a work insisting upon "Nietzsche's System."[43] Such tendencies, while still rather inchoate, may herald a more than accidental effort to forge a fin-de-siècle Nietzsche quite different from both the dominant Nietzsche of the 1930s and 1940s and the prevailing deconstructionist one. It is a reaction that reflects both the exhaustion of the postmodernist thematics of indeterminacy[44] and perhaps the reassertion of an incipient (redefined) liberal impulse.

The signs of a weakening of the postmodernist impulse will be accompanied, almost by definition, not by the disappearance of Nietzsche (we will address the sources of his perennial fascination shortly) but rather his re-invention. This reinvention, like Nietzscheanisms of previous times, will seek to interpret the philosopher (partly consciously, partly unconsciously) within the prism of these changing political and cultural circumstances and sensibilities.

Nietzsche's "postmodern" guise will almost certainly not be the last word.[45] In its history, Nietzscheanism has assumed an astonishing variety of often quite incompatible forms (vegetarian, warrior, expressionist, socialist, Zionist, feminist, Nazi and Fascist, anarchist, sexual libertarian, and so on). While we cannot predict its future contours, the legacy will, in all probability, live on as a dynamic force and assume new forms, dangerous as well as potentially liberating, responding to the dilemmas and needs of changing times, integrated into our own tentative self-definitions and representations.

Nietzsche, however understood, is not likely to leave us because of his almost uncanny ability to define—and embody—the furthest reaches of the general post-Enlightenment predicament; to encapsulate many of its enduring spiritual and intellectual tensions, contradictions, hopes, and possibilities. Admirers, opponents, and critics alike have always agreed that one did not simply read Nietzsche; rather as Thomas Mann put it in 1918, one "experienced" him.[46] More than any other modern thinker he has acted as a kind of seismometer of our spiritual and intellectual life, a personalized stamping ground and battlefield upon which its tensions, conflicts, contradictions, and possibilities have been played out.[47] From the 1890s through to the present, his life and thought have provided an acutely relevant prism through which to express and confront the changing meanings and problems of a fluid, always unclear, yet ultimate modernity, most radically conceived, in the words of Leszek Kolawkoski, as the belief "in the unlimited possibility of mankind's self-creation"[48] and characterized by the predicament of nihilism and its interconnected transvaluative liberating and cataclysmic potential. Because he has defined, stands so close to the center of, our ongoing concerns, Nietzsche has not been exhausted by—nor can he be reduced to—any particular political system or cultural movement or historical time frame. His legacy, and its immense capacity for creative renewal, will persist (as will the opposition to it). Our relationship to him will, surely, continue to confirm Ernst Bertram's dictum that "great men are inevitably our creation, just as we are theirs."

NOTES

1. I have explored this in detail for the German case in *The Nietzsche Legacy in Germany, 1890–1990* (Berkeley: University of California Press, 1992).

2. Ernst Bertram, *Nietzsche: Versuch einer Mythologie* (Berlin: G. Bondi, 1918), 5.

3. See chapters 8, 9, and "Afterword" in Aschheim, *The Nietzsche Legacy* (see note 1).

4. Walter Kaufmann, *Nietzsche: Philosopher, Psychologist, Antichrist* (Princeton, NJ: Princeton University Press, 1950).

5. Derrida has considered this question in detail in "Otobiographies: The Teaching of Nietzsche and the Politics of the Proper Name," in Christie V.

McDonald, ed., *The Ear of the Other: Otobiography, Transference, Translation*, trans. Peggy Kamuf and Avital Ronell (New York: Schocken, 1985); see esp. 23–24, 30–31.

6. Our culture is awash with this Nietzsche. All the above-named authors' works should be consulted. For typical examples of this genre among many see Clayton Koelb, ed., *Nietzsche as Postmodernist: Essays Pro and Contra* (Albany: State University of New York Press, 1990); and David B. Allison, ed., *The New Nietzsche: Contemporary Styles of Interpretation* (Cambridge: MIT Press, 1985).

7. On Kaufmann's denaturing of Nietzsche's power-political dimensions, see Walter H. Sokel, "Political Uses and Abuses of Nietzsche in Walter Kaufmann's Image of Nietzsche," *Nietzsche-Studien* 12 (1983): 436–442.

8. See Ernst Behler, "Nietzsche jenseits der Dekonstruktion," in Josef Simon, ed., *Nietzsche und Hegel*, in the "Nietzsche in der Diskussion" series (Würzburg: Königshausen & Neumann, 1985), 88–107.

9. For an interesting postmodernist exception, see Avital Ronell's application of Nietzschean immunological themes to current Californian problematics in "Hitting the Streets" in her *Finitude's Score: Essays for the End of the Millennium* (Lincoln and London: University of Nebraska Press, 1994), esp. 47–61.

10. "Introduction," in Koelb, *Nietzsche as Postmodernist*, 5.

11. See Jean-François Lyotard, *The Postmodern Condition: A Report on Knowledge*, trans. Geoff Bennington and Brian Massumi (Minneapolis: University of Minnesota Press, 1984).

12. Of Foucault's *Madness and Civilization*, Derrida wrote: "The attempt to write the history of the decision, division, difference, runs the risk of construing the division of an event or a structure subsequent to the unity of an original presence, thereby confirming metaphysics in its fundamental operation." Jacques Derrida, "Cogito and the History of Madness," in his *Writing and Difference* (London: Routledge, 1981), 40.

13. See Gregory Bruce Smith, *Nietzsche, Heidegger and the Transition to Postmodernity* (Chicago: University of Chicago Press, 1996).

14. Jacques Derrida, *Spurs. The Styles of Nietzsche*, trans. Barbara Harlow (Chicago: University of Chicago Press, 1979), 75.

15. Jacques Derrida, *The Ear of the Other* (Lincoln: University of Nebraska Press 1985), 84–85. On Derrida's relation to Nietzsche see Michel Haar, "The Play of Nietzsche in Derrida," in David C. Wood, ed., *Derrida: A Critical Reader* (Oxford: Blackwell, 1992), 52–71.

16. See the interesting volume edited by Richard Schacht, *Nietzsche, Genealogy, Morality: Essays on Nietzsche's "Genealogy of Morals"* (Berkeley: Univ. of California Press, 1994); and "Translating, Repeating, Naming: Foucault, Derrida, and *The Genealogy of Morals*" in Koelb, *Nietzsche as Postmodernist*.

17. Gottfried Benn, "Nietzsche: Nach Fünfzig Jahren," in Dieter Wellershoff, ed., *Essays. Reden. Vorträge* (Wiesbaden: Limes, 1965), 488–493.

18. Here the French connection to Georges Bataille comes to mind. That early most radically transgressive Nietzschean, a man of the left who flirted with and who was, for a time, attracted to the irrationalist Fascist thematic, displayed a radicalism, an attraction to the transgressive beyond, that parallels Foucault.

19. I have summed up the scholarship from a number of sources. The biography by Jim Miller, *The Passion of Michel Foucault* (New York: Anchor Books, 1993), is

basic here. See too Alexander Nehamas, "Subject and Abject: The Examined Life of Michel Foucault," in *The New Republic* (February 15, 1993).

20. See Mark Lilla's insightful remarks in "A Taste for Pain: Michel Foucault and the Outer Reaches of Human Experience," *Times Literary Supplement* (March 26, 1993), 3–4.

21. For a good survey and analysis of these trends, see Robert C. Holub, "Nietzsche and the Women's Question," *The German Quarterly* 68:1 (1995): 67–71.

22. Cf. Derrida, *Spurs / Nietzsche's Styles*, 101.

23. Paul Patton, ed., *Nietzsche, Feminism and Political Theory* (New York: Routledge, 1993), xi.

24. See Diana Behler, "Nietzsche and Postfeminism," *Nietzsche-Studien* 22 (1993): 354–370. For another recent consideration of the issue, see Peter Burgard, ed., *Nietzsche and the Feminine* (Charlottesville: University of Virginia Press, 1994).

25. For a recent example, see Kelly Oliver, *Womanizing Nietzsche: Philosophy's Relation to the "Feminine"* (New York: Routledge, 1995).

26. Throughout the history of this legacy the appeal to any number of (left and right) political positions has been the radical Nietzschean promise—present but never clearly articulated; this after all, was the job of individual self-creation—of personal and collective transvaluation going beyond all previously thinkable forms. What some feminists today regard as the necessary feminine transvaluations—the peace-loving, antiwar, nurturing feminine values—will not be easily reconciled with the kind of vitalist transvaluation Nietzsche so graphically outlined in many of his works.

27. Cf. Aschheim, *The Nietzsche Legacy*, 85–92.

28. Valentine de Saint Point, "Futurist Manifesto of Lust 1913," in Umbro Apollonio, *Futurist Manifestos* (New York: Viking, 1973), 70–74; and her "Manifesto of the Futurist Woman" (1912), in Karl Hulten, ed., *Futurism and Futurisms* (New York: Abbeville Press, 1986), 602–603. Emphasis original.

29. Mark Warren, *Nietzsche and Political Thought* (Cambridge, MA: MIT Press, 1988), 157.

30. In an acute review of my work, John Toews commented that it would have been better had I revealed the ethical and value-laden contours of my own construction of the historic constructions of Nietzsche. These, I should have stressed, were clearly marked by my quest to understand the murderousness of the Nazis and a sense that—no matter how parodistically—Nietzsche was somehow implicated in this. At the same time, I also believe that his thought is too rich and complex to be simplistically reduced to this one historical outcome. See John E. Toews's review of *The Nietzsche Legacy* in *Central European History* 26:3 (1993): 353–355.

31. Friedrich Nietzsche, "The Antichrist," in Walter Kaufmann, ed. and trans., *The Portable Nietzsche*, (New York: Viking, 1961), 592–593.

32. See my paper, "Nietzsche, Anti-Semitism and the Holocaust," in Jacob Golomb, ed., *Nietzsche and Jewish Culture* (London: Routledge, 1995), 3–20.

33. Jürgen Habermas, *The Philosophical Discourse of Modernity: Twelve Lectures*, trans. Frederick G. Lawrence (Cambridge: MIT Press, 1987).

34. Terry Eagleton, "Awakening From Modernity," *Times Literary Supplement* (February 20, 1987), 194.

35. See the "Introduction" to Richard Wolin, *Labyrinths: Explorations in the Critical History of Ideas* (Amherst: University of Massachusetts Press, 1995), 2. I

must point out that I do not concur with Wolin's rather undifferentiated onslaught on postmodernist positions.

36. This may be the place to situate myself within this problematic. As Eagleton has pointed out (in *Against the Grain*, 85) both metaphysicians and "wild" deconstructionists believe that unless you have the "whole truth" you have none at all. I would agree with Eagleton that radical contextualization for the historian does not mean the subversion of the truth but only adequate understanding of and tentative approach to it.

37. Cf. Koelb, "Introduction," *Nietzsche as Postmodernist*, esp. 6–8.

38. Haar, "The Play of Nietzsche," 57, 65.

39. Maudemarie Clark, "Language and Deconstruction: Nietzsche, de Man, and Postmodernism," in Koelb, ed., *Nietzsche as Postmodernist*.

40. Ken Gemes, "Nietzsche's Critique of Truth," *Philosophy and Phenomenological Research* 52.1 (1992): 49.

41. See Ted Sadler, "The Postmodernist Politicization of Nietzsche," in Paul Patton, ed., *Nietzsche, Feminism and Political Theory* (New York: Routledge, 1993), 225–243. See also Brian Leiter, "Perspectivism in Nietzsche's Genealogy of Morals," in Schacht, ed., *Nietzsche, Genealogy, Morality*, 334–357.

42. See Kaufmann, ed., *The Portable Nietzsche*, 42–47.

43. John Richardson, *Nietzsche's System* (New York: Oxford University Press, 1996).

44. For an instructive assessment see Walter Laqueur, "Fin-de-Siècle: Once More With Feeling," *Journal of Contemporary History* 31 (1996): 5–47.

45. See the interesting critical comments by Robert C. Solomon, "Nietzsche, Postmodernism and Resentment: A Genealogical Hypothesis," in Koelb, ed., *Nietzsche as Postmodernist*, esp. 291–293.

46. Thomas Mann, *Reflections of a Nonpolitical Man*, trans. Walter D. Morris (New York: Frederick Ungar, 1983), 13.

47. This has been recognized since Nietzsche-reception began. See Gerhard Hilbert, *Moderne Willensziele* (Leipzig: Deichert, 1911), 19. This was a very common theme adjusted to suit the proclivities of the particular commentator. Thus as one early commentator put it, Nietzsche's struggle against his own time and the Christianity of his age was the "anticipation of our own struggle," while "Nietzsche's inner tension, from which his spirit sprang, is our tension." Theodor Odenwald, *Friedrich Nietzsche und das heutige Christentum* (Giessen: Alfred Töpelmann, 1926), 17, 23. Nietzsche, Mann wrote in a similar vein, was a kind of incarnation, a "personality of phenomenal cultural plenitude and complexity, summing up all that is essentially European." Mann, "Nietzsche's Philosophy in the Light of Contemporary Events" (1947), in *Thomas Mann's Address: Delivered at the Library of Congress 1942–1949* (Washington: Library of Congress, 1963), 69. Most recently Ernst Nolte has revived this notion of Nietzsche as a personalized "battleground" (*Schlachtfeld*) in his *Nietzsche und der Nietzscheanismus* (Frankfurt a.M.: Propyläen, 1990). See chapter 9 of Aschheim, *The Nietzsche Legacy*, for a critical discussion of this work.

48. "On the So-Called Crisis of Christianity," in Leszek Kolakowski's *Modernity on Endless Trial* (Chicago: University of Chicago Press, 1990), 90–91. See also his fascinating reflections on the complexity of Nietzsche's modernity in the opening essay (from which the book takes its title), especially 8–9.

4
Anti-Semitism and the Judiciary in the Federal Republic of Germany
RAINER HERING

The judiciary in Germany is, in general, traditionally associated with conservative politics in the same way the issue of "law and order" is connected with conservative and right-wing political groups. A tendency of judicial leniency toward the extremist or radical right is frequently assumed by leftist organizations. While a full-grown right-wing bias has been documented in Germany during the Weimar Republic, very little work has yet been done on the judiciary in the Federal Republic of Germany, although it is a well-known fact that most of the members of the judiciary did not suffer a break in their careers after 1945, but continued in their careers much the same as before, or went into retirement on full pensions.

A few cases from the middle of the 1990s have currently heightened the sensitivity for undue leniency toward offences committed by persons with a right-wing background. In this connection it is important to realize that in German law there exists an offence called *Volksverhetzung* (translated below as "unlawful political incitement"), which makes the distribution of extremist right-wing propaganda concerning the Third Reich punishishable by law, especially if it is anti-Semitic. The offence includes denying the Holocaust and disseminating racist thought. As such it is a legal limitation of freedom of speech, which is causally related to German history in the first half of this century. This essay, while it takes up the recent cases, is mainly concerned with the situation in the late 1950s, especially with a judicial decision that led to major changes in legal requirements.

In 1994, judge Rainer Orlet in Mannheim made national and international headlines. Orlet had passed judgement on Günter Deckert, aged 55, leader of the National Democratic Party (*Nationaldemokratische Partei* [NPD]). In his verdict he showed an understanding bordering on agreement with the party's right-wing and anti-Semitic ideology and declared himself to be impressed by

Deckert's straightforward character. Günter Deckert joined the NPD in 1965 at the age of 25. From 1971 he worked as a high-school teacher until he was dismissed in 1988 for his unconstitutional political activities. In 1991, Deckert translated a lecture by Fred Leuchter, an American, who denies that Jews had been systematically killed with cyanide gas in German concentration camps during the Third Reich, and afterwards stated that he agreed with Leuchter's arguments. One year later the district court in Mannheim convicted Deckert of unlawful political incitement and sentenced him to a prison sentence of one year with probation.[1] In 1994 the federal supreme court reversed this verdict and the case was again referred to the district court for reconsideration. The judges came to the same conclusion and reinstated the former sentence of a year in prison with probation, but this time the grounds became a point of public interest. The verdict, mainly written by Judge Orlet, stated that Deckert was not an anti-Semite, but that he disliked the Jews' insistence on the Holocaust and their demand for political, economic, and moral compensation and atonement. It said the court felt sorry for Deckert and for his dismissal due to his unconstitutional political activities. Orlet declared himself impressed by Deckert's behavior during the trial, noting his straightforward character and responsible personality. Deckert was, according to Orlet, only fighting for his political goals energetically and with conviction; he was, the court said, trying to strengthen the German resistance (*Widerstandskräfte im deutschen Volk*) against Jewish demands. The court accepted it as a fact that fifty years after the end of World War II the Germans are still paying for the persecution of the Jews during the Third Reich politically, economically, and morally, while crimes of other nations are disregarded in comparison. Playing down the importance of Deckert's role in German right-wing extremism, Orlet concluded that the accused was a respectable family man whose only offence was to have uttered an unguarded statement.[2] This verdict and especially the grounds for it raised protests in Germany and other countries.[3] Chancellor Helmut Kohl joined the critics and called the verdict a "disgrace."[4]

So who is Judge Rainer Orlet? He is the son of an engineer and was born in Reichenberg (in the former Czechoslovakia) on March 29, 1935. In 1945 his family had to leave Reichenberg and went to Merseburg, in the territory of what four years later became the German Democratic Republic. From 1953 to 1954 he studied Slavic languages at the University of Halle/Saale, after which he studied law at the University of Heidelberg in the Federal Republic of Germany, graduating in 1958. Five years later he passed the second exam and was appointed judge. Orlet first worked at the district court in Heidelberg, and after 1975 in Mannheim (*Richter am Landgericht*).[5]

Orlet's decision has meanwhile been overturned by the federal supreme court and Deckert has been sentenced to two years in prison.[6] The parliament of Baden-Württemberg considered accusing Orlet of having perverted the course of justice, which would have been the first time for such an accusation against the German judiciary.[7] However, Orlet went into early retirement for health reasons in May 1995, so the case was dropped.[8]

In an unrelated decision in February 1995, the district court of Hamburg acquitted the operator of a "national" telephone information line that called into doubt the existence of death camps in Nazi Germany, referring to the "Auschwitz Myth." The judge found it impossible to treat the term "Auschwitz Myth" as the equivalent of "Auschwitz Lie," the use of which is punishable by German law. Many people could not see a difference and felt helpless and angry.[9]

Although these are isolated cases, they lead to questions about whether there are any overall ideological tendencies in the German judiciary. No judge or prosecutor has ever been sentenced for being involved in passing unlawful or cruel verdicts during the Third Reich. Was the continuity in the judiciary limited to personnel? Or is there a tradition of leniency toward right-wing agitators in the German judiciary even after 1945?

A major impact on legislation against unlawful political incitement was produced by a very influential case from the 1950s. In 1959 the case of Friedrich Nieland caused a scandal when a judge named Enno Budde refused to initiate legal proceedings against the author of an anti-Semitic pamphlet. This case is also important for the history of the judiciary, because here there is a rather obvious connection between the political behavior of a judge during the Nazi regime and his subsequent verdicts in postwar West Germany.[10]

In 1957 a timber dealer named Friedrich Heinrich Wilhelm Nieland (1896–1973) published a pamphlet entitled "How Many World [Money] Wars Will the Peoples Have to Lose?"[11] The thirty-nine pages were printed in the right-wing publishing house of Heimberg in Stade near Nieland's hometown of Hamburg.[12] Two thousand copies were sent out to all members of the federal and state parliaments and government. Friedrich Nieland warned of a Third World War, which some hundred Jews were preparing, and declared that the murder of the Jews in concentration camps by the Nazis had actually been organized and perpetrated by an international conspiracy of Jews. He demanded that no Jew should have a job with power and influence, neither in a government nor in political parties nor in a bank. He argued:

> The outrageous lie about the gassing and slaughtering of six million Jews by Germans under Hitler's power is in itself as absurd as possible. First and fore-

most, it is incontestably true that the organizers of this mass extermination of Jews were not Germans, but themselves Jews. . . .

No Jew must be allowed to occupy an influential position, whether in a government, in political parties, in banking or elsewhere.[13]

Maxim Kuraner (1901–1978), Social Democratic member of the parliament of Rhineland-Palatinate, made this pamphlet public and instituted legal proceedings. The prosecuting attorney in Hamburg brought charges against Nieland and Heimberg, but the first division for criminal matters of the provincial high court and court of appeal that had jurisdiction over political offences refused to open the trial. Instead there was a second investigation by the court. A psychiatrist analyzed Nieland and did not find him mentally ill.[14] The court under the chairmanship of Judge Enno Budde (1901–1979) closed the case without filing a charge or conducting a hearing. The court decided it would be impossible to prove that Nieland and Heimberg wanted to overthrow democracy:

> Against the accusation of having promoted antisemitic tendencies in their publication, the defendants defend themselves by stating they had had no intention of accusing the Jews as such, but only a closely circumscribed circle of Jews. . . . An intention to endanger the state cannot be established with sufficient certainty, especially as it seems questionable whether the publication can be said to be consistent, logically developed and sound in its inferences. . . . It is impossible to prove with sufficient certainty . . . that the defendants intended to replace the free democratic constitutional structure of the state with tyranny and despotism.[15]

The public prosecutor protested this decision but the first criminal divison of the court of appeal under the chairmanship of Dr. Otto Erich Herr (1893–1979) did not recognize the new arguments and upheld Budde's ruling. Hence it was subsequently impossible to institute proceedings against Nieland.[16] Herr's political past is interesting: son of a timber dealer, Herr was a member of a volunteer corps (the *Bahrenfelder Freikorps*) after the First World War and joined the National Socialist Party (NSDAP) on May 1, 1933. He was a friend of the Nazi senator Curt Rothenberger (1896–1959).[17]

Budde's decision caused particular public indignation and many individuals and organizations protested against it, e.g., the German Federation of Labor (*Deutscher Gewerkschaftsbund*) and the Central Council of Jews in Germany (*Zentralrat der Juden in Deutschland*). The Bundestag was called upon to create a law to prevent such decisions in the future.[18] Hamburg's mayor Max Brauer (1887–1973) visited Chancellor Konrad Adenauer in Bonn to discuss the incident on January 8, 1959. Six days later the Federal Cabinet passed the draft version of a "law against incitement of the people," which came into effect one year later.[19] It was considered extremely important to be able to follow up and punish anti-Semitic agitation.[20]

Although nearly every public statement concerning the case assumed that Judge Budde had strictly legal reasons for his decision, the magazine *Der Spiegel* and the Social Democratic newspaper *Hamburger Echo* made a connection between Budde's political behavior under the Nazis and the Nieland ruling. If one takes a closer look at his personnel and denazification files it is obvious that they were right: Budde had himself published anti-Semitic articles during the Third Reich. So who was Enno Budde? Born in 1901 and the son of a protestant pastor in Hamburg, Budde studied law and economics, finishing his dissertation in 1927. In July 1933 he became assistant judge in Hamburg, and in December 1934 he was appointed judge there.[21]

Budde started his political activities early. He joined the *Deutsch-Hannoversche Partei* in 1923, for which his father had been a candidate, running for a seat both in the Hamburg parliament and at the federal level without success. The *Deutsch-Hannoversche Partei* aspired to reestablish the Kingdom of Hannover; the so-called Guelphs (*Welfen*) aimed to break Prussian influence and power in Lower Saxony.[22] In 1927, Budde found himself on the wrong side of the bar and was fined 600 Reichsmarks—instead of six weeks in prison—because he had broken the law of protecting the Republic (*Republikschutzgesetz*). In a newspaper article Budde had referred to the Prussian colors as "foreign filth."[23] His later articles also had antidemocratic and anti-Prussian tendencies.[24] At that time Budde thought he would never be able to work in the civil service as a judge.

But times changed: on May 1, 1933, Enno Budde joined the NSDAP, and by 1937 he had been promoted to state judge. His political attitude during the NSDAP rule was called "perfect" (*einwandfrei*).[25] One might speculate that Budde's National Socialist activities had been aimed at getting himself a position in the judiciary, however, in 1933 he was not unemployed, and he even had a good position as secretary of a trade corporation. In addition to his party membership he also published anti-Semitic articles; thus one can assume that Budde enthusiastically supported at least the anti-Semitic racist parts of the Nazi ideology. In 1935 he emphasized the importance of keeping the (Aryan) race pure and free of Jewish influence, using Nazi terms like *artfremd*, *artzersetzend*, and *Blut und Boden*:

> . . . keeping the race pure is vital to its preservation . . . In the beginning of the 19th century, Jewish emancipation and the liberation of the peasants posed a new danger to blood and soil. . . . On the whole, blood and soil [proponents] in Lower Saxony have defied the liberalist tendencies of our time and have preserved their very own character, right up until National Socialism started its own

legislation to protect blood and soil. . . . Likewise, in the Aryan laws and the Act for the Prevention of Offspring with Hereditary Diseases, we re-find concepts from the old Lower Saxon law.[26]

In another article he argued that race and blood were a grace given by God: "Race and blood do not exist for or by themselves. Rather, they are a gift of grace entrusted to us by God. They are god-given greatness."[27] Budde also praised Adolf Hitler for the present national and racial reorientation in Germany.[28] All these facts were listed in Budde's denazification proceedings, but with the help of seventeen sworn testimonies (*Persilscheine*) he managed to present himself as part of the resistance against National Socialism and was categorized as "V—Persons Exonerated (*unbelastet*)" and in 1947 he was even promoted to director of the state court.[29]

The Hamburg parliament discussed the position of judges and the judiciary in the wake of Budde's decision. The Social Democrat senator Dr. Paul Nevermann (1902–1979) quoted several other of Budde's verdicts. For instance, a former prisoner of a concentration camp had instituted proceedings against a former guard for knocking out his teeth. During the trial Budde asked him why he had accused the guard—since they were both reserve officers they should have settled the matter out of court. Another former prisoner brought a charge of having been mistreated once during a series of ten interrogations. Budde refused to believe the accusation on the grounds that he thought it unlikely that mistreatment should have occurred only once in ten interrogations, and therefore decided that the man had probably not been mistreated at all. The federal supreme court reversed that decision and another judge sentenced the accused to one and a half years in prison.[30]

In the public debate that followed the Nieland ruling, Budde got prominent help from the well-known professor of protestant theology Helmut Thielicke (1908–1986). In his article with the suggestive title "Anti-Antisemitism in Hamburg," Thielicke maintained that Budde had been the victim of a smear campaign and disputed the right of the press to assume other than juridical arguments for Budde's decision. He pronounced the allusions to Budde's political past to be defamatory, without actually engaging any of the arguments. Thielicke's use of the term "Anti-Antisemitism" suggested the critique of anti-Semitism to be on the same level as anti-Semitism itself.[31] The head of the state press office, Erich Lüth (1902–1989), called Thielicke's article infamous and declared he was turning the truth upside down.[32]

As a consequence of the public debate about the "Nieland case," which was transformed more and more into the "Budde case," Enno Budde had himself transferred to a civil chamber where he worked until retirement in 1969.[33]

The "Nieland case" makes it obvious that research on the history of the judiciary should recognize continuities between the Nazi period and the Federal Republic of Germany (FRG). Whether one is dealing here with an isolated instance or a typical case can only be decided after further study. At the very least, however, it shows how important it is that the history of the judiciary analyze the texts of verdicts passed after 1945 in conjunction with the biographical background of the judges involved.

I would like to thank Katrin U. Grunwaldt and Gale B. Willcox for their help and encouragement with earlier versions of this essay.

NOTES

1. "Volksverhetzung in Tateinheit mit übler Nachrede, Verunglimpfung des Andenkens Verstorbener und Aufstachelung zum Rassenhaß" (Verdict of November 13, 1992, quoted in *Frankfurter Rundschau* 185 [August 11, 1995]: 10). On Leuchter cf. Deborah Lipstadt, *Denying the Holocaust. The Growing Assault on Truth and Memory* (New York: Plume, 1994).

2. Excerpts of the verdict are documented in *Frankfurter Rundschau* 185 (August 11, 1995): 10.

3. Cf. *Frankfurter Rundschau* 184 (August 10, 1994): 1, 3, 4; Jörg Friedrich, "Die wahre Auschwitz-Lüge," *die tageszeitung* (August 11, 1994); *Hamburger Morgenpost* 186 (August 11, 1994): 2, 3; *Frankfurter Rundschau* 185 (August 11, 1994): 1, 3; *Hamburger Abendblatt* 187 (August 12, 1994): 1, 2; *Frankfurter Rundschau* 186 (August 12, 1994): 1, 3; *Focus* 33 (August 15, 1994): 24–26; *Frankfurter Rundschau* 190 (August 17, 1994): 1, 3, 4.

4. *Frankfurter Rundschau* 188 (August 15, 1994): 4.

5. In 1976 Orlet finished his dissertation on the beginning of canon law during the first six centuries A.D. (*Die Anfänge kirchlicher Rechtssetzung bis in das sechste Jahrhundert*, published in Munich, 1976). The biographical information is given by himself at the end of his dissertation.

6. *Frankfurter Rundschau* 292 (December 16, 1994): 1, 3, 4; *Die Zeit* 52 (December 23, 1994): 4; *Frankfurter Rundschau* 94 (April 22, 1995): 1, 3, 4; *Hamburger Abendblatt* 94 (April 22, 1995): 4; *Frankfurter Rundschau* 251 (October 28, 1995): 1.

7. Accusing a judge finds its legal basis in Article 98 of the German constitution, but has never been used in the Federal Republic of Germany. Cf. Ernst Benda, "Ab ins Grundbuchamt? Richter Orlet sollte vor dem Bundesverfassungsgericht angeklagt werden," *Die Zeit* 12 (March 17, 1995): 10. Reprinted as "Antisemitismus in öffentlichen Konflikten. Kollektives Lernen in der politischen Kultur der Bundesrepublik 1949–1989" (Frankfurt and New York: Campus, 1997), 208–221.

8. *Frankfurter Rundschau* 109 (May 11, 1995), 1, 3; *Frankfurter Rundschau* 115 (May 18, 1995): 4. At that time, Orlet dissociated himself from his own verdict for the first time (*Hamburger Abendblatt* 105 [May 6, 1995]: 2; *Frankfurter Rundschau* 105 [May 6, 1995]: 5).

9. *Hamburger Abendblatt* 45 (February 22, 1995): 14; *die tageszeitung* (February 23, 1995): 5, 10, 21. The judgement is documented in *Frankfurter Rundschau* 54 (March 4, 1995): 16.

10. The original files of the "Nieland-Case" could no longer be found in the registration of the prosecuting attorney's office (phone call with Judge Peter Niemeyer, April 23, 1997). Although the Nieland case was very influential, it did not excite scientific interest for a long time. Two articles cited the case but did not go into detail: Klaus-Henning Rosen, "Vorurteile im Verborgenen. Zum Antisemitismus in der Bundesrepublik Deutschland," in Herbert A. Strauss and Norbert Kampe, eds., *Antisemitismus. Von der Judenfeindschaft zum Holocaust*, Schriftenreihe der Bundeszentrale für politische Bildung, Nr. 213 (Bonn: Bundeszentrale, 1984), 256–279, 266; Werner Bergmann, "Antisemitismus in öffentlichen Konflikten 1949–1994," in Wolfgang Benz, ed., *Antisemitismus in Deutschland. Zur Aktualität eines Vorurteils* (Munich: Deutscher Taschenbuch Verlag, 1995), 64–88, esp. 73–75. For a detailed reconstruction see Rainer Hering, "Der 'Fall Nieland' und sein Richter. Zur Kontinuität in der Hamburger Justiz zwischen 'Drittem Reich' und Bundesrepublik," *Zeitschrift des Vereins für Hamburgische Geschichte* 81 (1995): 207–222. For a sociological analysis, see Werner Bergmann, *Öffentliche Konflikte und kollektive Lernprozesse. Antisemitismus als Thema in der Öffentlichkeit der Bundesrepublik Deutschland 1949–1989*, Habil. ms., (Berlin 1995), 260–293.

11. Friedrich Nieland, *Wieviel Welt [Geld]-Kriege müssen die Völker noch verlieren? Offener Brief an alle Bundesminister und Parlamentarier der Bundesrepublik* (Stade: Heimberg, 1957).

12. Adolf Ernst Peter Heimberg (1881–1973) was one of the leading members of the anti-Semitic Deutschvölkischer Schutz- und Trutzbund (DSTB, 1919–1922), an association that was disbanded after the murder of Walter Rathenau. In 1921, Heimberg published a book by Alfred Roth (1879–1948), who was secretary of the DSTB, as well as several other national and anti-Semitic publications (cf. Hering, "Fall Nieland", 208).

13. Nieland, "Welt (Geld)-Kriege," 3–4, 32–33. All translations are my own.

14. Cf. Staatsarchiv Hamburg, Zeitungsausschnittsammlung A 752 (Budde), A 763 (Nieland); *Der Spiegel* (January 21, 1959), 20–25. The psychiatrist was Prof. Albrecht Langelüddeke (1889–1977) who joined the NSDAP on May 1, 1933, and gave a lecture on eugenics in 1933 (Hering, "Fall Nieland," 210).

15. *Der Spiegel* (January 21, 1959): 21–24.

16. Shorthand minutes of the parliament of Hamburg (*Stenographische Berichte der Bürgerschaft zu Hamburg* 2 [January 14, 1959], 48, and 7 [March 19, 1959], 250); *Welt am Sonntag* (January 11, 1959); *Frankfurter Rundschau* (February 2, 1959). In March 1959 the federal supreme court declared that Nieland's booklet was threatening the security of the state and withdrew the available copies (*Die Welt* [March 2, 1959]).

17. Staatsarchiv Hamburg, 241-2 Justizverwaltung-Personalakten, A 3288.

18. Cf. Staatsarchiv Hamburg, Zeitungsausschnittsammlung A 752 (Budde), A 763 (Nieland); *Der Spiegel* (January 21, 1959): 20–25.

19. *Die Welt* (January 15, 1959). This draft was controversial and was codified in connection with the sixth ruling to change the criminal law (Strafrechtsänderungsgesetz) on June 30, 1960 (§96a, 130 und 189 StGB; cf. *Bundesgesetzblatt* 1960, part I, 478; *Der Spiegel* [August 5, 1959]: 12–13, and *Der Spiegel* [March 30, 1960]: 17–18).

20. Cf. Bergmann, "Antisemitismus," 87.

21. Staatsarchiv Hamburg, 241-2 Justizverwaltung-Personalakten, B 3268, curriculum vitae February 23, 1925, and personnel sheet 72/1937. Enno Budde, *Der Kauf auf Abruf*, Diss. Jur., Hamburg 1927.

22. Hering, "Fall Nieland," 212–213.

23. Staatsarchiv Hamburg, 241-2 Justizverwaltung-Personalakten, B 3268, Beiakte 8 (verdict of September 12, 1927, Stade Court).

24. Enno Budde, "Wie aus einer Verteidigung eine Anklage wurde," *Deutsch-Hannoverscher Volkskalender* 35 (1932): 49–50. Cf. also the following by Budde: "Langenrehm," *Deutsch-Hannoverscher Volkskalender* 36 (1933): 49–50; "Das Land Hadeln," *Alt-Hannoverscher Volkskalender* 37 (1934): 55–57; "Ostfriesland unter preußischer Herrschaft," *Alt-Hannoverscher Volkskalender* 39 (1936): 67–68.

25. Staatsarchiv Hamburg, 241-2 Justizverwaltung-Personalakten, B 3268; especially subfile I B 823, 3; personnel sheet 72/1937, 5; and personnel sheet 1943.

26. Budde called the Guelphs the "saviors of blood and soil in Germany" ("Die Erhaltung von Blut und Boden in Niedersachsen," *Alt-Hannoverscher Volkskalender* 38 [1935], 50–51).

27. Budde, "Was sagt uns Langensalza heute?" *Alt-Hannoverscher Volkskalender* 39 (1936): 58.

28. Ibid., pp. 58–59.

29. Staatsarchiv Hamburg, 221-11 Staatskommissar für die Entnazifizierung und Kategorisierung, L 2161; 241-2 Justizverwaltung-Personalakten, B 3268.

30. Shorthand minutes of the Hamburg parliament (*Stenographische Berichte der Bürgerschaft zu Hamburg* 2 [January 14, 1959]: 50).

31. Helmut Thielicke, "Der Anti-Antisemitismus in Hamburg," *Die Kirche in Hamburg* 6.5 (1959): 3–4. Cf. Hering, "Fall Nieland," 219–221.

32. Erich Lüth, *Die Kirche in Hamburg* 6:7 (1959): 8.

33. *Hamburger Abendblatt* (January 17, 1959).

5
Germans and Jews Since 1945:
The Politics of Absolution, Amends, and Ambivalence
WILLIAM SAFRAN

I: DEALING WITH THE PAST

Germany's collective consciousness and much of its public discourse since 1945 have been marked by the mass murder of Jews. Few Germans now deny the Holocaust, but many deal with it in such a way as to retain their self-respect. Revisionists have argued that the Holocaust was one instance of "comparable" genocides; a sequel to Stalin's labor camps; a response to threats by Germany's foes—a preemptive genocide; and a policy for which the Germans were punished. Historian Ernst Nolte has insisted that the "so-called [sic] annihilation of the Jews during the Third Reich"[1] was an act of self-defense against Zionists and Bolsheviks who were fighting Germany.[2] For Andreas Hillgruber, another revisionist, a rough parity was reached when Germans paid the bill for the Holocaust in full with the defeat of their country, its division, and its loss of territory.[3] Others have compared the Holocaust to the nuclear bombing of Japan or the firestorm of Dresden.[4]

Some scholars, while condemning the Nazi regime and the Holocaust, have assigned some of the blame to Jews. Historian Friedrich Meinecke explained the rise of Hitler in part by alluding to the "immodest" behavior of Jews during the Weimar Republic.[5] Others have sought to excuse the murderers by focusing on the totalitarian aspects of the Nazi regime, in which Nazi murderers were mere cogs in a bureaucratic machine. The "systemic" approach is coupled with a tendency to depersonalize the murder of Jews. Chancellor Helmut Kohl in 1995 spoke of the "shame" of his compatriots about that "which was done to innocent people *in the name of* Germany."[6] Other Germans have thought of the crimes as the "deeds of National Socialism."[7] For some, the murder was on so large a scale that it becomes "banal"; for others, it was so far beyond the traditional experiences of Germany as to be "metahistorical."[8]

Between the end of the war and the 1970s the Holocaust was seldom discussed in German schools; references to it were brief and often ambiguous. The abnormality of the event was not the only reason for this; Germans were impatient with tales of Jewish victimization because they were busy bewailing their own fates. Today young Germans are more receptive to reports about the Holocaust because the accused are likely to be their deceased grandparents rather than their living parents; conversely, the event is more remote and therefore more abstract.[9] With the passage of time, consciousness of the Holocaust has receded; there has developed a new perspective, in which German sufferings have been equated with it. A controversial example was the visit of President Reagan and Chancellor Kohl to the military cemetery at Bitburg in 1985, during which fallen SS-men were mourned as victims of Nazism.

Comparing the fate of Jews under the Nazis with that of Germans under Soviet occupation has been a widespread practice. Such a comparison has been implicit in many of the remarks of Kohl and even in the treaty of German reunification. In gloss to that treaty he alluded to Germany's responsibility for World War II and the Germans' postwar traumatic experiences, but he said nothing about the Holocaust. Here he followed the example set a few years earlier by Chancellor Helmut Schmidt, who in listing a number of peoples who suffered at German hands ended his list with "etc." without mentioning Jews.[10]

One way of diluting the Holocaust as an event was the "recycling" of the *Neue Wache* in Berlin. This guardhouse was built in the nineteenth century to commemorate a Prussian military victory; after 1933, it memorialized Nazi heroes. In 1993 a new plaque was affixed to the structure in memory of "the victims of war and despotism." In short, it became an all-purpose place for laying wreaths, honoring all who died during the Hitler era. Kohl suggested that soldiers who fell for the fatherland deserved to be remembered as much as others who lost their lives during the same period.[11] Jewish victims of genocide were presumably also included; but the Käthe Kollwitz statue inside, which resembles a Pietà, has made it hard for Jews to identify with it.[12] Subsequently Kohl approved efforts to build a memorial dedicated specifically to Holocaust victims. However, when in 1995 the winning entry in a competition for such a memorial emerged, and it turned out to be a 100-square-meter monument, he rejected it as "too gigantic" or, as some critics commented, too visible.[13]

A number of German political leaders have oscillated between admission and rejection of collective responsibility. Sometimes there is a sort of division of labor: Kohl's remarks that the Holocaust has been overcome had to be "corrected" by statements from Presidents von Weizsäcker and Herzog affirming Germany's historical burden vis-à-vis the Jewish community. More recently,

Kohl balanced his relativizing acts with others that stress the uniqueness of the Holocaust. At observances on the fiftieth anniversary of the liberation of Auschwitz, he said that "the darkest . . . chapter in German history was written [there] . . . Auschwitz symbolizes the racial madness that lay at the heart of National Socialism and the genocide of European Jews . . . which is without parallel in history."[14] Such emendations have been met with suspicion, for they seem to be made at venues where they cannot be avoided.

One approach by Germans to auto-absolution has been to put themselves on a plane of moral parity with the Jews—a display of "Jewish envy," as a German observer has called it—by pretending that Germans were victimized as much as Jews because Hitler had "seized" their country in 1933 and "occupied" it.[15] An alternative approach has been the attempt to show that there was "another Germany." One such attempt was made in 1994 with an exhibit in the Library of Congress on the German anti-Nazi resistance that culminated in the plot against Hitler in 1944. But the exhibit did little to improve the German record, given the puny impact of the German resistance movement; and it did little to improve the image of Germany in the eyes of world Jewry, because the movement had saved no Jews from death and most of the plotters shared the anti-Semitic stereotypes of the period.[16] The exhibit took place in the wake of the opening of the Holocaust Museum in Washington, D.C., which "many German officials [have] perceived . . . as an attack, a betrayal of four decades of work toward reconciliation."[17]

Still another attempt to restore the German image has been to depict the Nazi period as a mere "parenthesis" of history that was rectified with the return to republican rule. This attempt has been transparent due to the continuities between the Hitler regime and the Bonn Republic. Ex-Nazis have served in that republic's institutions, especially the civil service and the judiciary. This phenomenon was considered transitory and was not expected to negate a positive view of German history or an optimistic prognosis of German democracy. The rethinking of history includes a focus on the country's liberal traditions and the place of Jews in them. Since 1945 many studies have attested to the presence of Jews in Germany for a millennium and their impact on German culture from the nineteenth century to the end of the Weimar Republic.[18]

The discussion of the Jews' contribution to German civilization has been informed by references to a German-Jewish "cultural symbiosis." The idea of such a symbiosis was spawned by a number of Jews who were deeply immersed in German culture and who were part of the German intelligentsia. They pointed to the Jewish enthusiasm for things German, the ease with which Jews entered German society, and their influence on German thought and science.

That view finds expression in the attempts by Jakob Wassermann, Hermann Cohen, and other Jewish intellectuals to prove that Germans and Jews coexisted happily because of strong cultural and spiritual affinities between them. But, as Gershom Scholem has pointed out, that relationship was "a fiction" because Jewish enthusiasm for German culture was not reciprocated.[19]

Since the end of World War II, many Germans have praised the Jewish role in their country's development and lamented its cultural impoverishment since the Holocaust. It is unclear how much conviction has lain behind such eulogies, and how relevant they are for the evolving postwar German-Jewish relationship. One writer has described that relationship as follows:

> Ironically, since Auschwitz . . . one can indeed speak about a "German-Jewish symbiosis." Of course, it is a negative one: for both Germans as well as Jews, the result of a mass annihilation has become the starting point for their self-understanding. It is a kind of contradictory mutuality, because . . . Germans and Jews have been linked to one another anew through this event. Such a negative symbiosis, constituted by the Nazis, will stamp the relationship of each group to itself, and above all, each group to another for generations to come.[20]

That kind of symbiosis is the theme of a novel by Romain Gary, in which the soul of a murdered Jew clings, like a *dybbuk*, to the body of a Wehrmacht officer who had taken part in the mass killings of Jews.[21] In real life, young Germans, when meeting a Jew, are often put on the defensive: they must define themselves in terms of their relationship to parents who might have played a role in the Final Solution.[22] It is as if the original sin with which Christians believe they are born is now complemented, if not eclipsed, by the original sin of being born a German. As President Herzog put it in a speech at Bergen-Belsen on the fiftieth anniversary of the liberation of that camp: "When we Germans mark this day of remembrance along with the victims, we are thinking of the words of the Old Testament, which is common to Jews and Christians alike: 'Our fathers sinned and are no more, and we bear the burden of their guilt.' These sins bear heavily on us Germans."[23]

Not all Germans accept the new "original sin." Some, like Helmut Kohl, reject the idea that children inherit the sins of their fathers. In his remarks about his good fortune of having been born too late to have taken part in Nazi crimes (*die Gnade der späten Geburt*) he seemed to imply that German history began in 1945, thereby attempting to erase any taint of guilt from Germans who were children, or were not yet born, when World War II ended. But as a devout Catholic he has done nothing to change the minds of some of his fellow believers about the collective blame of Jews for deicide, even a generation after Vatican II. The Oberammergau passion play still contains anti-Semitic references, and during his term as chancellor Kohl did not persuade its producers to eliminate them. Moreover, he has repeatedly refused to take to task politicians in his own party, the Christian Democratic Union (CDU), who have made anti-Semitic remarks.

II: APPROACHES TO *WIEDERGUTMACHUNG*

After the founding of the Bonn Republic, German leaders began to seek a way of "making up" for the crimes against the Jews and adopted a policy of reparations (*Wiedergutmachung*). The issue of reparations has been a sensitive one. The very term *Wiedergutmachung* is regarded by some as patronizing; it is also misleading because it means "making [something] good or functioning again."[24] While some proponents of *Wiedergutmachung* were inspired by an idealistic desire for reconciliation, others were motivated by a pragmatic aim: the regain of international acceptance. Chancellor Adenauer admitted this when he justified the policy before the Bundestag. Ironically, this statesman, despite his anti-Nazi record, did so in terms of a stereotype of traditional anti-Semites: "the great economic power of world Jewry."[25]

The moral payoff of *Wiedergutmachung* was limited because some of the reparations were symbolic, while others were "balanced" by acts that caused Jewish resentment. The reparations payment to Israel—used for resettling survivors—came to a fraction of the estimated Jewish material losses. But the money was very helpful to Israel, and the payments to individuals—about 75 cents for each day of incarceration—were helpful to Jews trying to rebuild their lives. Some survivors received monthly pensions, but these were often mere token payments, and there were many whose requests for pensions were turned down. The authorities of the Federal Republic were less generous in their payments to Holocaust survivors than to the widows of SS officers.[26]

This balancing has applied to other policies and acts as well. In order to limit expressions of historical revisionism, the Bundestag in 1986 enacted a law criminalizing the public denial of the Holocaust; however, the courts have been reluctant to enforce it. The law also makes it a felony to publicly question the cruel acts committed against Germans who fled or were expelled from Eastern Europe after the war, acts that no one has denied.[27] The statute of limitations for prosecuting war criminals was extended in 1965 and 1969 and finally lifted, but the courts have been loath to convict. Violence against Jews and foreigners is sometimes strongly denounced by politicians; but incidents of desecration of Jewish cemeteries have become so frequent that the police fail to arrest the culprits, and the courts, to punish them. It is difficult to determine how these ambivalences correspond to the attitudes of the general public. According to opinion surveys, anti-Semitism has declined; this is not because Germans have freed themselves from it but rather because it has been eclipsed by hostility toward "guest workers."

Balance is also apparent in Germany's dealings with Israel. Since the Bonn Republic formed diplomatic ties with the Jewish state, German politicians have reiterated that a "special relationship" existed between the two states. Israel has been the beneficiary of special grants from Germany, and Israeli institutions have received endowments from German sources. On many occasions, Germany has helped Israel in negotiations with the European Community. During the war of 1967 most of the public and leadership were pro-Israel. However, while German leaders professed an interest in the survival of Israel, arms were sold to Arab states. Government officials have argued that this was done by private firms illegally, but they have done little to bring the culprits to justice. During the Gulf war, Germany sent gas masks to Israel to help protect civilians against threats of poison chemicals in Iraqi missiles. Germany had been one of the countries supplying components for the chemical weapons.

There have been less-convoluted roads to reconciliation. These have included invitations by mayors of cities to former Jewish residents, visits marked by expiatory speeches, and the support of organizations devoted to Christian-Jewish cooperation. Since the early 1960s, a magazine, *Tribüne*, has been published that focuses on Israel and German-Jewish relations.

III: THE REVALUATION OF JEWISH CULTURE

One aspect of German-Jewish rapprochement has been the growing interest in Jews and Judaica. This is marked by the reprinting of works written by Jewish authors; the bestowal of literary prizes upon Jewish intellectuals; the publication of books on Jewish history and religion; and many lectures on Jewish themes. In the past two decades, institutes of Judaica have been founded in several German cities. However, these institutes have enrolled mostly non-Jewish students. Why do Christians enroll in such institutes? In the view of a staff member of one of them, they "discover an interest in Jewish studies as part of our German identity."[28]

There has also been an increase in popular interest in Jewish culture. Much of this has focused on the Eastern European elements of that culture. Jewish cultural festivals often feature *klezmer* music and Yiddish films and songs. This is ironic, since Yiddish culture, although tracing its linguistic roots to Middle High German, developed in a sense that was alien to the German spirit and was identified with a community that was almost totally wiped out by the Nazis. The irony is enhanced when one recalls that German Jews tended to denigrate Yiddish as a corrupted dialect of German and could hardly disguise their unease in the company of *Ostjuden* who spoke it.

During the nineteenth century, Christian studies about Jews focused largely on an unfavorable comparison with Christianity. Today Jewish studies focus not only on Jewish theology but also on Jewish history and society—in short, on Jews as members of a civilization.[29] Nothing could be more anachronistic: before Hitler, when there was a thriving Jewish community in Germany, Judaism was regarded as superseded and moribund; after Hitler, when Germany's Jewish community is little more than a relic, its living forces are being studied!

The "museum" aspect of the German interest in Jewish culture is evinced by the New Synagogue in Berlin in 1995. Destroyed in 1938, it was rebuilt, not as a house of worship, but as a "place of remembrance and encounters."[30] Another example is the rebuilt Rashi synagogue in Worms. Since the 1960s, that synagogue has held irregular services, not for the few Jews still living in the area, but for tourists. This concern with Jewish themes may be regarded as a posthumous "affirmative action," a kind of *Wiedergutmachung* accorded, not to living people, but to the memories of dead ones.

IV: GUILT AND RESPONSIBILITY: MORAL-THEOLOGICAL ACROBATICS

At the end of the war, the philosopher Karl Jaspers posited a delicate distinction between individual guilt, which applied only to active agents of the Final Solution, and collective guilt, which he rejected. However, there was the collective "shame" of Germans and their moral responsibility as individuals for their failure to criticize or resist.[31] Today the distinction between guilt and responsibility is obscured by those who argue that the killers, in carrying out murder, were not guilty in the legal sense because they were merely carrying out the law.

Young Germans reject the idea that they bear a personal guilt for the Holocaust. There are those who admit that, as Germans, they share the burden of their nation,[32] but it is unclear what that implies. For some it is the duty to atone to the survivors for the killing of their families by the previous generation; for others, to help prevent future genocides; for still others, to be tolerant toward minorities. Unfortunately, such feelings are rarely translated into action. Young Germans do not stage mass protests against the desecration of Jewish cemeteries or the acquittal of war criminals, nor do political leaders encourage them to do so; rather, the frequent violence against Jewish or foreign targets elicits little more than a perfunctory reaction. This is in sharp contrast to France, where instances of such violence are followed by big protest rallies in which political leaders participate. It is often argued that Germans do not often engage in street protests. However, it has been noted that "in no other country did so many demonstrations take place against the Gulf war as in Germany, where . . . some of the demonstrators even marched in Arab costumes."[33]

Germans have tried to restore their moral self-image by pitting German virtue against Jewish guilt. Germany's postwar share in the defense of the West has been regarded by many as a form of rehabilitation. Conversely, Jewish moral superiority is negated by the behavior of Israel toward the Arabs, which is often compared to that of Nazis toward Jews. Such a comparison offsets the philo-Semitism that one often finds among middle-aged intellectuals. The evocation of "Zionist" crimes, which is fairly common among the young, the New Left, and the Greens, is associated with a pro-Palestinian bias. This bias is accompanied by hostility to Israel whose anti-Semitic overtones are only thinly disguised. An especially obscene example was an article written during Israel's invasion of Lebanon that compared General Sharon to Adolf Eichmann.[34]

The equation of Zionist with Nazi behavior does not solve the problem. Even those Germans who reject the idea that they are guilty still *feel* guilty when they meet Jews, and they fault the Jews for generating that feeling by their very presence. This is a reversal of the age-old Christian belief that *Jews* are existentially guilty by virtue of their share in "the murder of Christ." One way out of this predicament is to practice mutual absolution. A manifestation of that approach was a sermon by Joseph Cardinal Höffner, delivered in Cologne Cathedral during an ecumenical service several days after the Bitburg episode, in which he declared:

> We should not, again and again, exhume past guilt and mutually committed injustices, in constant self-torment. We should not constantly weigh guilt against guilt and use it as a weapon, one against the other. All guilt is abolished in the mercy of Jesus Christ, who taught us in the prayer: "Forgive us our sins, as we forgive those who sin against us."[35]

It is arguable that Vatican II and other gestures of reconciliation, such as the dilution of the charge of deicide, were made in the hope that Jews would respond with their own acts of forgiveness. But that could not be done easily, because the memory of the Holocaust is still fresh among survivors. Moreover, the two main churches in Germany have not been consistent. On the one hand, church leaders have been examining the culpability of their flock, rethinking their relationship to Jews, promoting ecumenism, acknowledging a spiritual debt to Judaism, and referring to the "Judeo-Christian" tradition. On the other hand, among elements of the clergy one still finds a degree of ambiguity in efforts at reconciliation. An example is *Aktion Sühnezeichen*, a program sponsored by agencies close to the Lutheran Church, which sent young Germans to work in Israeli settlements. The work in Israel, inspired by a sense of moral duty toward Jews, began in the 1960s to be balanced by work in behalf of Palestinians, because "we . . . as the result of the mass murder of the Jewish people contributed to the escalation of the conflict between Jews and Arabs in Palestine and thus are involved in the guilt."[36]

The German approach to forgiveness is palpably Christological in pitting the morality of Judaism against that of Christianity. At the above-mentioned ecumenical service, Cardinal Höffner, while acknowledging the crimes committed against Jews "by many Germans, including some from our own ranks," hoped that God would forgive them; that forgiveness would come through belief in Jesus Christ, because "he died for us sinners . . . [and because] the redemption he has brought us is greater than all the calamity caused by man."[37] But the Jews, instead of forgiving the Germans, remind them of Auschwitz—a form of behavior for which Germans do not forgive *them*, and which feeds anti-Semitism. The tables are turned by means of a sort of theological acrobatics: instead of Germans asking the Jews for forgiveness for Auschwitz, Jews are held to be guilty of using Auschwitz against Germany. To many Germans, such a use confirms the difference between the revenge mentality of the Old Testament and the love and kindness of Christianity as preached in the New Testament.[38] A major change occurred during observances of the fiftieth anniversary of the liberation of Auschwitz: a number of Catholic bishops openly admitted that their flock shared responsibility for the Holocaust by failing to speak out against anti-Semitism, to protect Jews, and to resist Hitler's genocide, and in some cases, by helping to carry it out.

A complicating factor in German attitudes is the gradually increasing number of Jews in the Federal Republic. That increase is used by some as proof that after all the polemics about a Final Solution there are plenty of Jews left, and by others that Germany has become an attractive place for Jews because of its prosperity and tolerance. This makes Jews less apologetic about continuing to reside in that country than they had been for several decades after the war. Conversely, their growing presence is embarrassing to those who prefer to engage in friendly acts relating to Jews in the abstract rather than to deal with them as part of a living community, which constantly puts Germans in the dock by insisting that the Holocaust not be forgotten.[39] Luckily, most of the newly arrived Jews—perhaps a third of the Jews of Germany—hail from the former Soviet Union; they may be in a less accusatory mode than their non-Soviet fellow Jews because their knowledge of the Nazi regime is less direct and is eclipsed by their experiences with Soviet totalitarianism.

If there has been a growing admission of German responsibility for the Holocaust, it is due in large measure to the fact that a generation that had nothing to do with the event came to constitute a majority of the German people; this generation could approach its country's history more honestly. The change is also the result of Germany's division, which left that country exposed to constant inspection of its democratic behavior and its conduct vis-à-vis Jews. Now that unification has been achieved and outside pressure has let up, will the strivings for reconciliation continue? As their country gains power, will Germans of the new Berlin Republic act like a "normal" nation and rewrite history so that the consciousness of Nazi crimes will be effaced? Time may contribute to such a development; for with the elapse of years, the generation of Holocaust survivors will disappear, and with them, the vocal accusers of the Germans.

NOTES

1. Ernst Nolte, "Between Myth and Revisionism," in H. W. Koch, ed., *Aspects of the Third Reich* (London: Macmillan, 1985), 36.

2. Ernst Nolte, *Der europäische Bürgerkrieg 1917–1945: Nationalsozialismus und Bolschewismus* (Frankfurt: Ullstein, 1987).

3. Andreas Hillgruber, *Zweierlei Untergang: Die Zerschlagung des Deutschen Reiches und das Ende des europäischen Judentums* (Berlin: Siedler, 1986).

4. Rudolf Walter Leonhardt, *X-mal Deutschland* (Munich: Piper, 1962), 98–104.

5. Friedrich Meinecke, *The German Catastrophe* (Boston: Beacon Press, 1963; first published by Harvard University Press, 1950).

6. *Der Spiegel* (Jan. 24, 1995): 24.

7. Ralph Giordano, *Die zweite Schuld, oder, Von der Last Deutscher zu sein* (Hamburg/Zurich: Rasch & Röring Verlag, 1987), 258.

8. Hannah Arendt, *Eichmann in Jerusalem: A Report on the Banality of Evil* (New York: Viking, 1964); Gustav Seibt, "Historien der Deutschen: Ein Literaturbericht," *Merkur* 47.1 (1993): 47.

9. "Wie halten sie das aus?" *Der Spiegel* (April 3, 1995): 76–81.

10. Michael Wolffsohn, *Eternal Guilt?* (New York: Columbia University Press, 1993), 41.

11. See Peter Steinbach, "Der Historikerstreit," *Tribüne* 34.135 (1995): 120–133.

12. Sibylle Quack, "Das Bewahren des Grauens: Mahnwachen, Denkmäle und KZ-Gedenkstätten," *Vorgänge* 125 (1995): 35–47.

13. Jane Kramer, "The Politics of Memory," *New Yorker* (Aug. 14, 1995): 48–65.

14. Stephen Kinzer, "Germans Reflect on Meaning of Auschwitz," *New York Times* (Jan. 28, 1995).

15. Quoted by Jane Kramer, "The Politics of Memory."

16. Udi Chadash, "Der 20. Juli und die Juden," *Tribüne* 33.130 (1994): 62–64.

17. Mark Fisher, "The Rewriting on the Wall," *Washington Post* (July 24, 1994).

18. See for example Bernt Engelmann, *Deutschland ohne Juden: Eine Bilanz* (Munich: dtv, 1974).

19. Jack Zipes, "The Negative German-Jewish Symbiosis," in Dagmar C. G. Lorenz and Gabriele Weinberger, eds., *Insiders and Outsiders: Jewish and Gentile Culture in Germany and Austria* (Detroit: Wayne State University Press, 1994), 144.

20. Dan Diner, "Negative Symbiose," *Babylon* 1 (1986): 9; quoted in Zipes, "The Negative German-Jewish Symbiosis," 144.

21. Romain Gary, *The Dance of Genghis Cohn* (New York: World Publishing, 1968).

22. See Peter Sichrovsky, *Born Guilty: Children of Nazi Families* (New York: Basic Books, 1988).

23. German Information Center (New York), *Statements and Speeches* xviii:6 (1995).

24. Interview with Rolf Pauls, in Otto Romberg and Heiner Lichtenstein, eds., *Thirty Years of Diplomatic Relations Between the Federal Republic of Germany and Israel* (Frankfurt a.M.: Tribüne Verlag, 1995), 50–54.

25. Wolffson, *Eternal Guilt?*, 18.

26. See Jörg Friedrich, "Verbrechen, die sich auszahlen: Nazi-Opfer und Nazi-Täter vor dem Entschädigungsamt," *Die Zeit* (June 30, 1989): 15–16.

27. Giordano, *Die zweite Schuld*, 337.

28. *Intermountain Jewish News* (Denver: April 28, 1995): 9.

29. See Ulrike Brunotte, "Wissen über Glauben," *Die Zeit* (April 21, 1995): 18.

30. *Deutschland-Nachrichten* (April 21, 1995): 6.

31. Karl Jaspers, *Die Schuldfrage: Ein Beitrag zur deutschen Frage* (Zurich: Artemis-Verlag, 1946).

32. See Björn Krondorfer, *Remembrance and Reconciliation* (New Haven, CT: Yale University Press, 1995), 59–63.

33. Interview with Ignaz Bubis, in Otto Romberg and Heiner Lichtenstein, eds., *Thirty Years of Diplomatic Relations Between the Federal Republic of Germany and Israel* (Frankfurt a.M.: Tribüne Verlag, 1995), 75.

34. Helmut Schödel, "Bruder Eichmann, Bruder Sharon," *Die Zeit* (Feb. 4, 1983): 12.

35. Saul Friedländer, quoted in Krondorfer, *Remembrance*, 57.

36. Quoted in Wolffsohn, *Eternal Guilt?*, 149.

37. Quoted in Ilya Levkov, ed., *Bitburg and Beyond* (New York: Shapolsky, 1987), 191.

38. Michael Mertes, "The Germans and Historical Inhibitions," *German Comments* 37 (1995): 15–18.

39. Frank Stern, *Im Anfang war Auschwitz. Antisemitismus und Philosemitismus im deutschen Nachkrieg* (Gerlingen: Bleicher Verlag, 1991), 158 and passim.

6
The Decline and Fall of the German Mandarins: Intellectuals and Post-Reunification Germany

THOMAS A. HOLLWECK

In 1990, five states that had formerly comprised the German Democratic Republic (GDR) acceded to the Federal Republic of Germany. This historical event is generally referred to as "reunification." At the time, less than a full year had passed since the opening of the Berlin Wall and a moment of euphoria that has only two parallels in German history, neither of which conjure up pleasant memories: the beginning of World War I and January 20, 1933. Each of these three events signifies the beginning of a fundamental change. But whereas the earlier events appear to have disrupted the very continuity of German history itself, the opening of the Wall set in motion a course of events that led to October 3, 1990, conceived as the very reconfirmation of continuity, that is, not the continuity of Germany, but the continuity of the Federal Republic.

As we examine what has happened since it is hard to be too critical of the process itself, unless one is motivated by fundamental doubts concerning the dissolution of the GDR and the continued existence of two German states. Ultimately reunification seems to have been a success, and even Germany's European neighbors who had watched the enlargement of Germany with anxiety have, with different degrees of enthusiasm, hailed the bigger Federal Republic as a model of practical political and economic success. What appears to be somewhat less successful, however, is the process of Germany's self-understanding as a society that must not only bring together two different historical experiences but must do so in the light of their common political origin before 1945. Those whom I call the mandarins, the intellectual establishment and the political and spiritual representatives of the society, responded to the development of the past several years without much imagination and have made every effort to give the developments an air of normality. Something that in the mid-1980s would have been unthinkable must now appear as though it is the most normal development in the world. The reasons for this underreaction on the part of Germany's mandarins, self-evident as they seem at first sight, are nevertheless complex. One only has to look at Jürgen Habermas's recent collection of writings, called *Die Normalität einer Berliner Republik*,[1] to see some of the symptoms of this complex state of affairs. The underlying thesis of Habermas's reflections is a simple one: the historical significance of German reunification cannot be seen as an isolated event in the age of European integration and global interconnectedness. The question, as Habermas sees it, is whether the German *Sonderbewußtsein,* that German sense of having to play a special role in the concert of nations, would be revived in the wake of reunification or whether the sense of normality that had characterized the old Federal Republic would extend to the new republic. My own contention, and here I agree with a recent article by Manfred Henningsen,[2] is that this *Sonderbewußtsein* is by no means completely dead and its eventual disappearance will depend very much on how the citizens of the new German states, i.e., the old GDR, come to terms with their history of forty years with the Stasi and the Prussian version of socialism.

But precisely there lies one of the key problems. Anyone who followed the press articles on the occasion of the fifth anniversary of reunification came away with a sense that the growing together (*Zusammenwachsen*) of the two parts of Germany has turned out to be a far more painful process than anyone would have expected. It has at best become a *Zusammenwuchern,* a wild growing together, as it has been referred to in Germany recently—at worst, a great refusal, a breakdown of communication. If we look at the Germans as they have often done themselves, as a family that has to share one house, we must conclude that far too many of the family members stay in their rooms and refuse to come out to share the common German meal table. The Germans have become an unhappy family, and counseling does not seem to be working. Is this discontent going to be a permanent feature of the new Germany and what would this mean to the future of its citizens?

These questions have of course been the subject of extensive debates in Germany, and the nature of this new country composed of the not so new elements of the old Federal Republic and the defunct GDR has begged for some form of analysis; but, to everyone's surprise, the analyses have for the most part been conducted in terms of the self-understanding that existed on either side of the Elbe prior to 1990. What are some of their recurring themes? There is first of all the question of nationhood and its meaning after Germany's earlier attempts to articulate itself as a nation turned out to be political failures. This question must be seen in the context of the disappearing relevance of the nation-concept in the age of European integration. There is secondly the question of socialism versus free enterprise, and there are the lingering doubts in the minds of many Germans in the new states whether a communal structure had not been too hastily abandoned that protected the weaker members of society, from the children to the sick and the old, and that emphasized the notion of solidarity in all areas of the public life while disparaging individual differences. And there is, thirdly, the burden of German history and the question whether a country with such a history can ever really hope to achieve a kind of national normality and purpose that Germans, if not always correctly, sense in other societies, such as Scandinavia, the United Kingdom, France, and the United States. These being the central areas in which the debate has gone on and where it is still taking place, one could easily conclude that the debate is indeed mired down in issues that from the very beginning were chosen to lead to the kind of impasse the Germans currently experience, and one might be tempted to drop the subject altogether and mumble something about the Germans who always like to make things more complicated, more difficult than they already are. One might at last say something about time healing all wounds and not to worry, for the Germans are after all "the economic engine of Europe." We have heard these opinions frequently in the recent past, and yet I cannot say that they satisfy me; they strike me as half-truths, as easy answers to incorrectly posed questions. For as much as I am convinced that Germany indeed will find some form of normality as a nation and a partner in the European Union, I feel ill at ease with the muddled picture that all these different concerns I listed earlier really present. I believe that it is extremely important to unravel the different issues and to look at them in a dispassionate manner.

In an issue of *Merkur* that appeared in 1990 and was largely devoted to questions of German unity and nationhood, the philosopher Rüdiger Bubner[3] expressed his astonishment at the fact that the intellectuals appeared to have become speechless at the very moment when a revolution was taking place in the GDR and when history was moving again after decades of stalemate, something that in the days of Fichte and Hegel would with great certainty have elicited enthusiastic responses. Here, Bubner mused, a revolution was taking place in a German state reversing a pattern that had begun after the French Revolution. While other nations took to the street, the Germans accomplished their revolutions in thought; the "revolution of the spirit," to use Fichte's famous term, seemed to the Germans to be the more complete form of political revolution. The "booming silence" (*dröhnende Schweigen*) of the German intellectuals after November 1989 broke that pattern. Bubner saw two notable exceptions to the silence, Jürgen Habermas and Dieter Henrich. Let us follow him and take a closer look at these two thinkers and their reflections on the historical implications of 1989 and 1990.

Habermas, in his *Die nachholende Revolution* (1990),[4] speaks of the revolutions in Eastern Europe as revolutions intended to "catch up" with the developments in the West after World War II. The "catch-up revolution," intended to open the door to a return to the democratic *Rechtsstaat*, takes its bearings from models that had long before been overtaken by the revolution of 1917, if one follows the orthodox socialist interpretation of history. This, argues Habermas, may explain the nearly complete absence of any "innovative and future directed ideas" in this revolution. Is it possible to see the largely bloodless revolutions of 1989–1990 as a revolution that in fact concludes the age of revolutions, a revolution that represents the polar opposite to the French Revolution? Seen from the angle of a postmodern critique of reason, such an interpretation indeed possesses a suggestive logic that is not far removed from the free-enterprise apocalypse of Fukuyama's "end of history" that became the slogan of 1990 in the United States. Habermas himself stays away from such oversimplifications and offers a more subtle critique of both the consumer society and state socialism. The particular characteristic of the European mind—according to Habermas on November 23, 1989—lies in the way in which it restlessly creates its own alternatives and continues the tradition of modern rationalism, i.e., a self-criticism that always goes beyond what was before. At a time when Helmut Kohl already had the top-secret blueprint for German unification in his desk drawer, the philosopher still believed in the dialectics of the European mind. Bubner, who at the time of writing his essay must have already known how the German chancellor was chasing the elusive spirit of history, gives Habermas more credit than he deserves. The Hegelians celebrate a last, if quiet, triumph in Bubner's essay, for, in Hegel's words, it is the task of philosophy to grasp the life of its time in the idea. And this process Bubner not only sees in Habermas but also in Dieter Henrich's book *Eine Republik Deutschland* (1990).[5] Henrich, too, wants to stress the parallels between the way in which classical German philosophy had internalized the ideas and events of the French Revolution and the task confronting the philosophers of the Federal Republic in 1990. The constitution of a new republic is at the heart of Henrich's reflections, and the opportunity of the historical moment is seen as the challenge confronting all Germans to give themselves a truly republican constitution. Henrich shared this desire for a new constitution with a significant number of intellectuals in both parts of Germany, and the discussions surrounding the nature of such a constitution were perhaps the most gratifying development of the first half of 1990.

In retrospect, all these attempts to seize the historical opportunity to find a truly constitutional form for the German *Kulturnation* appear doomed from the start. And the fact that the so-called reunification was accomplished on the basis of the Basic Law of the old Federal Republic is too often seen as an all too practical solution to a very complex theoretical problem. It was, on the contrary, the only solution. For intellectuals on both sides, the dissidents of the Neues Forum in the east, and the mandarins of the old republic, be they Social Democrats or conservative nationalists, failed to see that the people who had really spoken were not they but the thousands who shouted: "We are the people" (*Wir sind das Volk*) and who cheered Helmut Kohl in Dresden. This is what Willy Brandt realized when he spoke of "what belongs together must grow together" and what people like Günter Grass und Christa Wolf did not want to accept.

But why were those whom I call the mandarins ultimately out of tune with the realities that led to the self-dissolution of the GDR and its incorporation into the Federal Republic? My contention is that the failure of the mandarins is to be sought in the way they perceived themselves and their respective societies prior to 1990—that is, they had created images of illusionary societies that they claimed to represent. For, ultimately, this is a question of representation, not in the practical political sense—there the process of representation works as well or as poorly as it always has—but in the sense that a society stands for something other than its mere physical existence. And the three issues I had listed at the beginning, nationhood, socialism, and German history, had long been settled in both German states, and those who settled them had become their representatives and guardians. Let us begin with the question of nationhood. Both the eastern and the western mandarins agreed that there was the German *Kulturnation,* and that this Kulturnation could very well be represented by two German states. One did not have to be a fervent partisan of "reunification" and revisionist revanche-politician of the old Adenauer Republic, or an antifascist, peace-loving *Nationalpreisträger* in order to live comfortably with the knowledge that there already was a German nation and that its political division was ultimately a blessing in disguise. The question of German nationhood was, if at all, to be treated as a nonpolitical question, for to raise it as a political issue meant to address the two other questions I have mentioned, socialism versus a democratic state and German history culminating in the Holocaust.

Wohin treibt die Bundesrepublik? was the title of a famous book that appeared in 1966 and whose author was none other than the philosopher Karl Jaspers.[6] In this critical polemic, Jaspers, at a time of considerable stability and prosperity in the old Federal Republic, relentlessly pointed out the illusions, paradoxes, and amnesia that informed German politics and policy in the mid-sixties. It was a time when politicians routinely held up reunification in "peace and freedom" as the ultimate goal of German politics, and the Oder-Neisse border with Poland was still a hotly debated topic. It was also a time, and this was the immediate occasion of Jaspers's book, of the great parliamentary debates about *Verjährung,* the necessity of lifting the statute of limitations regarding the murders and crimes against humanity committed in the name of Nazi Germany. In addition, there were the debates about emergency laws that were supposed to replace the empowerment of the Western Allies to act as ultimate sovereign in case of a national emergency in the Federal Republic. And in these times of highly emotional debates, Jaspers raised his voice to deplore the mediocrity and moral uncertainty of the parliamentarians and the German public in general. With a philosophical radicalism that may sound almost naive when we compare it with the contemporary way of speaking about politics and conscience, Jaspers asked his countrymen to turn around so that they would be able to bring forth leaders who would take responsibility and would act with conscience and without illusions. One could argue that a few years later one such politician arose in Willy Brandt, whose few years as chancellor restored credibility to the Federal Republic and gave its voice among nations a new moral weight that was a direct result of the admission of its historical guilt.

To the voices of Jaspers and Brandt one could perhaps add a few others who have made a difference over the years, those of Böll, of Günter Grass and Wolf Biermann, but on the whole one would have to say that the combination of realism and conscience is a rare thing among the German mandarins. Seen in the context of the events of 1989 and 1990, this circumstance assumes a renewed significance, because the situation now has become even more complicated. On the one hand, the most dire predictions of Jaspers's book have not become fulfilled: the Federal Republic has not become a military dictatorship, nor has it been overrun by the troops of the Warsaw Pact or annihilated in nuclear war. On the other hand, the peaceful revolution in the GDR proved the existence of a level of political maturity that should have blended well with the increased democratic maturity in the West. And yet, the intellectuals on either side were not ready to confront the question of German nationhood when it confronted them squarely after November 1989. "I was not prepared to be a German" ("Ich war nicht darauf vorbereitet, ein Deutscher zu sein").[7] This is how Christian Graf von Krockow quotes the writer Uwe Kolbe who together with his colleagues in east and west had as early as 1990 rejected suggestions that the writers would take any leading role in defining German nationhood any differently than it had been defined for over forty years: Germany, the *Kulturnation.* Tellingly, the volume of writer-responses is entitled "My Germany Is Not to be Found on Any Atlas" (*Mein Deutschland liegt auf keinem Atlas*).[8] Where does it lie? Does it lie in the heads of those who had found their niches in two separate societies but who still clung to the idea of the *Kulturnation* with its Luther, Goethe, Schiller, Marx, and Thomas Mann? One sympathizes with Günter Grass's impassioned pleas against the call for unity,[9] one wonders how Stefan Heym and Christa Wolf would have fared in a society informed by a democratic and humanistic socialism, but one must also ask the question: Why for them and many others on both sides the political entity called Germany remained and remains an ultimately unloved and maybe even unlovable parent—or, should we say, child? Some of the answers to this question are to be found in a small manifesto that appeared in 1992 and of which some 100,000 copies were in print that same year.[10] Among its contributors were Marion Gräfin Dönhoff, the publisher of the weekly *Die Zeit,* former chancellor Helmut Schmidt, a bank president from Hamburg, the chairman of the board of Daimler Benz and two representatives from the east, a professor at Berlin's Humboldt University, and the vice-chairman of the Socialist Democratic Party (SPD)in the German Bundestag. The manifesto reflects the frustration that had settled over the whole country by 1992, after the attacks on foreigners, after it became clear that the economy in the new states would sink into a deep recession, and social justice for the new citizens would remain a dream for a long time to come. The authors lament the lack of vision running through all levels of German society, from its politicians to its intellectual and economic leaders. While a tone of genuine concern for the plight of the Germans in the east is evident in the manifesto, and while there appears to be a deep-rooted belief in the democratic process that will eventually lead to an easing of existing tensions, there is also the usual expression of a social and political malaise that apparently transcends the more tangible and real problems caused by the breathtaking speed of reunification. The authors show themselves as liberal on immigration and the citizenship question in a chapter with the Grassian title "So That Germans Won't Die Out" (*Damit die Deutschen nicht aussterben*); they prove their economic expertise and their loyalty to the European concept to which they are totally committed. But this clearly liberal-conservative work ultimately confirms the point I am trying to make: the manifesto is really no manifesto, but it is, as the Germans say, a *Beschwichtigungsversuch,* an attempt by the mandarin elite to calm the emotions of their obviously upset countrymen and -women and to counsel good behavior. And once again, as the essence of German nationhood the contributors see the classical accomplishments of German philosophy, German literature, and German music that they hope will fit ideally into the greater mosaic of European culture from Oxford to St. Petersburg. The good German has always been the *Bildungsbürger,* while his less desirable brother, the proletarian and the general, finally have no more reason for existing. And everybody will live happily ever after.

It is precisely at this point that I would like to voice my strongest reservations. I must begin by asking the by no means rhetorical question: What would a thinker of the rank of an Ernst Bloch have said to all of this, and how would this utopian dreamer and combative political partisan have regarded the disappearance of socialism from German soil and the very real economic worries of the unemployed millions primarily in the east? While I do not believe that his analyses and polemics would have done justice to all the real problems facing the Germans today, I do think that he would have articulated these problems better, more angrily, yet more justly than those who do so today. And I cannot help wondering how the most ironic of all German *Bildungsbürger,* that reluctant *praeceptor Germaniae* Thomas Mann, would have judged the situation. He, who in the years of the Weimar Republic had told his fellow Germans that things would not be good in Germany until Karl Marx had read Friedrich Hölderlin,[11] went to Frankfurt and Weimar in the Goethe-year 1949 and earned the ire of many Germans in the west at the time. To him the *Kulturnation* was after all still a living reality, even after the catastrophe of the Nazi adventure. He was also ironist enough to settle in Switzerland after his return from America. Would he have joined in the chorus of the perplexed? It is idle to speculate in such hypothetical scenarios, but I must admit I find the question intriguing. "A broad area" (*ein weites Feld*), one could say with the pessimist Grass.

It is the latter who in his new novel[12] seems to have gone farthest in the direction of abdicating the mandarin position and who is working out his fears and his disappointment over the way the two Germanies were rejoined. One need not agree with his historical analysis to be sympathetic to his sentiments. Grass radically questions the viability of a German nation after Auschwitz, and in that we have to take him seriously. And, in a strange way, *Ein weites Feld,* in its stubborn refusal to be original, to be poetry, makes the point that certain things about being German are no longer possible, especially nationhood and intellectual pomposity. There is a real discontent in Germany and those who cry for new visions and concepts only disguise their own discomfort at the way things have turned out. The German mandarins had always thrived along the German Sonderweg. And now the *Sonderweg* has come to its end, in that almost everybody who is not on the far right agrees. But there the agreement ends. One has to read non-German analyses these days, such as a recent issue of *Daedalus,* to find not necessarily visions but clear assessments of the current political issues untainted by the kind of self-pity that all too often characterizes German writings.[13] But, then, these analyses are written by American, French, and English political scientists, historians, and sociologists and they do not reflect what I had alluded to before: the historical guilt. For them, and rightly so,

Germany is part of the multinational, multicultural Europe of today and its identity cannot be separated from the processes that will one day constitute the identity of Europe. For them, Germany can share the small triumphs on the road toward integration. But Germany today also shares the guilt and frustration of all Europeans in Bosnia, the tragic moment of the last years of this century, much of which has been dominated by the political inability of the *Kulturnation* to become a political nation in the concert of nations and thus too often retreated into its own brand of culture that was still defended in Thomas Mann's *Observations of an Unpolitical Man,* namely the culture of the *Sonderweg.* A society that has always been mortally afraid of internal political and social conflict now has to learn to cope with this fear and to make its conflicts into a productive element that could help shape its identity. There is already the dawning of a time when even German culture is no longer purely German; and that culture will have to be represented, too. I would venture the prediction that the *Kulturnation* will not be the representative symbol of the Germans and the nostalgic mandarins on both sides will no longer be of any importance. This process will take time and it will require the courage to endure, perhaps even seek public conflict. Only then could Heinrich Heine's admittedly utopian verses become part of the representative German reality:

> The Grundy generation now
> thank Heaven is slowly dying,
> it's for the grave, brought by its own
> hypocrisy and lying.
> [*Das alte Geschlecht der Heuchelei*
> *Verschwindet, Gott sei dank heut,*
> *Es sinkt allmählich ins Grab, es stirbt*
> *An seiner Lügenkrankheit.*][14]

Looking at this analysis of the German mood of 1995, I find it reflects some of the frustration that characterized the later years of the Kohl era and which was only in part a consequence of the often painful process of growing together. With the victory of the red-green coalition and the dawn of the Berlin Republic much of this frustration seems to have gone away. The intellectual climate in Germany has become more relaxed and at the same time more invigorating. At a time when the new chancellor has appointed a secretary of culture—with cabinet rank—it is becoming evident that the *Kulturnation* and the political nation are about to come closer than they have been in a long, long time. What this will mean for Germany and Europe is one of the more intriguing questions at the end of the twentieth century, which owes so much of its political and intellectual texture to the land in the heart of Europe.

NOTES

1. Jürgen Habermas, *Die Normalität einer Berliner Republik* (Frankfurt a.M.: Suhrkamp, 1995). All translations in this paper are my own.
2. Manfred Henningsen, "Der deutsche Sonderweg—am Ende?" *Merkur* 49.5 (May 1995). 379–389.
3. Rüdiger Bubner, "Philosophen und die deutsche Einheit," *Merkur* 44.10/11 (Oct.-Nov. 1990): 1018–1025.
4. Jürgen Habermas, *Die nachholende Revolution. Kleine politische Schriften VII* (Frankfurt a.m.: Suhrkamp, 1990).
5. Dieter Hendrich, *Eine Republik Deutschland. Reflexionen auf dem Weg aus der deutschen Teilung* (Frankfurt a.m.: Suhrkamp, 1990).
6. Karl Jaspers, *Wohin treibt die Bundesrepublik? Tatsachen—Gefahren—Chancen* (Munich: Piper, 1988).
7. Christian Graf von Krockow, *Die Deutschen in ihrem Jahrhundert. 1890-1990* (Reinbek bei Hamburg: Rowohlt, 1990), 346.
8. Françoise Barthelemy and Lutz Winckler, eds., *Mein Deutschland findet sich auf keinem Atlas—Schriftsteller aus beiden deutschen Staaten über ihr nationales Selbstverständnis* (Frankfurt a.M. Suhrkamp, 1990).
9. Günter Grass, *Deutscher Lastenausgleich. Wider das dumpfe Einheitsgebot. Reden und Gespräche* (Frankfurt a.M.: Luchterhand, 1990).
10. Marion Dönhoff et al., *Weil das Land sich ändern muß. Ein Manifest* (Reinbek bei Hamburg: Rowohlt, 1992).
11. Thomas Mann, "Kultur und Sozialismus," in *Werke. Das essayistische Werk*, vol. 2 (Frankfurt a.M.: Fischer, 1968), 165–173.
12. Günter Grass, *Ein weites Feld* (Göttingen: Steidl, 1995).
13. I am referring to the issue titled *Germany in Transition* in *Daedalus* 123.1 (Winter 1994), especially Heinrich August Winkler, "Rebuilding a Nation: The Germans Before and After Reunification," 107–127, and Anne-Marie Le Gloannec, "On German Identity," 129–148.
14. Heinrich Heine, *Deutschland. A Winter's Tale*, trans. T. J. Reed (London: Angel Books, 1986), 94; *Deutschland. Ein Wintermärchen* (Stuttgart: Reclam, 1977), 71.

Section II: Post-Holocaust Identity Debates

7
Afro-Germans: The Invisible Visible Germans
SUSANN SAMPLES

"I am German. I was born here and still am different. A Black. A mixture of black and white." ("Ich bin eine Deutsche, ich bin hier geboren und bin doch anders. Eine Schwarze. Eine Mischung von schwarz und weiß.")[1] This statement, made by a young Afro-German woman in *Farbe Bekennen* (1986), succinctly and poignantly describes the phenomenon of being a Black German in a predominantly white German society. Too frequently, the usually darker skin color of the Afro-Germans simultaneously accentuates the visibility of their racial—that is—Black heritage and the invisibility of their German nationality.

As many people are not even aware of the existence of the Afro-Germans, the purpose of this essay is to introduce this group of Germans of color to a wider audience and to examine the problematic relationship between these Black Germans and the white Germans. This essay will also look at Afro-Germans and the issue of diversity in terms of the redefining of the designation "German," since contemporary German society is now grappling with multiculturalism and multiethnicity.

While the designation "Afro-German" is fairly recent (mid-1980s),[2] Afro-Germans or Black Germans have been a presence in Germany for nearly a century, and four successive generations of Afro-Germans can be traced. In the past, the terms employed to describe these mixed-race individuals were almost all overwhelmingly pejorative: *Bastarde, Mulatte, Mischlingskinder, Besatzungskinder, Soldatenkinder, deutsche brown babys, dunkle Deutsche,* and *GI babys*, to mention a few.[3] The designation "Afro-German," however, originated from the desire and efforts of a few Black Germans to define themselves and to affirm their mixed racial ancestry:

> With Audre Lorde we developed the term "Afro-German," imitating Afro-American, as an expression of our cultural origin. "Afro-German" seemed obvious to us since we five have a German mother and an African or Afro-American

father. Meanwhile we have become acquainted with Afro-Germans whose parents both come from Africa or whose one parent is Afro-German and the other is from Africa. Consequently, it became clear to us that our essential mutuality is not a biological but rather a social criterion: life in a white German society.[4]

Consequently, "Afro-German" is now much more encompassing, referring to any German with some Black ancestry. However, when discussing the three earlier generations of Black Germans, "Afro-German" acquires a more narrow definition since these biracial individuals tended to have one German and either one African or African-American parent. As a designation "Afro-German" is slowly gaining acceptance, but it still elicits bafflement among the general German population—perhaps confirming the persistent "invisibility" of these Germans of color. Moreover, some of the Black Germans themselves have shown a reluctance to embrace this term unconditionally, arguing that it emphasizes the difference, not the commonality that they share with their fellow Germans. Perhaps, as the Afro-Germans develop a group identity, a consensus will emerge for one common and acceptable designation.

The existence of such a term as "Afro-German" is also indicative of the importance of race and color in German society. Other children born out of relationships with non-Germans have typically generated little or no attention. Contrarily, skin color has been the most decisive factor in singling out the Afro-Germans: "The German Negroes are now discovering that they have inherited from their American (Black) fathers not only the skin color but also the discrimination" ("Die deutschen Neger erfahren jetzt, daß sie von ihren amerikanischen Vätern nicht nur die Hautfarbe, sondern auch die Diskriminierung geerbt haben").[5] While this statement is directed at those Germans with Black American fathers, it can be easily expanded to include all Afro-Germans. To understand the condition and status of Afro-Germans in Germany, it is necessary to examine briefly the myth of blackness, which influences the average German's perception of Blacks and hence Afro-Germans.

First and foremost, the myth of blackness *is indeed a myth*, consisting of stereotypes, clichés, and misconceptions.[6] Blacks are viewed in contradictory terms: either they are brutes, lacking any cultural depth or they are naive or simple children in need of superior guidance. This latter misconception provided the justification for the colonization of Black Africa. The myth of blackness, in turn, has fostered persistent negative stereotypes about Blacks, who are typed as born athletes or as being either sexually overendowed or sexually uninhibited or both. For example, the August 3, 1995, edition of *Stern* featured an article about the seemingly invincible Kenyan runners, describing them thusly: "They race from infancy. They are ambitious, carefree and crazy about big victories" ("Sie rennen von Kindesbeinen an. Sie sind ehrgeizig, unbekümmert und wild auf große Siege").[7] While *wild auf* is an idiom, the employment of the word *wild* nonetheless conjures up images of a savage or primitive. In general, the image of the Black and Africa as portrayed in the media is also largely negative, reinforcing the myth of blackness: "The Africa image of the savage, lacking culture and history" ("Das Afrika-Bild des 'Wilden', 'Kultur- und Geschichtslosen' ").[8]

Not surprisingly, skin color is usually the sole factor in identifying race and evaluating achievement or worth. In *Black Skins White Masks*, Frantz Fanon observes, "As color is the most obvious outward manifestation of race, it has been made the criterion by which men [people] are judged, irrespective of their social or educational attainments."[9] Against this backdrop, the colors "black" and "white" have acquired an aesthetic, moral, and intellectual value: black embodies evil and ugliness, white, goodness and beauty. Blacks thus belong to the "savage universe," whites, to the civilized one.[10] Recent studies about German attitudes toward Blacks also confirm the persistence of racist perceptions about Blacks.[11] In his seminal study, *Toward a Final Solution: A History of European Racism*, George Mosse declares: "The story of racism is not pleasant to tell, and that is perhaps why it has been told so rarely in the fullness it deserves: not as the history of an aberration of European thought or as scattered moments of madness, but as an integral part of the European experience."[12] Sadly, the myth of blackness has become a reality for some Germans who project these racist stereotypes and misconceptions about Blacks onto the Afro-Germans. Therefore it is not surprising that because of their sometimes darker skin color, Afro-Germans have experienced problematic and uneasy relations with white Germans.

The first generation of Afro-Germans coincides with the German colonial period in Africa (1884–1918). Unfortunately, data about this generation is extremely scarce. One documented case in *Farbe Bekennen* is the account of the two sisters, Frieda and Anna, whose father was a colonial Black with German citizenship living in East Prussia.[13] Even though German male colonists faced harsh governmental and societal condemnation for having intimate relationships with Black women, some nonetheless fathered children. However, the strong social and racial taboo of miscegenation has, for the most part, erased awareness of their existence.

Hans Werner Debrunner's *Presence and Prestige: Africans in Europe* documents the fate of the few Africans brought to Germany by the North German Mission for apprenticeships in the late nineteenth century.[14] Since these students were carefully monitored and received "restricted training," it seems unlikely that they fathered any children while in Germany. The 1913 pseudo-scientific study of the African Rehoboth Colony is noteworthy since its conclusions about these colonists of African-German/Dutch/English ancestry reflected and reaffirmed the prevailing racial eugenics and hygiene arguments of that day. Consequently, a correlation was shown to exist between these individuals' whiteness of skin color and their level of civilization. The book concluded with a rather chilling assessment of the value of these mixed race colonists to German colonial interests:

> In spite of everything the pronounced verdict: *they are natives and must remain so and never should (such a) man or woman be accepted into our race.* It is hoped and expected that they will develop with good, correct, strict, not too forgiving treatment . . . In the future we will have a mighty and industrious native component in our colony—a complacent, small, loyal and devoted tribe that still also [will be] after generations: *the nation of bastards.*[15]

By far, the second generation of Afro-Germans is the most famous, consisting largely of the Rhineland Black Germans whose parents were German women and Black and part-Black French Occupation troops stationed in Germany shortly after World War I (1918–1923). Sally Marks and Gisela Lebzelter have convincingly demonstrated that the hysteria surrounding these children was largely external and ungrounded.[16] The local population's reaction to these Black-German children was in general not racist. Nonetheless, the Weimar government exploited the existence of these biracial children as a rallying call for racists in the United States and Great Britain. It was unthinkable that a white civilized nation such as Germany had to be subjected to the indignity of having "half-savage" French colonial troops on their soil. The racist propaganda masked a political agenda to humiliate France and thus to force the withdrawal of French troops from the Rhineland.

Reiner Pommerin has examined the public and political reaction to these children and has painstakingly documented their fate in the Third Reich.[17] With an overtly racist state policy, the Third Reich encouraged and condoned the discrimination, harassment, and persecution of non-Aryans. While Blacks occupied the lowest rung of the Nazi racial scale, biracial individuals did not fare much better. Miscegenation was viewed as an abomination since the mixing of inferior races with the superior Aryan race only led to the diluting or weakening of the latter. This sentiment was reinforced in the schools with such slogans as "God made all Whites and Blacks, the hybrid comes from the devil" ("Alle Weißen und Schwarzen hat Gott gemacht, die Mischlinge stammen vom Teufel"), or "The mixed breed can only have the bad traits of both races" ("Die Mischlinge können nur die schlechten Eigenschaften von beiden Rassen erben").[18] Naturally, the educational and professional opportunities of these Afro-Germans were severely restricted. Afro-German survivors of the Third Reich, such as the two sisters, Frieda and Anna, and Fasia Jansen, have recounted the hardship endured because of their Black ancestry: "The Hitler era was the worst that one can imagine. One cannot suddenly designate people as 'unworthy'. While they could not simply eliminate us, they did not want to tolerate us either."[19]

Public Nazi reaction to the Afro-German children was somewhat subdued; there was little or no media coverage. However, as early as April 13, 1933, these biracial individuals were the subject of ongoing secret discussions.[20] About to enter adolescence, the Afro-German children were perceived as a real racial threat to the Aryan race. The Nazi solution to this dilemma may offer some insight about the status of these Afro-Germans in German society. In contrast to the increasing isolation and public persecution of the Jews, the 1937 sterilizations of the Rhineland Afro-Germans were never given the veneer of legality and moreover were performed in absolute secrecy. Despite the propagandist rhetoric these children were still considered German, and thus the Nazi regime acted cautiously in order not to arouse any public indignation or condemnation. Three hundred eighty-five sterilizations were carried out.[21] Pommerin muses sadly: "Likewise it remains hidden to us whether this child or the rest of the hybrid children even knew what was happening to them at that time, whether they know it today."[22] The fate of these Rhineland Afro-Germans in post–World War II Germany is unknown; they appear to have vanished from German consciousness.

In addition to the Rhineland Afro-Germans, other Afro-Germans as well as Black colonials and Black foreign nationals resided in Germany during the Third Reich. They, too, suffered varying degrees of harassment and persecution. Ironically, the two sisters, Frieda and Anna, and a few Blacks actually enjoyed a fairly successful film career, appearing in a succession of *Afrika-* and *Kolonialfilme*.[23] Despite the good income and camaraderie such work provided, their life outside of the studio was harsh. No doubt, the most perplexing account is given by John Welch, an African American musician living in Nazi Germany, who claimed to have experienced no discrimination whatsoever.[24]

The famous designation "Year Zero" is a popular myth since it merely acknowledged the physical collapse of the Third Reich. Racism and racial stereotypes, especially prevalent during the Third Reich, did not suddenly vanish; people's perceptions *did not* and *could not* change so quickly. Thus, a kind of societal self-deception developed toward the Afro-German children born after the Second World War. Studies of the late fifties and early sixties revealed that the average German tended to be more sympathetic toward these children but more critical of their German mothers. The darker skin of the Afro-Germans highlighted the three perceived societal stigmas of that period: race, illegitimacy, and "consumption envy" (*Futterneid*).[24] The statement, "What can this child do about it, then?" reflects the racism of that period.[25] The pity is, of course, that these children are part Black. Here miscegenation is almost synonymous with racial degeneration: "Racial mixing is almost exclusively perceived as something negative, almost threatening."[25] To be less than white is to be perceived as "flawed." As late as 1981 Peter Schütt wrote about people shouting "racial disgrace" (*Rassenschande*) at him and his Black American wife on the street.[26]

The unprecedented size of this post–World War II generation of Afro-Germans (about 6,000) prompted a great deal of discussion about their social role in Germany.[27] This debate occurred against the backdrop of persistent racial stereotypes, most notably, the presumably lesser intelligence of Blacks. In fact, the 1960 study *Farbige Kinder in Deutschland: Die Situation der Mischlingskinder und die Aufgaben ihrer Eingliederung* deemed it necessary to state emphatically that Afro-Germans possessed the *same* intelligence level as their white German counterparts: "Do Negroes, on average, have less intelligence than whites? The supposition that it is so was proven false—at least for our experiment group."[28] However, the paucity of Afro-German children on the university track fueled the perception that they were indeed of lower intelligence, and thus capable of only menial or a few selective service-related occupations.

An important and often overlooked correlation existed between the support system of the Afro-German children and their performance in school. Too often, even their immediate families or guardians tended to have lower expectations based on erroneous perceptions about race: "Even Gisela's mother believed her daughter would possess little intelligence, and so she would always have difficulties."[29] Furthermore, the constant state of being "under siege"—in school, at home, and in society—could have also contributed to these children's low academic performance. These factors were at times overlooked or ignored, and these children's poor academic performance was attributed to their race.

While the Afro-German children were for the most part tolerated—they were often perceived as "sweet" (*süß*) or "cute" (*niedlich*)—as these children approached adulthood, their social role once again became problematic. Their social and professional integration in German society released latent racist fears among some Germans. More tellingly, their natural desire to date and to marry was met with open hostility and rejection. A sensationalist *Stern* series (1972), "My Son-in-Law—the Negro" (*Mein Schwiegersohn—Der Neger*) exploited the fears of the average German about biracial marriage.[30] Relatives, friends, and the couples themselves were queried about this social taboo.

Time and time again, skin color has played a key role. Although the skin color of Afro-Germans encompasses a wide spectrum (from dark brown to white), in the German media they were usually portrayed with the unmistakable Black features: coal-black with large, protruding lips so that there could be no mistaking their Black ancestry. Indeed, the black skin color became synonymous with the "Negro joke" (*Negerwitz*)—it alone could call forth a plethora of negative stereotypes. By the way, the *Negerwitz* was quite commonplace until fairly recently. Afro-Germans (as well as Blacks) are often subjected to having their skin color described in words normally associated with eating or drinking (for example, "coffee brown" (*kaffeebraun*). Such words, of course, function to stress the exotic aspect.[31] Regrettably, this tendency also persists in the United States. In the aforementioned segment about mixed-race Germans on National Public Radio's "All Things Considered," the reporter described an Afro-German man thusly: "But even his curly hair and café au lait complexion made him stand out."[32]

By their very existence, Afro-Germans confront Germans with the issues of German identity, race, and racism. First of all, the designation "German" is racial. Simply speaking, as long as you look German—that is—northern European, then you will be accepted. Thus, the Russian Germans, even though they speak little or no German, are acknowledged as Germans, but third-generation Turks, or for that matter Afro-Germans, are not. Throughout their existence in Germany, Afro-Germans have been the invisible Germans. Indeed, in the early fifties they were thought to be so alien to the German society that overseas adoptions—preferably in the United States or Scandinavia—were begun. Fortunately, this project was quickly abandoned, but it gives an indication of their problematic social role in Germany.

In 1993 Afro-Germans numbered about 300,000 out of a population of nearly 80 million. The most recent generation (those born after 1965) has assumed a more vocal and militant stance. Members of this generation were responsible for originating the designation "Afro-German," which celebrates and affirms their mixed-race origin. The last fifteen years have also witnessed the appearance of a number of books in which Afro-Germans or people of color have spoken candidly about their experience of "Being Other in white Germany" ("Andersartigsein im weißen Deutschland").[33] Their first-hand accounts describe the condition of being "Other" in Germany. Most have learned to endure the almost daily indignities. Not surprisingly, in some Afro-Germans an anger is discernible as they must continually prove their German identity. Coming to terms with their Black-white ancestry is too often an isolating and solitary experience, which may explain the difficulty of forging a group identity and consensus. That their situation is difficult is evidenced by the desire of some to "submerge" (*untertauchen*). While some Afro-Germans have sought out the companionship of Africans or African-Americans, others have journeyed to Africa in search of an identity. One often ignored fact is that while Afro-Germans share the bond of race, a multicultural dimension exists since their parents come from many different Black cultures. The voice of this German ethnic minority continues to be small; they do not seem to be a visible component of the mainstream German consciousness.

While the focus of this chapter has been the Afro-Germans, we cannot discuss them without also discussing foreigners living in Germany today, since many issues involving diversity in contemporary German society concern both groups. As recently as the late 1990s, one could still hear statements such as, "The FRG cannot be an immigrant country" and "a homogeneous nation with guests," which are troubling since they doggedly denied reality. Reality for the Germany of today is the presence of a large population of foreigners with differing cultures and ethnic backgrounds. As late as 1960, Germans tended to perceive their society as being free of racism: "There is still no ingrained prejudice against Negroes here as there is in the South in the United States or in South Africa."[34] However, evidence conclusively has shown that German society is racist. The heretofore overwhelmingly pejorative terms for these Black Germans reveal an insensitivity of the German mainstream society. How, for example, should one regard the persistence of such offensive bakery items as the *Sarotti-Mohr* or *Negerküsse*, or—more exasperating—the employment of the term *Neger*? The reaction of many Germans to Afro-Germans (or for that matter, any people of color) has been influenced by negative racial stereotypes that do not equate Black with German. Thus, Afro-Germans, like the foreign asylum seekers, are perceived as "Other," non-German, foreigner. While both of these groups have experienced racism, we must remember that Afro-Germans are German citizens and thus are entitled to all the rights of German citizenship.

Fortunately, grassroots organizations ("Parents With Black Children" ["Eltern mit schwarzen Kindern"] and "BAZ Black Germans Initiative" ["Initiative Schwarze Deutsche im BAZ"]) have arisen providing support for the Afro-Germans and their families. Yet, as good as these support systems are, they are no substitute for strong, decisive government commitment and intervention.

Germans and Germany need to redefine themselves by asking: "Who is German?" "Who should be German?" German nationality should not be based on race. Moreover, the social role of foreign immigrants also needs to be reexamined and defined. In order for that to occur, Germans must also critically reevaluate their perceptions of the developing world. The naturalization process, which now is lengthy and fairly costly, needs to be streamlined and accelerated. Above all, German society must confront and deal with its racist tendencies, and government support and commitment is imperative for this. Laws must be enacted that prohibit all forms of discrimination. Nearly fifty years ago during a 1952 *Bundestag* debate, the following entreaty was made: "The German people should show the world that in spite of [the] difference and color we see only the humanity in people" ("Das deutsche Volk sollte der Welt zeigen, daß wir bei aller Verschiedenheit und bei aller Farbigkeit im Menschen immer nur den Menschen sehen").[35] This plea is still relevant today. Eradicating racism is a formidable task, but a change in the general German population's perception is necessary in order for all inhabitants of Germany to be able to co-exist peacefully. Multiculturalism is, after all, the celebration of all cultures, including the dominant German culture.

NOTES

1. Dagmar Schultz, ed., *Farbe Bekennen* (Berlin: Orlanda, 1986), 107. Unless otherwise indicated, the translations are my own.

2. For more about its origin, see the introduction in Schultz, *Farbe Bekennen*, 9–12.

3. The translations for these words are: "bastards," "mulatto," "mixed-race children," "occupation children," "soldiers' children," "German brown babies," "dark Germans," and "GI babies."

4. "Mit Audre Lorde entwickelten wir den Begriff 'afro-deutsch' in Anlehnung an afro-amerikanisch, als Ausdruck unserer kulturellen Herkunft. 'Afro-deutsch' schien uns einleuchtend, da wir fünf eine deutsche Mutter und einen afrikanischen oder afro-amerikanischen Vater haben. Inzwischen lernten wir Afro-Deutsche kennen, deren Eltern beide aus Afrika stammen oder deren einer Elternteil afro-deutsch ist und der andere aus Afrika kommt. Dadurch wurde uns klar, daß unsere wesentliche Gemeinsamkeit kein biologisches, sondern ein soziales Kriterium ist: das Leben in einer weißen deutschen Gesellschaft" (Schultz, *Farbe Bekennen*, 10).

5. Karin Thimm and DuRell Echols, *Schwarze in Deutschland* (Munich: R. Piper, 1973), 100.

6. Sander L. Gilman, *On Blackness Without Blacks: Essays on the Image of the Black in Germany* (Boston: G. K. Hall & Co., 1982).

7. "Die Muskeln Afrikas," *Stern* 32 (1995): 28.

8. Manfred Paeffgen, *Das Bild Schwarz-Afrikas in der öffentlichen Meinung der Bundesrepublik Deutschlands 1949–1972*, Arnold-Bergstraeser Institut Materialen zu Entwicklung und Politik (Munich: Weltforum, 1976), 494.

9. Frantz Fanon, *Black Skin White Masks*, trans. Charles Markmann (New York: Grove Press, 1967), 118.

10. For more information, see V. Y. Mundimbe, *The Invention of Africa* (Bloomington: Indiana University Press, 1988).

11. See Sander Gilman and Rosmarie K. Lester, "Blacks in Germany and German Blacks: A Little Known Aspect of Black History," in Reinhold Grimm and Jost Hermand,

eds., *Blacks and German Culture* (Madison: University of Wisconsin Press, 1986), 113–134; and Rosemarie Lester, *Trivialneger. Das Bild des Schwarzen im westdeutschen Illustriertenroman* (Stuttgart: Akademischer Verlag Hans Dieter Heinz, 1982).

12. George L. Mosse, *Toward the Final Solution: A History of European Racism* (New York: Howard Fertig, 1978), xiv–xv.

13 Schultz, *Farbe Bekennen*, 66.

14. Hans Werner Debrunner, *Presence and Prestige: Africans in Europe* (Basel: Basler Afrika Bibliographien, 1979), 351–368.

15. "Trotzdem das ausgesprochene Votum: *es sind Eingeborene und müssen solche bleiben und nie sollte einer oder eine aufgenommen werden in unsere Rasse* . . . Falls sie sich dann bei guter, gerechter, strenger und sie nicht verziehender Behandlung, . . . wirklich so entwickeln, wie zu erhoffen und zu erwarten ist, werden wir in Zukunft in unserer Kolonie ein kräftiges und arbeitsames Eingeborenenelement haben, . . . ein sich wohlfühlender kleiner, uns treu ergebener Stamm, und noch nach Generationen: *die Nation der Bastards.*" Cited by Eugen Fischer, *Die Rehobother Bastards und das Bastardsproblem beim Menschen* (Jena: Verlag von Gustav Fischer, 1913), 304–305.

16. Sally Marks, "Black Watch on the Rhine: A Study in Propaganda, Prejudice and Prurience," *European Studies Review* 13 (1983): 297–334; and Gisela Lebzelter, "Die 'schwarze Schmach': Vorurteile, Propaganda, Mythos," *Geschichte und Gesellschaft* 11 (1985): 37–58.

17. Rainer Pommerin, *Sterilisierung der Rheinlandbastarde. Das Schicksal einer farbigen deutschen Minderheit 1918–1937* (Düsseldorf: Droste Verlag, 1979). While he is sympathetic toward the tragic fate of these Afro-German children, Pommerin betrays an insensitivity by employing the derogatory word *Bastarde* to identify them.

18. Schultz, *Farbe Bekennen*, 70.

19. "Die Adolfsche Zeit war die schlimmste, die man sich vorstellen kann. Man kann doch nicht plötzlich Menschen als 'unwertes Leben' bezeichnen. Sie konnten uns zwar nicht einfach liquidieren, aber dulden wollten sie uns auch nicht." Schultz, *Farbe Bekennen*, 71. See also Peter Schütt, *Der Mohr hat seine Schuldigkeit getan . . . Gibt es Rassismus in der Bundesrepublik? Eine Streitschrift* (Dortmund: Weltkreis, 1981), 151–158.

20. Michael Burleigh and Wolfgang Wippermann, *The Racial State: Germany 1933–1945* (New York: Cambridge University Press, 1991), 129.

21. Pommerin, *Sterilisierung der Rheinlandbastarde*, 72.

22 . "Und ebenfalls bleibt uns verborgen, ob dieses Kind und die übrigen Mischlingskinder überhaupt gewußt haben, was damals mit ihnen geschah, ob sie es heute wissen." Ibid., 82.

23. Schulz, *Farbe Bekennen*, 77–78.

24. John Welch, "Twelve Years Under Hitler," *Pittsburgh Courier* (May 6, 1944).

24. Lester, *Trivialneger*, 92.

25. Klaus Eyferth, Ursula Brandt, and Wolfgang Hawer, *Farbige Kinder in Deutschland. Die Situation der Mischlingskinder und die Aufgaben ihrer Eingliederung* (Munich: Juventa Verlag, 1960), 105.

25. Ibid.

26. Schütt, *Der Mohr hat seine Schuldigkeit getan*, 12.

27. For example, see Eyferth, Brandt, and Hawer, *Farbige Kinder*; and Hermann Ebeling, "Zum Problem der Deutschen Mischlingskinder," *Bildung und Erziehung* 7.10 (1954): 610–630.

28. Eyferth, Brandt, and Hawer, *Farbige Kinder in Deutschland*, 8.

29. Thimm and Echols, *Schwarze in Deutschland*, 100.

30. Eva Windmöller, "Mein Schwiegersohn, der Neger," *Stern* 39 (1972): 80–87.

31. Indeed, the various food-drink related terms are products usually associated with Africa or the tropics.

32. "All Things Considered," National Public Radio (October 9, 1995).

33. See Schultz, *Farbe Bekennen*; Thimm and Echols, *Schwarze in Deutschland*; Schütt, *Der Mohr*; and Gisela Fremegen, *Und wenn du dazu schwarz bist. Berichte schwarzer Frauen in der Bundesrepublik* (Bremen: Edition CON, 1984).

34. "Es gibt bei uns noch keine bereits verfestigten Vorurteil gegen Neger, wie im Süden der Vereinigten Staaten oder in Südafrika." Cited by Eyferth, Brandt, and Hawer, *Farbige Kinder*, 7.

35. Fremegen, *Und wenn du dazu schwarz bist*, 99.

8
Else Lasker-Schüler: The "Small Drama" of Subjectivity

SYLVIA HENKE

Translated from the German by Valerie Ammon

In 1919, Kurt Pinthus asked Else Lasker-Schüler for a short biography for reprinting her poems from the lyrical anthology "Menschheitsdämmerung" (Twilight of Humanity). This is what he received from the poet, who was fifty years old at the time: "I was born in Thebes (Egypt), even though I came to the world in Elberfeld in the Rheinland. I went to school through age eleven, became Robinson Crusoe, lived for five years in the East, and since then I have been vegetating."[1] Lasker-Schüler always decorated her biography with fantastic legends—she changed locations, falsified dates, and gave herself fabulous names: she was Jussuf, the prince of Thebes, Tino of Baghdad, the Black Swan, Robinson Crusoe, the Blue Jaguar of the Indians. She was either a thousand or two years old, was now male and then female, of this world or perhaps not. Even her own death, which she incorporated into her poetry with the death of Jussuf at the end of her Malik novel, became in her autobiographical writings and letters a playful insertion: "Hang me up often in the night, I just can't find the tree again early in the morning.—Please don't reveal my bad luck. I would rather be a shepherd than a pitied Prince of Thebes."[2]

The fictionalization of her own biography goes so far that the name Else Lasker-Schüler almost stands as a legend in itself. The countless self-stylizations, with which she made fun of her critics and friends, the legendary veils in which she wrapped herself, did, of course, not remain without consequences for the reception of her work and her life. For legends arise at the cost of the concrete story that disappears in them. That is how the memory of the exiles of 1933—who were expelled by the Nazis—could quickly fade in Germany to an anecdote for reminiscence. For example in Gottfried Benn's speech about Else Lasker-Schüler from 1952:

> Ms. Else Lasker-Schüler lived at the time (that is, 1912) in Halensee in a furnished room, and from that time until her death, she never again had her own

apartment; only cramped rooms, stuffed with toys, dolls, animals and various odds and ends. She was short; boyishly thin; her hair, black as pitch, was cut short, which was rare at that time; she had animated eyes, black as ravens, with an evasive, inexplicable look. You could never cross the street with her without the whole world stopping still to look at her: she wore extravagant wide skirts or pants and outrageous robes, her neck and arms dangled with conspicuous, fake jewelry, chains, earrings, with fake gold rings on her fingers, and since she was always brushing strands of hair away from her face, these "servant girl's rings," one has to confess, were plainly visible to everyone. She never ate regularly, she ate very little, she lived on nuts and fruit for whole weeks at a time. She often slept on benches, and she was poor at all stages of her life and at all times. She was the Prince of Thebes, Jussuf, Tino of Baghdad, the Black Swan.[3]

Seven years after 1945, the "great" German poet, Benn, was able to conjure up this fairy-tale picture of the small, constantly poor, constantly homeless girl and thereby allow the historical dates to disappear—1933 (flight from Germany), 1939 (final emigration to Jerusalem), 1945 (death)—these dates that cut through her fantastic life like inflamed monuments of actual history. That Benn ignored these dates with exemplary historical forgetfulness in order to lovingly and bemusedly remember the nonsense and "servant girl's rings" has its own logic, because the next sentence of his speech is: "And this was the greatest woman poet that Germany ever had."[4] Even if, therefore, she disappeared from Germany in 1933, and under puzzling circumstances, still she had to be repatriated (*eingemeindet*) that much more emphatically in 1952.

BETWEEN HOMECOMING AND MARGINALIZATION

The placing, and/or repatriation of the exiled poet into literary history is a problem that decisively contours the postwar reception of her work. Jakob Hessing's examination from 1933 gives the most recent critical representation of this reception history. His concern in viewing the mythologizing tendency of Lasker Schüler reception in postwar Germany as part of a displacement of historical reality is also, partially, a well-justified rejection of the dominant postwar German studies method of *Werkimmanenz,* with its fading out of historical facts. However, when Hessing takes the reception history of Lasker-Schüler as an example of a German-Jewish historiography, in order to anchor the Jewish poet in historically concrete Judaism by means of a sharp division of literary self-portrayal and real biography, then a dubious repatriation has been attempted— a repatriation or "homecoming," which conceals the fragmentary nature of her literary "Jewishness." For every act of placing, be it into a Jewish, a Catholic or a German community, overlooks the conflict that accompanies any reading of Lasker-Schüler's texts.[5]

Else Lasker-Schüler "app-lied" Jewish tradition in her poetry, as in the sense of twisting tradition, just as she did with Christian myths, Oriental stories, and modern fairy tales. In wilful usages, splinters of tradition from the Torah and the cabala surface, which to be sure *remind* one of a Jewish textual tradition, but do not restore it. When, for example, she regularly embellishes the letters in her handwritten works with stars and moons, this reminds one of a cabalistic letter-mysticism in which the letters of the Torah are decorated with little crowns and crosses, but by expanding to a cosmic emblematic she attaches at the same time her own wilfulness, with which she masks the old tradition and therefore renders it foreign.

Not surprisingly, a controversy developed between her and the "recognized cabalistic scholar," Gershom Scholem, whom she sought out in 1934 (during her first stay in Jerusalem) to discuss the cabala. Concerning their meeting she noted in *Land of the Hebrews*: Scholem tried hard "with the poison of logic" to "demystify" the legends of holy Israel, to uproot Papyrus: "I say 'to wed the miraculous with schoolmaster's logic creates a misalliance.' I moved on angrily." [6] This misalliance, however, is mutual; in a letter to Walter Benjamin, Scholem writes about this meeting: "My latest guest currently in Palestine, which I may have already told you, is Else Lasker-Schüler. A ruin, in whom insanity not so much resides as haunts." [7]

Nothing about a "religious dispute," then, as she describes it; insanity is the only thing that the Jewish scholar can ascribe to Else Lasker-Schüler with her poetic application of Jewish legends. Kafka, as well, another Jewish contemporary, could not express himself otherwise at an earlier time about the texts of Lasker-Schüler: he could not stand her empty and artificial poems, her prose was "onerous" to him, in it worked "the indiscriminate twitching brain of an eccentric big city woman." [8] Kafka's attack on the "brain" of the writer was not really original. After all, already in 1910 her poem "Quietly Speaking" (*Leise sagen*) had been laid open to the ridicule of the middle-class readers of the *Hamburger Zeitung* by the literary establishment, which dismissed the poem as "complete brain mush." [9] In view of such stigmatizing, any repatriation—even a repatriation to the Jewish community—would have seemed problematic, at the very least.

EFFORTS AT DE-MYTHOLOGIZATION

The stigmatizing of Else Lasker-Schüler's work and person as insane can be seen not only as a premise for the later mythologizing—it is also, in a manner of speaking, simply the flip side of this mythologizing. It accounts, moreover, for the efforts both of scholars and of her estate to achieve an "*undamaged* image" of the poet.[10] However, the determination to construct an "undamaged image" of her from her work led to the selection and censorship of the extant texts as undertaken at the end of the 1950s by the Catholic Kösel publishing house in Munich, which published what is still the only collected edition of Lasker-Schüler's texts, containing only 60 percent of her texts. The philological quality of this edition is obviously poor with regard to the versions and chronology of the texts included: whole letters and passages of letters are omitted from the two-volume edition of her correspondence, and the edition as a whole has no notes. This will change with the critical edition of her collected works that is currently being produced: in commemoration of the fiftieth anniversary of her death; the first of eleven volumes that appeared in 1996. These volumes are being jointly edited by research groups in Wuppertal and Jerusalem, and the Jewish Press (*der Jüdische Verlag*) at Suhrkamp has applied for the rights to publish them. With two volumes of correspondence, and one volume of drawings and scattered writings, the edition will provide an overview of the actual breadth of Lasker-Schüler's artistic production. This thorough philological assemblage of the texts will also finally allow for a demythologizing of the person without attempting to normalize and correct the texts.

LITERARY NOMADISM

"I have never made a system for myself, the way smart women do; have never fastened myself to a world view, the way even smarter men do, have not built myself an ark. I am unattached. Everywhere lies a word of mine, everywhere a word came from me."[11] To take Else Lasker-Schüler's texts seriously is to read them as testimonies of a literary nomadism: lacking a world view and with words strewn here and there, her texts are as persistently written *between* traditions, nations, and religions as they are between genres. In her application of genres, she is indeed a nomad, in the sense of someone who "participates without belonging."[12] Many, like Benn, would have preferred to keep the lyricist Else Lasker-Schüler, accept the autobiographical prose, dismiss the dramas as unsuccessful, and ignore her letters. Yet, thank God, it is not so easy. Lasker-Schüler not only moved within all genres, but—unconcerned with rules—she blended genres as well. In that she composes her prose in epistolary form, incorporates drawings and typeface into her letters, dramatizes her poetry by reciting it in exotic costumes, and yet calls her drama "pacing poetry" (*schreitende Lyrik*), all of her texts tend to leave their genre—and in so doing they form their own genres. It is in this sense that she said of her first drama, *Die Wupper*, that it was "not simply a fairy tale or a play or a drama . . . , but at most a ballad of the city, with smoking chimneys."[13] In this way, a new genre was established alongside those that already existed—and this new genre had its share in the greatest of all genres, the drama, which remains without affiliation.

ICHUNDICH—DRAMA OF VULNERABLE SUBJECTIVITY

Of the three plays that Else Lasker-Schüler wrote, the "theatrical tragedy" *IchundIch* is the most disputed. It appeared in 1940–1941 in Jerusalem, was long regarded as a testimony of the aging poet's mental derangement, and to avoid disgracing the image of the lyricist (according to Ernst Ginsberg in 1961) remained banned from the official edition until 1980. As a result, unsuccessful aspects of this posthumously published and, in many respects, dreadful play were largely seen as resulting from its form; no consideration was given to the fact that the fragility of form is interconnected to the material weight, which the piece brings to the poet's "stage of the heart." For as a "living stage," she is unwilling in her dramatic poetry, and especially in *IchundIch*, to withdraw herself into an objective *Textinstanz*. Contrary to the first modal genre rule of drama, which holds that the *Erzählinstanz* in drama is empty, a complex structure of subjectivity is revealed in the very title of the piece, as is, of course, a beginning of modern drama in the sense in which Gerhart Hauptmann described it: "The beginning of the drama is the I—split two, three, four, five, multiple times."[14] Appropriately, the dramatic "I" in Lasker-Schüler's piece has not vanished into the stage, but appears in the figure of the "poet." In a complicated prologue, the poet explains to the public the occasion for and plot of her piece, which is performed on her "stage of the heart": it is a monstrous story, it is a "murder" story and everything but a private one. Because the characters of her *IchundIch* configuration are Faust, Mephisto, Marthe Schwerdtlein, Göring, Goebbels, Hitler, Himmler, Nazi soldiers and servants of Satan, it could be said that the entire weight of former German political and theatrical history is placed on the fragile stage of the heart. Indeed, it is one of the very first dramas that attempts to come to terms with the German catastrophe of Nazi terror. As a dramatic climax, Göring, Goebbels, Hess, Hitler, and an entire army of soldiers who are advancing into hell to negotiate an oil monopoly and thereby gain the final victory, are received by Mephisto and Faust and submerged in a stream of lava. And yet the piece, despite its "big" subject-matter, did not become an antiwar or anti-Nazi piece; it remained, in other words, "small." Why?

At first glance, the plot of Lasker-Schüler's tragedy seems childlike. In fact, Lasker-Schüler's theater has in some ways the features of children's theater. Yet precisely the label of childlike—which has also repeatedly caused belittling interpretations of Lasker-Schüler's entire oeuvre—is not sufficient to write off this play. Clearly, Lasker-Schüler writes in a direct relationship to the child that she was, and certainly also to the child that she had: childhood memories, children's stories, children's games, and children's words can be found in almost all her works, whether they are about handwriting, drawings, experiences, solar systems in people, stories or faces. It is always about little ones and the grown-ups; the child's face always shows up in the adult face, and small figures in big ones. Let me clarify this with an example from *IchundIch*: Goebbels explains to his wife Marthe that the Hitler of the ancient Germans was named "Wotan"; Marthe, who is hard-of-hearing, understands *Truthahn* (meaning turkey) and is surprised.[15] This is a type of comedy that trivializes the extremely weighty political context. This trivialization, however, can be understood as Lasker-Schüler's attempt to bring the incomprehensible closer into her own proximity and—at the cost of historical accuracy—to bring it into some relationship to herself: in this passage she makes Hitler small—something I would characterize as a departure from history and representation. But in doing so, the political is not simply rendered banal, it is instead brought into relation with the personal and thereby reduced; placing it in reference makes it less violent to the personal. At the same time, the stage loses the power to represent that which, from a subjective point of view, is unimaginable. The violence of representation—which always lies in its ability to objectify things completely—cannot be realized in the play's content; the power of the political cannot be mastered theatrically. Thus *IchundIch* reminds us that the political violence of the world theater cannot be easily dramatized on the "heart stage" of an "I"-theater. In Lasker-Schüler's subjective theater and poetry, a drama of radically open and therefore vulnerable subjectivity is always quietly taking place, a subjectivity that is so obsessed by the other person that it now and then gets lost in him (or her). In her epistolary novel *My Heart* (*Mein Herz*), she writes: "I have never experienced people other than as a frame in which I placed myself; sometimes, to be honest, I lost myself in it."[16]

When this frame, however, becomes the dramaturgy of a mass murder, as in *IchundIch*, she not only loses herself in it, but also dies from it. It is thus only fitting that the poet, who herself appears on her "heart-stage," is killed by the probing questions of theater critics in the last act.[17] This again is also childlike, yet it is at least peculiar that the one who wrote the play should also die in it. It is peculiar and has the melancholy characteristic of a work that, aware that it will not outlive the story, must fear for the survival of its own art. And this melancholy is quite justified, with respect to the history of Lasker-Schüler's drama and the destruction of her books in 1930s Germany. The death in the drama is only a more radical form of the vulnerability in a poetic program, in which "the self" can never remain itself, opening itself to constant unstopping transformation into the Other, and endangering itself without the possibility of return.

With its continual transposing of work, person, and character, the inside and outside of the text, age and gender, with invented traditions and masquerades, as well as ancient poetic motifs that her texts convey into modern lyric (heart, stars, blood, gold, nights, and sky), Else Lasker-Schüler's work was alien in its day and at the same time detached from any positive indigenous past. It remains nomadic, if the nomadic (like the Jewish) is that which goes beyond myth to remind us of the challenge of the unfamiliar. This unfamiliar quality must be protected when interpreting her texts, particularly against certain approaches to literary studies that are based on the unity of work, author, and world view. Not until the last few years, therefore, have the texts of Else-Lasker Schüler been interpreted satisfactorily, in my opinion. This reception is not concerned with distinguishing art from biography, central from marginal texts, but instead with reading her work as *poetography*,[18] that is, as a constant transformation of real into a poetic existence, as an in-between-world in which poetry and life are continuously translated into one another—in the balance beyond all ideology, incorporation, and territorialization.

NOTES

1. Kurt Pinthus, ed., *Menschheitsdämmerung. Ein Dokument des Expressionismus* (Hamburg: Rowohlt Verlag, 1959), 302.

2. Else Lasker-Schüler, "Letter to Fritz Engel (1914)," *Wo ist unser buntes Theben. Briefe von Else Lasker-Schüler* (Munich: Kösel Verlag, 1969), 2: 63.

3. Gottfried Benn, "Rede auf Else Lasker-Schüler" (1952), *Gesammelte Werke*, vol. 4, *Reden und Vorträge* (Wiesbaden: Limes Verlag, 1968), 1102.

4. Ibid.

5. Jakob Hessing, *Die Heimkehr einer jüdischen Emigrantin. Else Lasker-Schülers mythisierende Rezeption 1945–1971* (Tübingen: Niemeyer, 1993).

6. Else Lasker-Schüler, *Gesammelte Werke*, vol. 2, *Prosa und Schauspiele* (Munich: Kösel Verlag, 1962), 802.

7. Walter Benjamin and Gershom Scholem, *Briefwechsel 1933–1940* (Frankfurt a.M.: Suhrkamp, 1985), 136.

8. Cited by Jörg Drews, ed., *Dichter beschimpfen Dichter* (Leipzig: Reclam, 1994), 111.

9. The scandal and trial ensuing around this poem are documented by Erika Klüsener, *Else Lasker-Schüler* (Hamburg: Reinbek/Rororo, 1980), 72.

10. Letter of Ernst Ginsberg (September 2, 1958) to Manfred Sturmann, Nachlaßarchiv Jerusalem. Cited in Else Lasker-Schüler, *Ichundich*, ed. Margarete Kupper (Munich: Kösel Verlag, 1980), 84. In her afterword to this edition, Kupper documents the history of the battle over the literary quality of *Ichundich*. The latest stage in this critical discussion is found in Hessing's study.

11. Lasker-Schüler, *Gesammelte Werke*, 387.

12. In his essay "The Law of Genre," on the relation between law and genre/gender, Jacques Derrida speaks of the law of genre as a generative motif of literary production—a law that is yet always correlated to the transgressing of itself, even as it denies the mixing of genres. In this respect, it is never simply restrictive, but instead permissive or even itself generative. Derrida, "La loi du genre," *Glyph* 7 (1980): 184.

13. Lasker-Schüler, *Gesammelte Werke*, 944 and 658.

14. Gerhart Hauptmann, *Gesammelte Werke*, ed. Hans Egon Hass (Berlin / Hamburg: Fischer, 1966), 6: 1036.

15. Lasker-Schüler, *Ichundich,* 35.

16. Lasker-Schüler, *Gesammelte Werke,* 387.

17. Lasker-Schüler, *Ichundich,* 74.

18. Cf. especially the study by Meike Fessmann, *Spielfiguren. Die Ich-Figurationen Else Lasker-Schülers als Spiel mit der Autorrolle. Ein Beitrag zur Poetologie des modernen Autors* (Stuttgart: M&P Verlag für Wissenschaft und Forschung, 1992), 3ff.

9
Some Thoughts on the Tenuous and Precarious Relationship Between Feminism and German Studies

RUTH-ELLEN B. JOERES

This is not the first time that I have concerned myself with the vexing tensions between feminism and German studies. At the 1991 San Francisco annual meeting of the Modern Language Association (MLA), I presented what Sara Lennox has since called a "manifesto" to the field of *Germanistik*—both in Germany and the United States—as a field whose roots are still located in the depoliticization and pessimism that arose as a result of the horrors of World War II.[1] A field that, to my jaundiced eye, bore as much resemblance to feminist inquiry as elephants to parsley.[2] At that time, I hazarded a guess that if German departments continued to ignore the momentous challenges presented by feminist scholarship, they would find that their feminist colleagues and their students interested in feminist inquiry would be apt to abandon them, heading instead for women's studies and gender studies programs, or for the more welcoming atmosphere of other literature departments.

A year later, at the annual meeting of the German Studies Association, I once again chose to respond polemically in a commentary on three papers that reacted in various ways to that initial talk of mine. Although the general topic was still the uneasy relationship between German studies and feminism, this time I focussed on how gender as an analytical category critical to feminist inquiry has in a number of instances begun to lose its central position when it is placed in relationship to other analytical categories—in this particular instance, to sexuality. One of the three papers seemed to me to have followed that pattern in its discussion of the ways in which lesbians and gay men find points of connection and tend to view that connection as more compelling and more important to them than that of gender, which would, after all, separate them.[3] The displacement of gender in this instance struck me as marking a possible move away from feminism on the author's part, or at the very least as further evidence of the problematic ways in which gender is being viewed at present.

These talks have emerged from a period in which I spent five years as one of two editors of *Signs: Journal of Women in Culture and Society*, a particularly interesting location for me, an American feminist Germanist, given the scarcity of German studies–related submissions to, not to mention publications in, *Signs*. In that position I have found myself increasingly in a place of between-ness: between German studies and feminism, between my own interests in U.S. feminist work and the literary and social history of German women, between two countries, two nationally based literary approaches, two often very different worlds. But given my geographical location in the United States and the concentrated focus of my work with *Signs*, I have tended during this time to see the German side of my activities from a different vantage point, from a distance and through a different lens.

In the meantime, however, German studies in the United States has continued to undergo inevitable transformation as the post-*Landeskunde*, post–World War II generation has begun to establish itself in the profession. Issues not only of feminism but also and increasingly of multiculturalism have more and more been reflected in the discussions swirling around revisions in the field. The *Women in German Yearbook*, the central voice of U.S. feminist German studies, has acquired an editorial board and has left the relative obscurity of the University Press of America, assuming a heftier and increasingly professional scope in its new location at the University of Nebraska Press. Sara Lennox, who like me has occupied herself considerably (and with more optimism than I) with the connection between feminism and German studies, is emphasizing the obvious growth in that connection—from the current make-up of most of the MLA divisional executive committees in German, to the increasing number of conferences that emphasize the interdisciplinary nature of German studies and acknowledge the importance of feminist inquiry in the process, to the ongoing importance and influence of the Women in German (WiG) organization.[1]

Even I, the inveterate pessimist, can acknowledge that the tone of my 1991 talk in San Francisco was perhaps too grim. Even I can occasionally ignore the small, insistent voice in me that points out the capricious nature of MLA divisional executive committees, the dwindling number of jobs available for those post-*Landeskunde* new Ph.D.s, the veritable ghettoization of feminist work in the WiG *Yearbook*, and the continuing traditional understanding even in U.S. German studies of the meaning of the term "women."[5] It is, after all, clear that the numbers of German studies graduate and undergraduate students interested in feminist work remain high—that Women in German and its *Yearbook* are prospering—that the powerful influence of American feminist inquiry on U.S. and German feminist work is continuing.

In the discussions of feminism and German studies, there is a necessary distinction made between German as it is taught in the United States and German as it is taught in Germany. Although the separation is indeed self-evident, the *connections* between the two also cannot and should not be ignored. German literature and culture are, after all, the common basis of both areas of inquiry: we are all concerned with a particular geographical and linguistic location, its history, its social, political, cultural parameters. It is one thing to point out progressive developments in this country while continuing to deplore the backwardness of German-based *Germanistik*: to give up on the latter as a lost cause, to engage, in other words, in a self-fulfilling prophecy. It is another to acknowledge the strong, albeit problematic connections between U.S.- and German-based German studies and to suggest possibilities for transformation and change that could indeed emerge from the feminist work that is now under way, especially in this country. In that light, I want to begin on a more optimistic note than I have in the past by making a suggestion that has, in fact, to do with that commonality, a way in which feminist inquiry and German studies might benefit from each other.

German feminist work of the second wave has, it seems to me, always been fairly derivative, dependent in large part on French, British, and American feminist inquiry for its own discussions and debates. First, it seems, there were Hélène Cixous and Julia Kristeva, whose writings were translated and discussed by German feminists; now, the interest seems to have moved more in the direction of Teresa de Lauretis and Judith Butler. Such appropriations obviously involve a spin of originality: German feminists select texts that speak especially to them and revise and comment on them as they expropriate them. Nevertheless, although Blackwell's can publish anthologies on French, Italian, British, and American feminism, it does not seem likely to include a volume on German feminist inquiry anytime soon. And the 1980s collections of translated German feminist work, *German Feminism: Readings in Politics and Literature* (1984) and *Feminist Aesthetics* (1985),[6] have not been followed by any marked increase in interest on the part of U.S. feminists in the work of their German counterparts. What does get done in the matter of "German feminism," in literature and culture studies, at least, is largely confined to U.S. feminist/Germanist work.

There has also been very little in the way of successful combinings: that is, German feminists may borrow extensively especially from U.S. and French feminist work, but the useful ways in which those and other national feminisms either pull in other analytical categories such as class or race or ethnicity, or successfully incorporate other modes of knowledge production such as psychoanalysis and Marxist/socialist inquiry, have not been supplemented by any specifically German take. How, then, can German feminists and U.S. Germanist/feminists think together about issues of gender and, on the basis of their particular subject matter, contribute an approach that would benefit both? Is there a way in which German studies, wherever it is taught and studied, could also benefit in the process?

Current history might play a useful role in this respect. In that vein, I want to mention an experience I had in 1995 in connection with a visit to Leipzig, where I had been invited to do that which best characterizes me nowadays, namely, to give a lecture on the so-called mother of German feminism, Louise Otto-Peters, a nineteenth-century German social activist and writer about whom I have written, and a second lecture on aspects of current U.S. academic feminism.[7] Both papers were delivered to a feminist audience consisting primarily of women from eastern and western Germany who represented a variety of interests, ages, professions, and political positions. I suspect that most of them had an interest in feminism even if their understandings of "feminism" varied widely. But whereas my lecture on Otto-Peters elicited a response that delved into the literary/critical and historical aspects of what I had asserted, the second lecture produced a quite different reaction.

By the time I delivered that paper, I was familiar with my audience, which consisted mostly of people who attended both events. It therefore did not take me long to realize that they had more or less divided themselves on either side of the aisle into east and west. When I had completed my talk, a discussion of current issues of theory and practice among U.S. feminist academics, the literal split of the room was reflected in the split of the discussion, in which my role ultimately became that of facilitator rather than respondent. It is too facile to conclude that the east saw itself on the "practice" side of the discussion, the west on the "theory" side, but I am nevertheless convinced that there were aspects of such a split in evidence in that room: eastern women who are losing their jobs in great numbers, who are seeing the gender-specific benefits of daycare centers and abortion rights with which the socialist state provided them rapidly fading away, who are increasingly turning to activist tactics that are specifically related to their status as women; western feminists, mostly academics, who may smart at the limitations that continue to be imposed upon them because of their gender and their location in a country that has never been very progressive in its understanding of gender roles, but who have been engaged in open feminist debates for some time and have read so extensively for so long that they now have a store of theoretical information on which to base their debates. I came away from that discussion both shaken and stimulated. I felt connections there, and conflicts, and differences, not only between the obviously varying positions expressed by the eastern and western women, but also among all the groups represented, that is, including *me* as the U.S. feminist who had opened up this can of worms.

I also came away from the excitement of that session with a strong conviction that here might be the germ of a discussion that could indeed involve many of us and that might, in time, lead to a particularly valuable and specifically German contribution to feminist inquiry. For whereas the French feminists have shown how psychoanalysis can be fruitfully brought into the feminist discussion, and the British and Italians have contributed notably to the socialist-feminist debates and the discussion of class, and the Americans have emphasized the critical importance of adding analytical categories such as race and ethnicity to undifferentiated investigations of gender—it has become increasingly clear to me that the category of gender could be immensely enriched were it to be brought more analytically into the particular political, national context that arises when we begin to examine the differences between eastern and western German feminisms: between two separate countries, that is, who share a language and a common history, but who, at least during the forty-year period of 1949–1989, developed increasingly as discrete national entities precisely at the time that the so-called second wave of feminism was emerging in Europe and the United States.

Although the topics of nationalism and nationhood have already been raised in the matter of gender and sexuality,[8] the specific situation that has developed over the years both since and before 1989 in reference to attitudes in eastern and western Germany is particularly fraught when the topic is that of the legal, political, and social (not to mention mythological) location of women. I am speaking less in terms of straightforward comparisons, and far more about broader theoretical questions concerning the relationship between nationalism, politics, and gender when they are examined in the case of the old and new German states. For what is especially notable about Germany currently are the ways in which reunification has become increasingly problematic—with the disparate communities that make up the combined German republic united only by "economic jitters."[9] And although the alienating factors creating separations between the former German Democratic Republic and Federal Republic of Germany emerge from many sources, the connections between nationalism and gender are especially apparent. I think, for example, of the inevitable differences in nationalist ideologies, but also of feminism as now a publicly discussed topic in eastern Germany, as well as the acknowledgement that feminism—understood quite differently in east and west—has material as well as theoretical ramifications for both eastern and western German women.

I am not the first to point out such connections. But I am less concerned here with the growing body of work that is appearing both in the academic and trade press on the status especially of eastern German women, and also more recently on the relationship between women in the eastern and western halves of the country—and far more intent upon pointing out what seems to me to be a possible meta-topic that could benefit German studies, wherever it is undertaken.[10] Unlike Sara Lennox, who has rightly asserted that U.S. feminists have influenced U.S. feminist-Germanists who have in turn forced issues of multiplicity and multiculturalism upon the field of German studies,[11] I am choosing a different point of departure by designating a uniquely German experience, namely, the clashes and misunderstandings and differences between the understanding of feminism in the nationalist blocs that eastern and western Germany have represented, and asserting that this may well be a way in which Germanists on all fronts could indeed make an important contribution—could, in fact, give a profile to German feminism that it has lacked before, a theoretical framing that has immense potential.

I have never doubted that feminism could enrich the field of German studies—that indeed it has already done so in important ways. But the two questions that I posed earlier about how U.S. and German feminists could think together and, by means of their work on gender, become acknowledged by and included more centrally in German studies, cannot be answered by a single suggestion. I feel, in fact, a continuing skepticism about a positive and constructive response to such questions, based in part on my own cultural location as an American woman who has been a witness to and participant in U.S. feminist developments since the 1970s, but who has also spent much of her adult life studying the often depressing stories of nineteenth-century German women and their struggles with the patriarchy. It is almost always distressing to think in terms of the status of German women in their society, both now and at earlier times. It is also easy to feel cocky about the far more privileged place of U.S. feminists, within and outside of the academy. But there continue to be uneasinesses in me that cause me to conclude my thoughts with some polemical statements that concern the conference at which these remarks were originally presented.

For a meeting whose title emphasized the "changing faces" of German studies, I found it ironic to see this session entitled "Women's Voices" followed by one called "German Intellectuals," with its exclusively male speakers and male subjects. This could be read as an implication that women are in some other category besides intellectuals, that they are therefore marked not as writers, poets, Jews, and that their primary characteristic is and remains what is still generally understood to be a biological designation. Women as subjects were not only located in "Women's Voices"—they were included in the papers of other sessions as well. But feminist inquiry itself appears to have remained marginal or unproblematized, and hardly the vital element that it deserves to be.

In addition, although I am always pleased to be involved in discussions of how we might transform German studies, I must wonder at the dates that were chosen for this conference. The meeting might indeed have had a very different make-up, brought forth a very different set of debates, had it not—perhaps inadvertently—been scheduled on precisely the same days as the annual meeting of Women in German. In Florida, the feminists were convening to discuss interdisciplinary connections to German feminist work, connections between cultural theory and feminism, and pedagogic methods for teaching diversity. The German studies people were in Boulder, thinking about the Holocaust, German intellectuals, and "women's voices." And the twain do not seem likely to meet. However unintentional this simultaneity may have been, its symbolic significance is certainly to be noted.

What this indicates for me is an enacting of the very split I continue to see in German studies between it and feminist inquiry. And there is, I believe, an analysis to be drawn from this situation. For a very long time, feminist scholars—here and in Germany[12]—have debated the pros and cons of meeting by themselves or joining together with others: a debate that has, by extension, led to a discussion of institutionalizing women's studies versus so-called mainstreaming, or separatism versus integration. When I have been asked a question around such binaries, my standard answer has always been that we need and benefit from both locations. At the same time, I myself am learning to think beyond the binaries in other ways, partly because of an essay by the Latina feminist philosopher Maria Lugones that we published in 1994 in *Signs*. I had asked three lesbian women of color to provide their impressions on the concept of separatism, as it might be viewed today. Lugones's piece is the most startling of the three, in part because she never uses the word *separatism*, instead choosing to focus, as her title says, on "Purity, Impurity, and Separation."[13] Her point of departure is deceptively simple and concrete, a detailed description of what happens when an egg white is separated from an egg yoke, which concludes by asking whether separation is "always or necessarily an exercise in purity."[14] From that example, Lugones moves the egg on to its role in the production of mayonnaise, when it is added to the other ingredients, and when adding more than a certain amount of oil will lead to another sort of separation. And with that, she has reached her operative image, curdling.

By the time she concludes her essay, curdling has become an answer of sorts to problems of separation and purity whereby "separation as curdling, an exercise in impurity" is to be seen as different from "separation as splitting, an exercise in purity."[15] Her choice of curdle-separation, as she calls it, allows curdling to become a tactic: "[A] haphazard technique of survival as an active subject, [but also] an art of resistance, metamorphosis, transformation."[16] She provides examples of such curdling, including the following: "bi- and multilingual experimentation; . . .categorial blurring and confusion; . . . practicing trickstery and foolery; . . . withdrawing our services from the pure or their agents whenever possible and with panache; . . . marking our cultural mixtures as we move." And she leaves her readers with the thought that "although we will not be acknowledged, we have been seen as threatening the univocality of life lived in a state of purity, their management of us, their power over us."[17] In other words, separatism, as it has been traditionally understood by feminists, is no longer an issue for her. And separation, at least curdle-separation, can no longer be connected for her with its purifying meaning.

Does all of this have anything to do with my thoughts on the simultaneous holding of the Boulder German Studies conference and the Florida Women in German conference, or on what I still consider to be the tenuous and precarious relationship between German studies and feminism? Surely, Maria Lugones is writing primarily from her position as a woman of color, with the emphasis neither on her gender nor her sexual orientation, but on her ethnicity: although the request to her was for a position paper on a specifically gendered issue, namely whether the separation of the sexes has any validity as an idea today or is indeed still a part of feminist debates, she chose instead to write above all as a Latina. I think she nevertheless has a suggestion applicable to Germanist feminists like me who continue to feel the problematic nature of their relationship to German studies. The "women's voices" separation that has so often been imposed by others upon us smacks almost of a separation of purity and splitting. Still, the fact that those of us who are feminists made a choice to go to Boulder rather than Florida to meet with other feminists is not necessarily an illogical step on our part. For actually, we belonged in both locations. We certainly see the connections and the contradictions between German studies and feminism: we live them. And if our presence leads to curdling and not to purity, to the curdling of stirring things up and not to the purity of True Womanhood that is implied by a label like "women's voices," then that is all to the good. We need, of course, to maintain our own discrete identities as feminists, but as practicing German-studies people interested and invested in the future of our academic field, we can also provide links, seeing to it that our voices are heard in all sorts of settings, threatening the "univocality of life" along the way.

I am especially grateful to Susanna Ferlito and Joan Raisner for offering constructive suggestions on an earlier draft of this paper.

NOTES

1. Sara Lennox, "Feminismus und German Studies in den USA," typescript, 11.
2. Cf. Ruth-Ellen B. Joeres, " 'Language Is Also a Place of Struggle': The Language of Feminism and the Language of American *Germanistik*," *Women in German Yearbook 8: Feminist Studies in German Literature and Culture* (1993): 247–257.
3. "Commentary: Thoughts on *Germanistik* and Feminism," German Studies Association annual meeting, October, 1992.
4. Lennox, "Feminismus und German Studies," 1–2.
5. Such appears to be the case in Reinhold Grimm's interpretation of that term, for example, as evidenced in his 1992 *German Quarterly* special issue "Focus on Women"; the almost total lack of acknowledgment of feminist literary/critical work by any of the included articles is startling.
6. Cf. Edith Hoshino Altbach et al., eds., *German Feminism: Readings in Politics and Literature* (Albany: State University of New York Press, 1984); Gisela Ecker, ed., *Feminist Aesthetics*, trans. Harriet Anderson (Boston: Beacon Press, 1985).
7. Ruth-Ellen B. Joeres, "Louise Otto-Peters: Grenzen und Grenzüberschreitungen," keynote address at the conference "Louise Otto-Peters: politische Denkerin und Wegbereiterin der deutschen Frauenbewegung," Universität Leipzig; "Theorie und Praxis im heutigen amerikanischen akademischen Feminismus," Amerika-Haus Leipzig, March, 1995.
8. Cf. Andrew Parker et al., eds., *Nationalisms and Sexualities* (New York: Routledge, 1992).
9. *New York Times* (October 3, 1995), A5.
10. Cf. for example two recent books appearing in the trade press: Katrin Rohnstock, ed., *Stiefschwestern: Was Ost-Frauen und West-Frauen voneinander denken* (Frankfurt a.M: Fischer, 1994); Ulrike Helwerth and Gislinde Schwarz, *Von Muttis und Emanzen: Feministinnen in Ost- und Westdeutschland* (Frankfurt a.M.: Fischer, 1995).
11. Lennox, "Feminismus und German Studies, 2.
12. I have given a number of lectures in Germany in recent years on aspects of American feminism; two of them have appeared in revised form in *Feministische Studien*: "Von Frauenstudien zur Frauenforschung: Neuere Trends im akademischen Feminismus in den USA," *Feministische Studien* 6.1 (November 1988): 129–135; "Sisterhood? Jede für sich? Gedanken über die heutige feministische Diskussion in den USA," *Feministische Studien* 12.1 (May 1994): 6–16.
13. Maria Lugones, "Purity, Impurity, and Separation," *Signs* 19.2 (Winter 1994): 458–479.
14. Ibid., 458.
15. Ibid., 460.
16. Ibid., 478.
17. Ibid., 478 and 479.

10
Germans and Jews After the Fall of the Wall: The Promises and Problems of Hybridity

TODD HERZOG

Mixed identities seem to be making a comeback. In response to intense pressure, at least a dozen states have adopted a "multiracial" category on various registration forms and the U.S. government has tested a similar category for inclusion on the 2000 census, already prompting widespread complaints that the African-American community will lose numbers if people choose to label themselves "multiracial."[1] And even Betty Crocker, that icon of American domesticity, is going hybrid: General Mills is reportedly assembling seventy-five pictures of women of various ethnicities in order to combine them into a new image for Ms. Crocker. Finally, by anyone's estimation, hybridity is the theoretical flavor of the day. Contemporary cultural criticism has resurrected the hybrid as an icon of political resistance to colonial power, repeating a fascination that captured the West's imagination at the end of the nineteenth century.[2]

At the forefront of this critical movement is Homi K. Bhabha, who has developed a powerful model of cultural hybridity that seeks to interrogate colonial discourse by focusing on the point "where cultural differences 'contingently' and conflictually touch,"[3] in order to problematize a nation's claim to a homogeneous identity:

> Hybrid hyphenations emphasize the incommensurable elements—the stubborn chunks—as the basis of cultural identifications. What is at issue is the performative nature of differential identities: the regulation and negotiation of those spaces that are continually, *contingently*, "opening out," remaking the boundaries, exposing the limits of any claim to a singular or autonomous sign of difference—be it class, gender or race.[4]

Such a hybrid strategy, for Bhabha, tends to articulate itself at historically transformative moments and "opens up a space of negotiation . . . that is neither assimilation nor collaboration," but rather "makes possible the emergence of an 'interstitial' agency that refuses binary representation of social antagonism."[5]

Neither comfortably "inside," nor reassuringly "outside" of the dominant culture, hybrid agencies are able to construct new "visions of community, and versions of historic memory." [6]

Bhabha's model of cultural hybridity, developed ultimately in an English context, is a positive one—the hybrid position is a good position to occupy. His model seems to provide a means by which to get beyond the body as a marker of difference and gives the hybrid the tools with which to accomplish this. What happens, however, when one historicizes Bhabha's model? In this chapter, I want to apply Bhabha's model of hybridity to an event that seems to beg for such a reading: the reemergence of a united German nation after 1989–1990 and the simultaneous reemergence of a vibrant German-Jewish culture. As they seek to justify life in the German diaspora, it seems as if the third generation of German-Jewish writers—such as Maxim Biller, Esther Dischereit, Barbara Honigmann, Irene Dische, and Raphael Seligmann—have been attentively reading their postcolonial criticism. There is a marked tendency among these authors, as they attempt to reconcile German and Jewish identities and carve out a space for themselves in the German diaspora, to adopt and thematize an "impure" identity, and occupy a hybrid position vis-à-vis German society. Since Jews trace their lineage through the mother and Germans trace their lineage through the father, the children of "mixed marriages" that one continually finds in third-generation writings are the corporeal manifestations of the problem of reconciling Jewish and German identities.

I have two projects here: first, I want to look at the cultural element of the contemporary German diaspora, examining the ways in which third-generation writers articulate an identity that is both German and Jewish in an attempt to create a place in Germany for the German Jew; second, by historicizing theories of hybridity, I want to interrogate these theories, testing whether they actually effect the cultural transformations that proponents claim for them.

Hybridity is certainly not a new issue in German-Jewish relations. As I mentioned above, hybridity was as fascinating to cultural critics at the end of the nineteenth century as it is at the beginning of the twenty-first, and contemporary constructions of hybridity are continually fouled by this old model. The model I am referring to is that of the *Mischling*, which constructed the hybrid as a pathological character and held the floor in German racial science from the late 1800s until 1945. As Sander L. Gilman has demonstrated, fin-de-siècle racial science, seeking to come to terms with arguments about the supposed death of the Jewish race through assimilation, argued that not only are the offspring of German-Jewish marriages Jews, they are, in fact, Jews "in heightened form, who bear all the stigmata of degeneration that exist in incestuous or inbred families."[7] The degeneration of the Jew, the argument runs, manifests itself especially in the *Mischling*, who, according to Werner Sombart, "even though they are so very beautiful and so very talented, seem to lack a psychological balance that is provided by pure racial stock. We find all too often intellectually or morally unbalanced individuals who decay ethically in suicide or madness."[8] Lacking the balance of a "pure" center to his/her identity, the *Mischling* is a pathological character, marked by degeneration, insanity, and hysteria. The *Mischling* might be able to "pass" as a "pure" German for a while, but, "hidden within the name and Germanic lineage of the child is the true corruption of the race, the maternal lineage of the Jew."[9] As a 1920s anti-Semite said to Jakob Wassermann: "Jewishness is like a concentrated dye: a minute quantity suffices to give a specific character—or, at least, some traces of it—to an incomparably greater mass."[10] In all cases of "mixed" marriages (of hybridity) the argument runs that "the Jew will out." In fact, he/she returns with a vengeance, degenerate, pathological and hysterical: ". . . the exemplary hidden Jew waiting to corrupt the body politic."[11]

How does hybridity, with the legacy of the *Mischling* model, fare as it returns to the new German nation? I want to look at just one representative case study: Esther Dischereit's two novels, *Joëmi's Table* (1988) and *Merryn* (1992). *Joëmi's Table* and *Merryn* are surely the most radical attempts at hybridity in contemporary German-Jewish literature. *Joëmi's Table* opens with an explicit decision to become Jewish: "After twenty years as a non-Jew, I want to become a Jew again."[12] The narrator, Hannah's Daughter, is a textbook hybrid: Jewish mother, non-Jewish father. Or, as she succinctly puts it: "Mom's dead, dad's a goy."[13] What follows her decision to convert is a complex and radically decentered narrative that traces her search for a hybrid Jewish identity. *Merryn* records the journey of a teenage girl who runs away from home and travels throughout France and Germany in search of her identity.

Neither search ends in Israel, for both characters reject the Jewish State as a site of Jewish identity. Hannah's Daughter explicitly critiques the concept of national homogeneity: "One country is no country," she says to explain why she has no desire to visit the Promised Land—it is an artificial construct, she argues, built with bullets and bulldozers.[14] Dischereit makes a similar critique of Israel in a recent essay: though she admits to taking comfort in the escape route offered by the possibility of an Israeli passport, she nonetheless "fail[s] to associate anything positive with the idea of a nation-state based on a homogeneous people."[15] Like her character in *Joëmi's Table*, she refuses to define her Jewish identity within the boundaries of a nation, and consequently refuses to see dealings between Germans and Jews as "the kind of normal state of affairs that exists between the citizens of two nations."[16] This is precisely the state of affairs that has characterized German-Jewish relations since 1945, as can be seen in such philo-Semitic publications as the special 1992 issue of *Der Spiegel* titled "Jews and Germans," which constructs the two groups as separate and parallels a study of German attitudes toward Jews with a study of *Israeli* attitudes toward Germans, "as if there were no Jewish Diaspora in Germany to ask."[17]

Having rejected spatial separation in the Promised Land as a route toward finding a Jewish identity, both Dischereit and Hannah's Daughter choose a path that is precisely the opposite of settling in a *home*land: they adopt a migratory position toward Germany and other societies, choosing to be "unhomed." *Joëmi's Table* is perhaps best read as a sort of travelogue, the record of a complex series of trips across national borders, temporal borders, and personal borders (those between individual voices and individual bodies).

What sort of travelogue is this? I have been referring to *Joëmi's Table* as a narrative and to Hannah's Daughter as a character, but I am not sure that either term is appropriate. I have not yet met anybody who can tell the story of *Joëmi's Table* or even enumerate its characters. All attempts at constructing even a simple family tree fail. Names, dates, places, relations, and events seem to proliferate and overlap in a manner that lacks any logical consistency, as the narrative moves back and forth between the past and the present, between first-person and third-person narration. Hannah's Daughter is now the assimilated Jew who decides to register with the authorities, now the young mother who travels through North Africa, visiting the graves of diaspora Jews of Spain's Golden Age, now the widow who visits a German soldier's grave in France, now the child who eats a sandwich during a break in the school day. She calls herself "Hannah-Ruth" and "Meta, Heidi, Elke," pointedly rendering both hybrid constellations of names in the singular: "Finally—after three, four further streets—Hannah-Ruth buys Meta, Heidi, Elke this apple."[18]

Who, then is Hannah's Daughter? She is an interpersonal, intertemporal, interspatial *history*—located in a communal space where individual identities are fragmented into countless pieces and reassembled across time and space to form a hybrid voice situated, to adopt Bhabha's terminology, "in-between"—in-between nations, in-between times, in-between people. Hannah's Daughter is an endlessly hyphenated, endlessly fragmented, endlessly mobile identity. As such, she would seem to be a model of Bhabha's enunciation of hybrid agency,[19] refusing to cast herself as Other in German society, while at the same time maintaining an opposition to it. She becomes, in effect, *in-betweenness* per se; more pointedly, she is the *per se of in-betweenness*.

This in-betweenness, however, turns out to be an illusion. As she crosses the border between Germany and France, Hannah's Daughter reflects upon her identity and its visibility:

> But what if they demanded that I disrobe—why should they demand that—what if they demanded that I disrobe and I did. They would see the star, through the clothes—they can't see it—through my clothes, burned into my skin—it's not burned into my skin, I was never there—burned into my skin and the dogs would attack me.[20]

Significantly, these thoughts occur at a border crossing, the *locus classicus* of a hybrid identity. But it is precisely here that she questions her status as a hybrid: she can dress in German clothing, but her body remains Jewish; underneath her "disguise," she is indelibly marked as a Jew. I noted earlier that *Joëmi's Table* opens with a *decision* to become Jewish. But in the novel's opening scene, at the very point this decision is made, when to be Jewish seems to mean simply registering with the authorities and paying an additional 800 Deutsche Mark tax for the *Gemeinde* (community), the question of citizenship is broached. When questioned about her nationality, the narrator has difficulty responding: ". . . should I say German? Of course, one would have to say German, BUT would then follow . . . what BUT? But Jew. There it stands thick and heavy, the word that had been imprinted on the back and hung with cords around my neck."[21] What seems to be a question of dual citizenship is already in tension as "German" and "Jew" appear on two sides of a medallion hung around the narrator's neck, and the back side always threatens to reveal itself. As the marked body of the border-crossing passage seems to argue, there really is no decision at all: one can dress up in the clothes of the dominant culture, but underneath one is marked by what the narrator elsewhere calls "the birthmark of Cain."[22]

In one scene, Hannah's Daughter's schoolmates ask her about her religion and she answers that she is "Protestant," which is technically true, since that is how she was raised. But the children refuse to accept that answer: "You lie, you lie," they shout: "She's a Jew, I know that for sure."[23] Here we see where contemporary notions of hybridity are fouled by the historical model of the *Mischling*: the Jew can "pass" as a German for a while, but will ultimately reveal his/her Semitic markings, and even the children know that "for sure." Merryn's journey ends with a similar disappointment: though one character describes her as "the one living plural," she closes the novel by proclaiming herself to feel like an "integrated foreign body" and appends the rhyme of Humpty Dumpty, the hopelessly fragmented character who can never be put back together again.[24]

At this point, I would like to turn to the reception of Dischereit's two novels to see how their hybrid constructions are read.[25] Reviewers of *Joëmi's Table* are nearly unanimous in praising the novel as a whole and also nearly unanimous in pronouncing it difficult to comprehend. Gabriele Winter's review in *Auftritt* is exemplary in its faulting the novel for "too many chained together fragments" and "too many undecodable mysteries."[26] This fragmented language is, however, appropriate and justified, according to Winter, in those passages that deal with Hannah's Daughter's survivor mother, who is, in fact, responsible for the "difficult, fragmentary, and irresolute" nature of the book. Jewish survivors, she claims, cannot articulate their suffering. The book Dischereit should have written, according to Winter, is a book about her mother: "Esther Dischereit would have to write another book, one that deals only with her mother." Winter had started her review by complaining that the Jew is often cast too easily as the Other—"The past captures the present. Too often is 'Jew' (this scapegoating function is interchangeable with other minorities) perceived and spoken of as the Other"—but she ends with a reference to the specifically Jewish nature of the text: the Jewish mother becomes the key to all events in the narrator's life and the cause for its difficulty and its strangeness. The hybrid is an undecodable chain of fragments, a hysteric incapable of telling her story, who can ultimately only be understood through her "repressed" identity.

The reviews of Dischereit's second novel, *Merryn*, are even more explicit in their condemnation of the hysteria of mixed identities. Hanna Rheinz, writing in *Freitag*, notes Dischereit's difficult, fragmented style that somehow holds disparate elements together and explains it thus: "[I]t is the language of the inhuman, the crippled language of events, activities, and orders. It is the language of bastard children, whose suffering remains mute, without reflection, without having been heard."[27] Rheinz explicitly points to hybridity (*Bastardkinder*) as the source of Merryn's/Dischereit's (Rheinz, like most reviewers of Dischereit's work, continually identifies author with protagonist) inability to communicate; the hysterical *Mischling*, lacking a center to his/her personality, is incapable of telling his/her story. However, according to this reviewer, Merryn finds her voice when she comes upon the apartment of her grandparents, who were victims of the Holocaust. Similarly, Rheinz sees Dischereit finding her voice through another victim of the Holocaust, Anne Frank, whose diaries provide the inspiration for *Merryn*. The "real" story behind all the messiness and difficulty of hybrid fragmentation turns out to be, as in Winter's review of *Joëmi's Table*, a "Jewish story."

Gerhard Schulz's thoroughly negative review of *Merryn* in the *Frankfurter Allgemeine Zeitung* picks up on the same themes as Rheinz's review, criticizing the book as "one big puzzle" and asking whether "Humpty Dumpty can be compared with reality as the basis of literature."[28] Only one thing legitimizes this book, according to Schulz, and it can be found on the book jacket: the fact that Merryn's grandparents were deported to a concentration camp: "[T]hat is the only information that can be taken away from the book, and even this requires effort."[29] Like Winter in her review of *Joëmi's Table*, Schulz would like Dischereit to have avoided the confusing "Humpty Dumpty" routine and written a different book: "Especially today it would be interesting to take part in the experiences of a young German-Jewish woman, who is searching for her place between past and present, religion and nation."[30] Which is, of course, precisely the two books Dischereit has written! However, Schulz objects to the fragmentation and messiness of this search; in short, to its hybridity. What he wants is a voyeuristic look into the exotic world of the contemporary German Jew, a world that he explicitly casts as markedly different from his own. In the end, it is once again the "Jewish story" that matters.

The reception of Dischereit's novels reveals the point at which hybridity fails: hybrids lack a center to their personality; they are unbalanced, fragmented, and unable to communicate. The hybrid is, in short, the *Mischling*, whose "repressed" identity makes him/her a pathological character. And, in the end, that element returns to dominate, as the confusion of fragmented identity is cleared away to reveal the real "Jewish story" that it masks.

It is not only at the level of reception that hybridity breaks down in Dischereit's novels. Like her characters, Dischereit is a hybrid: Jewish mother, non-Jewish father. She initially appears to write from a politically hybrid position, announcing her program to disrupt the very concept of a homogeneous nation. All nations come in for the same treatment she gave Israel:

> It may be better for a Jew to be conscious of the temporality and evanescence of any kind of belonging to a nation—to forego the certainty of any set locality, to accept it as long as it lasts, but not to be too attached to it, or to believe in it . . . if ever we become part again of an existing order; despairing, deceived like the Jews of the Weimar period—or wouldn't it be more sensible and dignified to find one's place outside, alongside, the order—to be a disorder and create a new order?[31]

What might this new order look like? A glimpse can be seen in Hannah's Daughter's vision of a community constructed around the symbol of the "Also-Person" (*Auch-Mensch*). After overhearing a conversation in which a father tells his incredulous son that the Jew is "also a person," the narrator considers an alliance of "Also-People": "On the other side of the street live the Turkish Also-People. Should we build a community of Also-People, a class division into Person and Also-Person? . . . Can one simply become a Jew again? I will become a Turk at the very least. Then at least we could populate our other side of the street quite well."[32] But here we see the limits of Dischereit's hybrid pluralism: to become a Jew in Germany means to "come out" and move to the other side of the street, making oneself visibly different like the Turks, who are in a very different position from the Jews in contemporary German society, being much more often the targets of violent hate crimes and not being able to claim German citizenship. Dischereit's hybrid does not disrupt the notion of nationness as a liminal figure, but rather by casting herself (problematically) as explicitly and visibly Other. The "in-between" position is not an inhabitable position.

Can one, then, simply become a Jew again? In an interview with the *Allgemeine jüdische Wochenzeitung*, Dischereit answers this question thus: "The question of whether one can do it doesn't really present itself. One perhaps must do it, whether one wants to or not. It is not only a positive identification, but also a negative one, it is a curse—the curse of not forgetting. I have perhaps done nothing other than admit that it exists."[33] She rejects the notion, which she labels as American, that "he is a Jew who dresses himself as such" and echoes her character in *Joëmi's Table*, claiming that "there are people and there are Jews." Hence, Dischereit sees herself as ultimately a Jewish writer in the German language, writing for a foreign audience from a position as Other. She articulates her position in vivid terms: "To write in Jewish in front of a German-German audience has a slatternly prostituting air about it—like a woman getting undressed in front of the eyes of men, I know. But I see no alternative."[34] The hybridizing hyphen is rendered powerless when both sides are occupied by the same identity, as in the phrase "German-German." Dischereit sees herself as a foreign body writing in a foreign language ("Jewish"). And here, once again, we come across the metaphor of undressing: the German-Jewish author takes off her German clothes in front of the German reading public to reveal that "birthmark of Cain" that she has been hiding.

Hybridity ultimately fails in the case of Esther Dischereit, as the German-Jewish hybrid is read at all levels as the Jew in hiding who suddenly becomes visible. Dischereit's case is representative of much contemporary German-Jewish writing,[35] in which the disjunctive element in hybridity—the dash that pulls apart even as it draws together—continually comes to dominate, as it is fouled by the old model of the pathology of the *Mischling*. In fact, contemporary theory seems to repeat this fascination with the monstrosity of the hybrid, referring to him/her as an "unstable element," a "terrifying, exorbitant object," and "a disturbing question" that "speaks in tongues," to cull a few phrases (not entirely fairly) from Bhabha's *Location of Culture*.[36]

I will close with a brief anecdote. I was recently discussing this essay with a Germanist unfamiliar with the term "hybridity," so another person at the table (a distinguished academic whose liberal credentials are impeccable) translated it for her: "The hybrid is a *Mischling*." This translation, which we have seen being continually applied in the case of German Jewry, points directly to the problem.

NOTES

1. See Clarence Page, "What Color Are You?" *Chicago Tribune* (September 9, 1995).
2. For an illuminating discussion of the history of theories of hybridity, see Robert J. C. Young, *Colonial Desire: Hybridity in Theory, Culture and Race* (New York: Routledge, 1995).
3. Homi K. Bhabha, *The Location of Culture* (New York: Routledge, 1994), 207.
4. Ibid., 219.
5. Homi K. Bhabha, "Culture's in Between," *Artforum* (September, 1993): 212.
6. Ibid., 212.
7. Sander L. Gilman, *The Case of Sigmund Freud: Medicine and Identity in the Fin De Siècle* (Baltimore: The Johns Hopkins University Press, 1993), 195.
8. Werner Sombart, *Die Zukunft der Juden* (Leipzig: Duncker und Humblot, 1912), 44. Quoted in Gilman, *Case of Sigmund Freud*, 195.
9. Sander L. Gilman, *The Jew's Body* (New York: Routledge, 1991), 102.
10. Jakob Wassermann, *My Life as a German and Jew* (London: George Allen & Unwin, 1933), 72. Quoted in Gilman, *The Jew's Body*, 175.
11. Gilman, *The Jew's Body*, 102.
12. Esther Dischereit, *Joëmis Tisch* (Frankfurt a.M.: Suhrkamp, 1988), 9. All translations are mine.
13. Ibid., 9.
14. Ibid., 102.
15. Esther Dischereit, "No Exit From This Jewry," in Sander L. Gilman and Karen Remmler, eds., *Reemerging Jewish Culture in Germany*, trans. Michael Roloff (New York: New York University Press, 1994), 274.
16. Ibid., 274.
17. Gilman and Remmler, *Reemerging Jewish Culture*, 9–10. See also Katharina Ochse, " 'What Could Be More Fruitful, More Healing, More Purifying?' Representations of Jews in the German Media after 1989," in the same volume, 113–129.
18. Dischereit, *Joëmis Tisch*, 26.
19. In fact, *Joëmi's Table* shares many similarities with Toni Morrison's *Beloved* (1987), to which Bhabha continually turns when laying out his theories of postcolonial hybridity. See, for example, *The Location of Culture*, 9–18, and "Culture's in Between," 212. My reading of the pluralized voice in *Joëmi's Table* owes a debt to Bhabha's reading of *Beloved*.
20. Dischereit, *Joëmis Tisch*, 35.
21. Ibid., 9.
22. Ibid.
23. Ibid., 21.

24. Esther Dischereit, *Merryn* (Frankfurt a.M.: Suhrkamp, 1992), 117–118.

25. My examination of the reception of Dischereit's novels owes a large debt to the work of Sander L. Gilman. See his *Jews in Today's German Culture* (Bloomington: Indiana Univ. Press, 1995), esp. 64–69.

26. Gabriele Winter, "Suche nach Identifikation," *Auftritt: Rhein-Main-Illustrierte* (March 1989).

27. Hanna Rheinz, "Bitterkraut," *Freitag* (July 10, 1992).

28. Gerhard Schulz, "Die Steppenwölfin schnuppert," *Frankfurter Allgemeine Zeitung* (May 23, 1992).

29. Ibid.

30. Ibid.

31. Dischereit, "No Exit From This Jewry," 277.

32. Dischereit, *Joëmis Tisch*, 23.

33. "Es gibt Menschen—und es gibt Juden," *Allgemeine jüdische Wochenzeitung* (September 8, 1989).

34. Dischereit, "No Exit From This Jewry," 281.

35. See, for example, the hybrid constructions in Maxim Biller's "Verrat," in *Wenn ich einmal reich und tot bin* (Cologne: Kiepenheuer & Witsch, 1990); Irene Dische, "Eine Jüdin für Charles Allen," *Fromme Lügen: Sieben Erzählungen*, trans. Otto Bayer and Monika Elwenspoek (Frankfurt a.M.: Eichborn Verlag, 1989); Barbara Honigmann, *Eine Liebe aus nichts* (Berlin: Rowohlt, 1991); and Raphael Seligmann, *Rubinsteins Versteigerung* (Munich: dtv, 1989).

36. Bhabha, *Location of Culture*, 17, 26, 113.

II
Challenging the Status Quo: Michael Wolffsohn's Views on German-Jewish-Israeli Relations

ANDREAS MICHEL

In the recent *Festschrift* for Harry Zohn, *Brücken über dem Abgrund,* Andrei S. Markovits writes despairingly about the new Germany.[1] In his view, Germany's return to nationhood represents a kind of "normalization" that makes him question the future of Germany's relationship to its catastrophic past:

> Germans will become less guilt-ridden as well as less responsible vis-à-vis Jews, meaning that the Jews, too, will become "normalized." This in turn, means that Jews will become even more abstracted and "musealized" than they had already been in the Bundesrepublik. . . . This means that the Germans will never be able to come to terms with the Holocaust no matter how good their intentions have been or might still be.[2]

There is evidence today that Markovits is right, i.e., that a process of "normalization" is currently occurring in Germany. As I would like to show, however, such "normalization" is a welcome development if it leads to a reconsideration of the relationship between Germans and Jews. In presenting the ideas of Michael Wolffsohn, I would like to point out that "normalization" does not have to mean forgetting, repressing, or overcoming the past. Indeed, Markovits's own choice of words ("coming to terms") has a most likely unintended ring of finality to it that I believe incompatible with the event of the Shoah. The issues raised by Wolffsohn's provocative analyses of German-Jewish-Israeli relations, however, suggest a differentiated approach to the memory of the Shoah as well as a critical reassessment of over forty years of German politics in its shadow.

My thesis is that Wolffsohn's writings are indicative of the changes in the intellectual climate of the new Germany. For almost fifty years, the notion of collective German guilt overdetermined the role of the German intellectual. If it is true that, at least in modern times, intellectuals have conceived of themselves as the moral conscience of the society to which they belong, then recent German history is a case in point. After 1945, German intellectuals spoke within the forbidding frame of the Shoah, which they saw, and still see, as a *Zivilisationsbruch*, a caesura of such proportions that it forbids mere politicking (i.e., the struggle of opinion and interpretation) to any morally sensitive person. The Shoah thus prescribed the parameters of morality and of politics. With the enormity of the caesura came the enormity of German guilt, which resulted in the erection of taboos that informed public discourse and political decisionmaking. For progressive German intellectuals—the only ones public opinion would tolerate—questions of nationalism, patriotism, and, above all, Germany's relation to Jews and to Israel, were saturated with taboos. These taboos remained in effect up until and beyond the "historians' debate."

It is the context of these taboos that the writings of Michael Wolffsohn address. His analyses provoke because they challenge long-held moral convictions. He has therefore been attacked by representatives of all parties concerned: the German-Jewish community, German intellectuals, members of the Socialist Democratic Party (SPD) and *Grüne* (Greens) in Bavaria, and last but not least, the political right which, in Wolffsohn's words, showers him with hate mail. This latter fact should give some of his progressive critics, who see him only as the conservative German intellectual, pause. While it is true that Wolffsohn embraces (and is in turn embraced by) the Christian Democrats, the challenge that his analyses pose to the intellectual status quo extend far beyond the limited range of party politics.

Wolffsohn calls himself a "GermanJewish" patriot (*einen deutschjüdischen Patrioten*)—without a hyphen between *deutsch* and *jüdisch* because he sees himself as living proof that the two identities are not incompatible.[3] While nationalism has been anathema in German intellectual circles ever since the Nazi regime, patriotism before the fall of the Wall fared no better. To be sure, Jürgen Habermas made Sternberger's notion of constitutional patriotism acceptable, but the notion itself had more to do with a rationalist argument than with an emotional identification with one's country.[4] Wolffsohn is, of course, keenly aware of the multiple provocations that his confident self-description elicits. In his defense, he maintains that this description has basis in fact. Born in Tel-Aviv in 1947 as a son of German-Jewish immigrants, he returned to Germany with his parents in 1954 and there received his formal education at the Gymnasium and the university. Between 1967 and 1970 he returned to Israel to complete his military service. Since 1981 Wolffsohn has been professor for contemporary history at the University for the German Army (*Universität der Bundeswehr*) in Munich. In January 1992, he refused to cooperate with the newly appointed dean of the social sciences because the new dean had repeatedly performed public readings from *Mein Kampf* on the day of Hitler's anniversary. In the ensuing scandal, the president of the university, who had backed the dean, was forced to resign.[5] In 1989, Wolffsohn was nominated to head the *Zentrum für Antisemitismusforschung* (Center for Anti-Semitism Research) at the Technische Universität in Berlin but withdrew his candidacy when it became clear that he was considered too controversial by too many parties involved. As should be clear from these few biographical remarks, Wolffsohn is a person between worlds, in the midst of a highly charged territory. He calls his GermanJewish patriotism *cosmopolitan*, in order to defend himself against attacks by leftist politicians and Jewish critics alike who identify him with older German nationalist traditions. What he means by cosmopolitan ought to become clear during the following exposition of his ideas.

The most urgent question is perhaps, how can Wolffsohn call himself a GermanJewish patriot in the face of the catastrophic German-Jewish past? Wolffsohn's identification with the *Bundesrepublik*—and now with united Germany—is based on two fundamental observations: first, that post–World War II Germany has for the time of its existence proven qualitatively different from Nazi Germany, for which it deserves credit, and secondly, that a generational shift has occurred between perpetrators and victims of the Shoah on the one hand, and their children on the other—a shift that, in his view, ought to fundamentally alter the relations between Germans and Jews today.

While the positive assessment of the *Bundesrepublik*'s dealing with its past informs Wolffsohn's view of West German politics in general and of Israel and the Jewish diaspora in particular, his argument concerning the generational shift is foremost a moral and personal one. With respect to this question, Wolffsohn is reluctant to assume "the inherited martyrdom, without having suffered," and "to misuse the genocide to my personal advantage and adorn myself with the suffering of others."[6] He believes false martyrdom to be a desecration of the victims of the Shoah. To the same extent that he does not see himself as martyr, he does not view Germans of his generation and younger as marked by eternal guilt. Like him, a majority of Germans today has no direct experience of the Hitler state and is therefore not *criminally* responsible and cannot be held eternally guilty for the Shoah. This recognition does, however, not absolve Germans from their *historical responsibility* for remembering what happened in the name of Germany. On the contrary, just as Jews born after the catastrophe ought to insist on memory, it is incumbent upon Germans not to erase the part of their history that more than any other defines their relation to the world community. Commonsensical as these perceptions might seem, they have radical consequences. For this common-sense position enables Wolffsohn to come to conclusions about German-Jewish-Israeli relations that are quite unlike those held by the majority of German intellectuals whose positions are, for understandable reasons, overdetermined by taboos.

Because of his biography, Wolffsohn is in a unique position to step beyond these taboos and to practice a "detached" approach that allows him to distinguish different levels in German-Jewish-Israeli relations. He identifies two sets of oppositions that structure his interpretations. The first, that of *Tagespolitik* versus *Geschichtspolitik*, enables him to distinguish pragmatic from historical considerations in German policy decisions. The second opposition, between public opinion (*öffentliche Meinung*) and publicized opinion (*veröffentlichte Meinung*), registers the difference between opinion *polls*, on the one hand, and opinion *pieces* by German intellectuals, on the other. On the basis of these oppositions, Wolffsohn examines the history of German-Jewish-Israeli relations and comes to the conclusion that, all in all, the *Bundesrepublik*, as successor state to the Nazi crimes, has seriously attempted to assume its historical responsibilities vis-à-vis the Jews and the Jewish state.

Wolffsohn's favorite example is Konrad Adenauer's restitution policy toward the state of Israel that, according to Wolffsohn, was based not on *Tagespolitik* alone, but to a similar degree on moral and therefore historical considerations (what he calls *Geschichtspolitik*). According to Wolffsohn's research, Adenauer pushed his policies through against American indifference (they were more interested in German rearmament), against opposition in his own government, as well as against overwhelming German public sentiment. In 1952, almost 50 percent of West Germans polled were opposed to restitution payments to Israel.[7] Pitting Adenauer's governmental policy against public opinion, Wolffsohn gives Adenauer credit for his personal investment in historically informed *Tagespolitik*. One of the effects of Wolffsohn's thesis is that an assessment of German *Vergangenheitsbewältigung* in 1952 and thereafter must differentiate between the levels of actual policies, public opinion, and political culture. One of these levels alone cannot capture the complexity of German perspectives on restitution.

Wolffsohn's positive reading of official West German policy vis-à-vis restitution influences his position with respect to the emotionally charged topic of the Shoah. In *Eternal Guilt?* (1993, German original 1988), Wolffsohn claims that the Shoah has assumed the function of a political instrument perpetuating an anti-Germanism whose nature is entirely divorced from what he calls "the real Germany and the real Germans."[8] And he makes a provocative comparison:

> The instrument of anti-Germanism is as effective as anti-Judaism, which is also divorced from its object. Anti-Judaism, too, has little or nothing to do with real Jews and Judaism. Anti-Germanism draws upon, distorts, and exaggerates the

Germany of today just as, in earlier times, the Jew was portrayed only as caricature. For thousands of years, Jews have had to live with anti-Judaism. For better or worse, Germans will also have to learn to live with the omnipresence of anti-Germanism, and it will continue to generate difficulties, not just in the sphere of German policy toward Israel and the Middle East. . . . In the case of the Jews the conditioned reflex was: "Christ-killers"; in the case of the Germans it is, and will long remain: "Auschwitz." Collective historical memory apparently cannot do without distorting generalizations.[9]

This is strong stuff, and perhaps Wolffsohn overstates his case. Regardless of whether or not Wolffsohn's argument is overstated, however, I believe that his assessment is correct with respect to what, in *Verwirrtes Deutschland* he calls "*die guten Deutschen.*"[10] The good Germans are those who, with good intentions, accepted the idea of German collective guilt and of an essential flaw of the German character. I am referring here to a consensus among left-leaning West German intellectuals who were the spokespersons for a moral Germany for over forty years. One need only remember Günter Grass' writings during 1989–1990, where he invoked "Auschwitz" as a political instrument against unification.[11]

The issue that Wolffsohn is raising is not only whether such instrumentalization of the memory of the Shoah really has the victims in mind, but also, and primarily, whether reactions such as Grass's, based as they are on an assumption of collective national guilt over generations to come, are really in the best interest of the political realities within Germany and without. This issue is an urgent one because younger Germans will react (and are already reacting) with increasing irritation to the idea of being stigmatized by birth, especially so, as Wolffsohn believes, because "serious and honest efforts have been and continue to be undertaken to build and maintain an anti-fascist Germany."[12]

With respect to Israel, the instrumentalization of the Shoah has yet another function. In Wolffsohn's view, Israel needs the Shoah to maintain a sense of Jewish identity. Like the Western states, Israel underwent a process of secularization as a result of which historical events are no longer interpreted in a religious but in a worldly manner. Emblematic for this process is the "symbolic-sacred"[13] character of the commemoration of the Holocaust, one week before the Jewish Independence Day:

> The Holocaust summarizes and symbolizes the entirety of the sufferings of the long and often sorrowful history of the Jewish people. It has become the abbreviation for Jewish history. In the process, a development took place which can be regarded as typical of all groups that have dissolved the bonds with their religious traditions in the course of an increasing secularization. Suffering, which was perceived as divinely ordained in an era dominated by religion has come to

be viewed as the product of secular history, as the work of man rather than God.[14]

In Wolffsohn's view, the symbolic memory of the Shoah lends a sense of "negative" identity to the Jewish secular state—"negative" because its identity is defined by an event imposed from outside the Jewish tradition. In order to sustain its identity, Israel needs to maintain this outside, which guarantees its existence. Thus Wolffsohn's provocative conclusion: the memory of the Holocaust and a sense of anti-Germanism must be maintained by Israel and the Jews for reasons of Jewish identity. This mechanism, however, locks Germans, who want to be accepted as *different* from their past, and Jews, who, in some regards, need Germans to be *similar* to their past, in a very unhealthy, destructive interrelationship.

It is at this point that the different aspects of Wolffsohn's theses on German-Jewish-Israeli relations converge, and they might be summed up as follows. Wolffsohn's main concern is to lay out as clinically as possible the complex *political mechanics* in which Germans and Jews are interlocked because of the Shoah.[15] The destructive interrelationship just mentioned above is reinforced by another antithesis. While the majority of Germans, according to Wolffsohn, has largely been successful in espousing the slogan "Never Again Perpetrators" (*Nie wieder Täter*), the state of Israel is founded on the slogan "Never Again Victims" (*Nie wieder Opfer*). Over the last forty years, these differing convictions led to a less military and aggressive attitude in West Germany at the very moment when the Jewish state, in a number of wars, demonstrated its resolve to leave the role of victim behind. What follows from Wolffsohn's diagnosis is that, on an intellectual and pragmatic level, Germans and Jews have undergone a period of nonsynchronous (*ungleichzeitig*) development at the same time that they have been structurally locked together as never before. The merit of his work is the attempt to understand this complex interrelationship in as objective and detached a mode as possible.

Wolffsohn is aware that not everyone is able to share his detached attitude. Andrei Markovits is a case in point. In a footnote to the article from which I quoted in the beginning, Markovits says:

> By being an American Jew of Central European origins and a child of Holocaust survivors and a Holocaust-ravaged family, my criteria for German contrition, reparation, and restitution are completely unreasonable and unfair. In a sense, whatever the Germans did, are doing, or might have done will always remain inadequate for me. In a sense, the Germans simply cannot win with me. There is nothing wrong with my having such impossibly exacting standards as long as they are explicitly stated and clearly understood as informing my approach and analysis.[16]

I accept and respect this statement and this position. I accept it, although I disagree with its equation of Nazi Germany with post–World War II Germany, for two reasons. First, there cannot be any adequate restitution for what happened between 1933 and 1945. Therefore, the Nazi crimes cannot be forgiven. Secondly, I respect this statement for being candid about its status as an opinion, as an *interested* judgment that does not disguise itself as objective, scientific, and therefore true. In this manner, Markovits leaves room for the kind of position that Wolffsohn argues for.

I myself prefer Wolffsohn's more detached approach, an approach—I want to stress—that never absolves the German state from historical responsibility for the Shoah. I believe that his "provocative interruptions" (*provokative Zwischenrufe*; subtitle of one of his books) open up, for later generations of Germans and Jews alike, a new manner of relating toward each other. "By the grace of [his] birth," Wolffsohn is able to transcend encrusted antagonisms between Jews and Germans.[17] The big difference that Wolffsohn enters into the discussion on German-Jewish-Israeli relations is *differentiation*. A German and a Jew himself, he differentiates between victims and successor generations, perpetrators and successor generations, states and successor states. He claims a position as a German Jew whose identification with Israel and Judaism is in critical sympathy. Furthermore, with respect to the analysis of German political culture, he distinguishes between public opinion and publicized opinion, between *Tagespolitik* and *Geschichtspolitik*, and reduces neither one to the other. His grasp of German-Jewish-Israeli relations thus adds a degree of complexity to our deliberations that has oftentimes been missing.

In this respect, it is to be hoped that Wolffsohn's writings will have an impact on the normalization of intellectual discourse in the united Germany. I believe the time has come not to label someone a reactionary just because s/he challenges, on the basis of rational arguments, the status quo in German-Jewish relations. It is of course no accident that it takes the work of a Jew who is also a German to mount this challenge. Wolffsohn's analyses point to unhealthy mechanisms between Germans and Jews that first need to be recognized before they can be confronted.

NOTES

1. Andrei S. Markovits, "The Politics of Memory: The Predicament of German-Jewish Relations in the Former Bundesrepublik and in Post-Wall Deutschland," *Brücken über dem Abgrund. Auseinandersetzungen mit jüdischer Leidenserfahrung, Antisemitismus und Exil. Festschrift für Harry Zohn*, ed. Amy Colin and Elisabeth Strenger (Munich: Fink, 1994), 63–78.

2. Ibid., 76.

3. Michael Wolffsohn, *Keine Angst vor Deutschland* (Erlangen: Straube, 1990), 42. All translations are my own.

4. Jürgen Habermas, "Yet Again: German Identity—A Unified Nation of Angry DM-Burghers," *New German Critique* 52 (1991): 84–101. See in particular pp. 99–101, which are a direct answer to Karl Heinz Bohrer's article in the same issue (72–83) entitled "Why We Are Not a Nation—And Why We Should Become One."

5. See Michael Wolffsohn, "'Mein Kampf?'—Mein Dekan?—Mein Präsident? Eine Dokumentation," in his *Verwirrtes Deutschland? Provokative Zwischenrufe eines deutsch-jüdischen Patrioten* (Munich: Ferenczy bei Bruckmann, 1993), 193–230.

6. Wolffsohn, *Keine Angst vor Deutschland*, 13.

7. See Michael Wolffsohn, "Vergangenheitsbewältigung," in his *Keine Angst vor Deutschland*, 95–148.

8. Michael Wolffsohn, *Eternal Guilt? Forty Years of German-Jewish-Israeli Relations* (New York: Columbia University Press, 1993). Substantially revised version of the German original, *Ewige Schuld? 40 Jahre deutsch-jüdisch-israelische Beziehungen* (Munich: Piper, 1988).

9. Wolffsohn, *Eternal Guilt?* 64–65.

10. See for instance "Juden ja, Israel nein? Wider die guten Deutschen!" in Wolffsohn, *Verwirrtes Deutschland?*, 53–58.

11. "I want—in closing—to confront the break in civilization epitomized by Auschwitz with the longing for reunification. Auschwitz speaks against every trend born of manipulation of public opinion, against the purchasing power of the West German economy . . . and yes, even against the right to self-determination granted without hesitation to other peoples. Auschwitz speaks against all this, because one of the preconditions for the terrible thing that happened was a strong, unified Germany." Günter Grass, *Two States—One Nation?* trans. Krishna Winston with A. S. Wensinger (San Diego: Harcourt Brace Jovanovich, 1990), 122.

12. Wolffsohn, *Eternal Guilt?* 65.

13. Ibid., 75.

14. Ibid., 75–76.

15. Ibid., 64–67.

16. Markovits, "The Politics of Memory," 77.

17. Wolffsohn, *Ewige Schuld?* 7.

Section III: Poetry and Images After Auschwitz

12
Paul Celan and the German of the Non-German
ADRIAN DEL CARO

In my title, the phrase "the German of the non-German" is deliberately ambiguous. Today people associate speaking German with being German, and it is this profound misconception that I want to explore. Points I have to make are that non-Germans have for centuries had a right to speak German, that non-Germans have "ownership" of this language, that nationalistic Germans have pursued their myths of German "racial purity" by cultivating the myth of an exclusive "German" German, and that Paul Celan is a particularly revealing example of why all of us should learn to think of German as a language, not as a national identity.

I believe Paul Celan teaches us to appreciate German in its history, its social history, its etymology, and its communicative potential as, ultimately, a language of humans, a humane language, a language of poetry—despite the absolutely sordid, criminal, and genocidal applications of the German language as they erupted, but were not invented, during the Third Reich.

It might be self-evident to some that a German professor would take an interest in this topic, but most of my students and colleagues at the university take a far different view: German is German, and poetry written in German is German poetry—most would accept this tautology. But as Americans, Australians, and Canadians do not accept the logic that they are "English" poets because they write in some form of English, so too we should guard against the facile reduction of speaking German to being German. This reasoning can get us into trouble, I think, because the direct equation of a language with a nationality opens up the negative, nationalistic dimensions of that language, such that "non-native speakers" of the language are not accepted as full dialogue partners. In other words, this chapter is about what happens to a language, to its people, and to other peoples when its speakers declare sole ownership of that language for the purpose of elevating themselves and putting others down. I realize with some despair that my topic is complex; I offer this not as a simplification, but as a continuation of a dialogue Paul Celan himself joined in the 1950s and 1960s, when he published his award-winning volumes of poetry in German.

Paul Celan was an Eastern European Jew whose native language (*Muttersprache*) was German. When we use the German term *Muttersprache*, we should also understand that for Celan this term was particularly painful, because his mother and father were victims of the Holocaust and many Celan poems contain disguised personifications of his mother. His hometown of Czernowitz, Bukovina, a region now in Romania and Ukraine, was the easternmost city of the Austro-Hungarian Empire until 1918, when it became part of Romania. Amy Colin tells us that Czernowitz "produced a variegated German, Roumanian, Ukrainian, and Yiddish literature, and poets fluent in several languages." Moreover, she continues, "so strong was the impact of the Austro-German tradition upon the Bukovina that even Roumanian and Ruthenian authors wrote their first texts in German."[1] The intimate relationship between the Bukovina and the Austro-German language and culture that nourished it is even more strongly stated by Edith Silbermann, a childhood friend of Celan's, in her recently published *Begegnung mit Paul Celan. Erinnerung und Interpretation* (1993). Silbermann offers some reasons why Austro-German figured so prominently in the lives of Celan and his generation. During the 150 years of Austria's rule over Bukovina, Eastern European Jews were rapidly assimilating under the auspices of the Hapsburg Empire, with encouragement from Austrian authorities who feared the Slavs would establish themselves in this region. The German language was encouraged here, and the Jewish population of Bukovina was given greater rights and privileges than in other Habsburg crown lands. When the Romanians took Bukovina, this only intensified the German-language loyalty of the Jewish population, which identified itself with Austria and rejected Romania's German-inspired nationalism.[2]

Other biographers and commentators have remarked on Celan's close association with Austro-German.[3] It is important to make and remake this point, however, because some commentators have overlooked this fact in favor of the myth that Paul Celan never lived in a German-speaking region and experienced nothing but linguistic deprivation and isolation as a user of German, both before he left Czernowitz and afterwards, when he lived in France.[4] Silbermann dispels this misconception in her book,[5] and those who knew Celan personally or who were from the same region consistently relate that Celan was remorseful that Austro-German-speaking Bukovina became lost in history.

Celan's acceptance speech for the City of Bremen literature prize, awarded in 1958, alludes to Martin Buber, a philosopher from the same region as Celan and much venerated by him.[6] Martin Buber represented the same cultural background of what Celan called this "former province of the Hapsburg monarchy," which by 1958 "had fallen victim to the loss of history."[7] The word Celan used was *Geschichtslosigkeit*, which literally means "lack of history" or "historylessness." The point he stressed to his German audience was that German, as a language, was not unknown to him and to Martin Buber, even though Bukovina, like Celan's parents and the millions of other Jews exterminated in the Holocaust, disappeared from history. Without detailing his own experiences during and immediately following the Holocaust, Celan told his German audience, with irony, "you know how things were through the years," and he related that although Bremen, far in the north of Germany, was not a reachable reality for him, Vienna was, and so he ended up at first in Vienna. Celan explained further that he and his language had to "go through" periods of answerlessness, terrible silence, and "the thousand darknesses of death-bringing speech."[8] Silbermann does a fine job of linking this highly confessional passage with the history of the Jewish people: Celan repeated the word *Hindurchgehen* or "going through" seven times to invoke the trials of the Jewish people, their forty years of wandering in the desert, their 2,000-year diaspora, and most recently the Holocaust.[9]. When he spoke in German to Germans who were honoring him for his poetry, Celan made sure to educate his audience to the fact that German had been spoken in Czernowitz, continued to be spoken in Vienna, and that the one thing he had not lost during the darkness was his language—his Austro-German. This context has to be kept in mind whenever commentators insist on painting Celan as a helpless, depressed victim of Germans and their language who had no choice but to write in German: it was Paul Celan's right and his destiny as a poet to write in German, since German was his *Muttersprache*, too. Besides, who better to address and reform the hateful permutations of "German" German than one whose German was formed and informed by the multicultural ethos of the Hapsburg empire?

Celan was deliberately aggressive and affirmative in claiming his Austro-German heritage on the occasion of his speech to German listeners. On the most significant level, however, Celan asserted his non-German German throughout his poems, so that one can argue that he undertook a critical project every bit the equal of the survival of poetry after Auschwitz, namely what I call the rescuing of language from the clutches of hate speech, from oppression per se, from violent death by genocide. Before we humans mobilize as armies we mobilize as nations, and before we mobilize as nations, we cement our exclusivity and identity through language. Whatever is hated and despised in the Other, we have formulated in our respective languages. Celan understood this as a long historic;al process.

The Gospel of John begins: "In the beginning was the Word, and the Word was with God, and the Word was God." However, in the Old Testament, in Genesis, the beginning is otherwise: "In the beginning God created the heavens and the earth. The earth was formless and empty, and darkness lay upon the face of the deep, and the Spirit of God was moving over the surface of the waters." The revision of the Old Testament beginning has had world-historical linguistic consequences, inasmuch as the equation of "the Word" with God and with Jesus Christ forces a relationship between language, i.e., the Word, and salvation through Jesus Christ. It is no secret to religion scholars that Christianity is anti-Semitic, and it should not surprise anyone that Christians have learned, over the years, to exploit the perceived relationship between the Word, the Word of God, of Christ, and salvation per se. This habituation emerges in Joel Carmichael's recent book, *The Satanizing of the Jews*, in which Martin Luther is revealed in all his raging glory as a man preoccupied with the extermination of Jews once he learned that the Jews would not accept Christian scriptures even after he, Luther, translated them into German. And on a related point, Carmichael continues, Luther's famously abusive and crude language, with which he called the Jews "venomous and virulent" and "disgusting vermin," became fatal to the Jews when Luther's popularity increased.[10] Jerry Glenn was among the first scholars in the English-speaking world to point out the high incidence of anti-Christian and anti-Judaic blasphemy in Celan's poetry, which he documents in his excellent 1973 introduction to the poet.[11] What I am trying to avoid is pitting one religion against the other, since all proselytizing religions limit salvation, but what Celan reminds us about in his poetry was that Christians insist on the supremacy of the Word, and the equation of the Word with Christ. In the most basic terms, therefore, those who do not share the Word do not share in salvation. Celan reminds us that any word is a product of one's language: those who do not share that language are always in danger of being denied salvation by virtue of being denied that language, that word—the despised Others may not take part in the dialogue, and ultimately a dehumanizing through speech takes place. "Hate speech" is historically more subtle than the slander scrawled on walls and distributed in pamphlets.

When the spirit of Genesis is altered to appear as the Word, and when Christ becomes the fulfillment of that Word as God's incarnation on earth, an act of violence has been committed against all language, which was originally only a diversity of words, and this linguistic act of violence later encouraged acts of physical violence against those who were not of the Word. I think this is at stake, for example, in Celan's poem "Argumentum e Silentio," found in the 1955 volume entitled *From Threshold to Threshold*, wherein Celan presents a poetic history of speech.[12] Night, we are told, lies chained between gold and forgetting; both reach for the night, and the night lets both of them touch her. Now the human element enters the picture, with the simultaneous emergence of dawn and speech, only speech has two sides: one side is lucidity, representing consciousness and life, the other is darkness and concealment, representing unconsciousness and death. Once these elements rise, the ambiguous generosity of the original night is troubled by strife: each word competes to be the Word, and Celan brings in images of persecution. The night would gladly tolerate the touch of both gold and forgetting, but instead, when the original image is populated by speaking humans, neither side wants to remain silent, each side wants to prevail with its Word. Celan adds a mildly hopeful image to this poem, suggesting in conclusion that night, in the river basin of her tears, displays seeds again and again to submerging suns. The final image is completely silent, yet it is brimming with fertility despite the fact that night has wept a river basin of tears: this fertile plain might eventually yield a crop, meaning that the waters of concealment will work with the suns of light, forgetting will work with gold, and there is hope for a dawn without word-strife.[13]

What I have rendered in clumsy prose Celan of course gave us in exquisite images couched in his characteristic mystic and sometimes surrealistic style, but even a casual reader will remark that "the Word" (*das Wort*), is mentioned in five of the poem's seven short strophes, but has no place in the opening or closing strophes. It is too difficult to treat these poems as they deserve in this context, and I wish to assure my readers that Celan's poems received much more careful attention in a book I have written on this topic,[14] but for the moment, another attempt at a reading will help us see how Celan used poetry to focus on the exclusionary dimensions of the German language. The poem is called "The Mighty Fortress" (*Die feste Burg*) and is from the 1952 volume *Poppy and Memory*. The title directly addresses Luther's popular poem and hymn by the same name ("Ein feste Burg"), in which he refers to the God of Protestants as a "mighty fortress" and "a good defense and weapon."

Celan tells us that he knows "the most evening of all houses" or "the most occidental of all houses," using the German *abendlich* or "of the evening" in its double meaning of evening and occidental, or of the west. This locution is perfect for describing Germany and the role of the German language in the Western ethos, because the West is associated with Christianity à la Martin Luther. In this most occidental of houses, a much deeper eye than yours, we are told, holds watch. We are presented here with the citadel of Protestant Christian faith, inhabited by a deeper eye that keeps watch. Celan sees a green banner waving from the gable of this westernmost house, which he describes as a banner of grief, and says: "you do not know that you wove it." The green of the banner connotes hope, life, as the Jews hoped they would be assimilated by Christians, and Celan expresses this failure to accept the Jews by writing: "And it flies so high, as if you hadn't weaved it." The next line reads: "The Word, from which you took leave, welcomes you at the gate." The Jews had to stop at the Word, because accepting the Word would mean denying their own faith and entering Luther's instead. What had once touched Celan merely in passing—namely straw, heart, and flower symbolizing the holy trinity of father, son, and holy spirit—long ago became a guest of this house, but they no longer touch him. He completes the visit to the westernmost house by stepping in front of a mirror in the house; instead of his reflection Celan sees the flower, the heart, and the straw, and concludes: "And that deeper eye, it drinks your deep eye."[15] This poem recounts Celan's encounter with Christians as a parable of the Jewish encounter with Western, Christian Europeans, up to the point where the Jews are completely displaced by the image of the holy trinity. The Jews are of the East, and after the Holocaust, their image can no longer be reflected in the westernmost house, in Luther's mighty fortress, since the "deeper eye" that stands watch has swallowed them.

I have given only two examples of Celan's use of German to controvert the German of Germans, but there are dozens more. It is now time to establish why Celan was so interested in exposing the Christian-nationalistic aspects of German, and this I do using the writings of J. G. Fichte in particular. Fichte practiced precisely the kind of ideological appropriation of the Word of scripture to which Celan passionately objected. Jürgen Gebhardt explains that when Fichte became concerned about the lack of perfectibility of his *Wissenschaftslehre* or "science of knowledge," his writings became "exegesis of an ascent to the light, to the absolute, to the absolute reason or God."[16] Fichte is known for his nationalism during the years of the Napoleonic occupation and following, but it is not so widely known that he used the Gospel of John to propagate his new message. Gebhardt describes Fichte as a zealot who preached that "the incarnation of the logos corresponds with the ascent of the Ich to absolute knowledge,"[17] or for those less versed in idealist philosophy: Fichte believed that Christ, as the Word incarnate, was the culmination of his (Fichte's) own brand of philosophizing, which in turn was the culmination of all philosophy. In other words, Christianity, German philosophy, and German nationalism were blended into one and the same thing—absolute truth, infallibility, and exclusive salvation.

Fichte's *Reden an die deutsche Nation* put his Johannine zealousness into an even more negative light. In this work he claimed that Germans had achieved an evolution of the spirit that would usher in a new age.[18] Germany, moreover, had retained its original language, unlike the "neo-Latin" peoples of Europe who had no mother tongue;[19] the German people therefore spoke a vital language flowing from the power of nature, while other Europeans spoke superficially from a language whose roots were dead. Not yet finished with the linguistic superiority of German, Fichte maintained that when Germans learned Latin, they also learned the neo-Latin languages and therefore enjoyed a unique perspective in the European language family: Germans actually learned and knew foreign languages better than the native speakers of these languages, which enabled them to "oversee" foreigners and understand them better than they understood themselves.[20] The greatest gift the Germans gave to the "neo-Latin" peoples was what Fichte called "the improved doctrine" of reformed Christianity, since "true religion in the form of Christianity was the seed of the new world" whose mission was to spiritualize and sanctify the ancient world—which the Germans had accomplished.[21] The natural and indispensable drive of humans, Fichte argued, is to find heaven on earth, and as long as the German people exist, all further revelations of the divine will occur and take shape among them "without interference and corruption by anything foreign and not belonging to the whole of their laws."[22] This language, all of it, points to the exclusivity of German as a discourse favored by the divine, and the exclusivity of Germans themselves as keepers of the divine and teachers to the West. It does not take much imagination to leap from the earliest years of the nineteenth century to the 1930s and 1940s, when Germans felt similarly inspired or in-spirited by prophets such as Novalis, Kleist, Hölderlin, Fichte, Hegel, even Nietzsche, and when they translated their language into genocidal deeds. I do not mean to imply that Nietzsche's message was identical to the nationalism espoused by the earlier Romantics, but as Steven Aschheim has shown in his recent book on Nietzsche, Nietzsche's language was plundered by Germans in the spirit of Fichte's plundering of the spirit of Christianity.[23]

I could go on about Fichte, about how he blasted the Old Testament and Genesis in particular as "the absolute basic error of all false metaphysics and theology." [24] But my point has been made: since Martin Luther, Germans have celebrated a historical orgy of privileging themselves and their language at the expense of others. Paul Celan was an educated man, a teacher, a poet, a scholar, and in his poems he frequently refuted thinkers like Hölderlin and Fichte while giving voice to others like Heine.

Paul Celan's poetry represents a watershed in the history of consciousness because it ushers in a post-Holocaust consciousness. His German is antithetical to German nationalism and German nationalism's inherent Christian anti-Semitism, and it can be read as a style of German constantly at odds with

German, as non-German rebuilding its home in German, as the effort to render German humane and not merely "of and for Germans." Celan's German cautions us, at every turn, that a language may be hijacked, enslaved, and perverted by demagogues and ideologues, and this enslaved language may contribute to the genocide of those who are not "of the Word." Celan's German underscores the horrors inherent in language when it is divorced from humanity and elevated to the privileged discourse between mortals and God. Celan's mystic and surrealistic German alienates from the everyday in order to humanize speech, and the uncanny properties it displays are a deliberate, post-Holocaust strategy to address the fact that millions of innocent Jews and others will never have a resting place in the earth because of the fanatic hatred of a people bent by, and bent upon, having the last Word.

Celan's German speaks for the utterly homeless, the utterly speechless, commemorating and re-membering the dismembered using the "same" language that inspired and justified the Holocaust. Ultimately this means that German is not identical with being German, that German is not identical with being Nazi. When we teach German, in whatever venue and using whatever style or approach, let us make some room in the curriculum for Paul Celan and the German of the non-German. This does not mean merely including a token Austrian or Swiss writer in the pantheon of German writers: it means instilling in our students an appreciation for the dangers lurking in any language when the authority of the written word is chauvinistically draped in the authority of the "Word" that supposedly was at the beginning.

NOTES

1. Amy Colin, *Paul Celan: Holograms of Darkness* (Bloomington: Indiana University Press, 1991), xiii.

2. Edith Silbermann, *Begegnung mit Paul Celan. Erinnerung und Interpretation* (Aachen: Rimbaud, 1993), 7–8.

3. Gerhart Baumann, *Erinnerungen an Paul Celan* (Frankfurt a.M., 1992), 109. For Celan and his place in Austrian tradition, see also Amy Colin, "Paul Celan's Poetics of Destruction," in Amy Colin, ed., *Argumentum e Silentio: International Paul Celan Symposium*, (New York: Walter de Gruyter, 1987), 178; and Colin, *Paul Celan: Holograms of Darknes*, xix.

4. Some who may have contributed to the notion that Paul Celan had always been linguistically isolated are Michael Hamburger, his major English translator, who writes: "Paul Celan was a learned poet with an outstandingly rich vocabulary derived more from reading than from practice in the vernacular—inevitably, considering how little time he spent in German-speaking countries" (*Poems of Paul Celan*, trans. with introduction by Michael Hamburger [London: Anvil Press Poetry, 1988], 26); Katherine Washburn, another translator, who writes: "He spent his life in Paris as teacher, translator, and poet in a linguistic cocoon, spinning poems from a language nour-

ished chiefly by the letter and cut off at the source" (*Paul Celan: Last Poems*, trans. Katharine Washburn and Margret Guillemin [San Francisco: North Point Press, 1986], ix). See also Silbermann, *Begegnung mit Paul Celan*, who refutes the account of Alfred Margul-Sperber that Celan " 'had lived exclusively in a non-German language environment'," 8.

5. Silbermann, *Begegnung mit Paul Celan*, 8.

6. Ibid., 30–32.

7. Paul Celan, "Ansprache anläßlich der Entgegennahme des Literaturpreises der Freien Hansestadt Bremen," in *Paul Celan. Gesammelte Werke in fünf Bänden* (Frankfurt a.M.: Suhrkamp, 1983), ed. Beda Alleman and Stefan Reichert, 3: 185. All translations are my own.

8. Ibid., 3: 185, 186–187.

9. Silbermann, *Begegnung mit Paul Celan,* 15–16.

10. Joel Carmichael, *The Satanizing of the Jews: Origin and Development of Mystical Anti-Semitism* (New York: Fromm, 1993), 81, 84.

11. Jerry Glenn, *Paul Celan* (New York: Twayne, 1973), 23–25, 57–58, 72, 81–83, 121–26.

12. Celan, *Paul Celan: Gesammelte Werke* 1: 138–139.

13. Ibid.

14. Adrian Del Caro, *The Early Poetry of Paul Celan: In the beginning was the word* [sic] (Baton Rouge and London: Louisiana State University Press, 1997).

15. Celan, *Paul Celan: Gesammelte Werke* 1: 60.

16. Jürgen Gebhardt, *Die Revolution des Geistes. Politisches Denken in Deutschland 1770–1830. Goethe—Kant—Fichte—Hegel—Humboldt* (Munich: List Verlag, 1968), 93.

17. Ibid., 94.

18. J. G. Fichte, *Reden an die deutsche Nation*, vol. 7, *Johann Gottlieb Fichte's Sämmtliche Werke* (Berlin: Veit und Comp., 1848), 306.

19. Ibid., 324.

20. Ibid., 326.

21. Ibid., 351 and 354.

22. Ibid., 379, 381, and 382.

23. Steven E. Aschheim, *The Nietzsche Legacy in Germany 1890–1990* (Berkeley: University of California Press, 1992), 148, 235–243.

24. J. G. Fichte, "Die Anweisung zum seligen Leben," *Johann Gottlieb Fichte's Sämmtliche Werke* (Berlin: Veit und Comp., 1848), 5: 479–480.

13
Uncanny Holograms of the Past:
Recent German Poetry and Writing After Paul Celan and Theodor Adorno

ERK GRIMM

In recent years a growing number of young German poets have contributed to a poetic discourse that, by and large, focuses on the role of new media as a force that reduces the sensible mind to simple matter, thus relegating human memory to electronic storage. At the same time these authors, now mainly in their thirties, allude to figures and events of German history or everyday life that lie beyond their own subjective experience. Interestingly enough, Paul Celan seems to represent one of the most prominent figures of reference, even though the context of the Shoah is not mentioned. The immediate question arises as to what extent these poets are related to Adorno's well-known verdict on writing poems after the Shoah and also how they define their relationship to the poet who was able to express perennial suffering in the most subtle and moving way. To discuss this complex relationship, the term "hologram" will serve as my entry because it accommodates conflicting interpretations. The hologram is at the junction of three semantic strands, each of them representing quite different connotations. Most prominently, Amy Colin, in her study *Paul Celan. Holograms of Darkness*, chose this metaphor to describe the *uncanny* dimensions of Celan's poems that, like these photographic plates, produce often-changing "disturbing shapes, depth, and colors."[1] In contrast, in Jean Baudrillard's *Cool Memories*, all metaphorical meanings of this notion collapse. In one of his quirky aphorisms, the French philosopher tries to render the recent development of the postmodern cultural industry. He triggers a metonymical short circuit that conflates two distinctive images: "From the holocaust to the hologram: a fine programme."[2] A simple pun denigrates the vision of the Shoah and defiles the scene of horror with the obscenity of high-tech simulation. The presence of a haunting past touches upon our notion of memory whereas the techniques of reproduction, storage, and telematic distribution counterfeit the reality of pain. Not vision, but language itself is foregrounded in order to convey a sense of cynical humor that, for Baudrillard, seems to befit our apocalyptic age. Lastly, the hologram stands more generally for the fascination with simulation and communication technologies in German poetry. The abundance of technical terms, as we will see, is far away from Celan's ironical usage of this vocabulary in *Light Compulsion* (1970). Moreover, recent German poetry no longer shares Hans Magnus Enzenberger's concerns regarding the manipulation by mass media; instead, an interest in the materialities of communication prevails.

The reappropriation of history and simulation of "worst-case scenarios" in contemporary poetry, as means to overcome a purely "biographical" mode, is inextricably linked to the evaluation of an adequate linguistic representation. In a current intellectual debate in the *Merkur* on the appropriateness of metaphorical language in considering the Holocaust, it became evident that poetry, despite Adorno's verdict, is still seen as the most appropriate form of subjective representation, even though the participants in that debate widely disagree on the possibility of metaphorization in historiography. The dispute between Amir Eshel and Jakob Hessing actually originates in George Steiner's essay concerning the Shoah, "The Long Life of the Metaphor." Steiner emphasized a metaphysical interpretation of the Holocaust. For instance, he stated that Celan's poems—quoting his "Radix, Matrix" as an example of God's indifference—cannot be approached by rational analysis. "We are in a sphere of the living metaphor, of language which stands beside itself." [3] He explains this paradoxical image by pointing out that Jews, after the Shoah, were confronted with the question of how to communicate with God; this was the first time that such a hermeneutical dilemma was raised, a truly theological problem that had not existed before. More recently, in 1992, Hessing elaborated on one of the implicit assumptions in Steiner's plea for a metaphorical interpretation of Celan, namely that a single death camp, Auschwitz, can stand for the experience of the Shoah.[4] Hessing's essay, "Poems After Auschwitz,"[5] is clearly indebted to Adorno's dictum; it insists that Auschwitz fully represents the experience of the Holocaust and could thus only be adequately understood by Jews. Finally, in a harsh response to Hessing's essay, entitled "Auschwitz as Metaphor," Amir Eshel argues against Hessing's thesis while reproaching him for his "transhistorical" references to the extermination of Jews because neither his solemn tone nor a religious ideology would be permissible. Hessing's ideology, according to his critic, presupposes a confidence in the identity of the Jews as the chosen people despite the fact that the obligation to read the Holy Scripture was often neglected in modern times. Regarding Hessing's figurative speech—"For a moment, Hitler lifted the globe of the world"[6]—Eshel demurs at such an interpretation of the infamous Final Solution because of its hyperbolic and quasi-mythic qualities. In his opinion, the mosaic belief is not the sole legitimate criterion to speak about poetry and the Holocaust, rather, one would have to provide clear categories of literary interpretation.[7] In general, Eshel pleads for an appropriate analysis of poetry rather than confusing literature with history. For him, the metaphor of "Auschwitz" does not render history at all since the single name does not appropriately render historical causality and other indelible names. As a matter of fact, scholars of German literary historiography would want more or less history illustrated by poems. It is in this context of "theological-mythological explanation patterns," to use Eshel's phrase, that Paul Celan emerges as the paradigmatic poet for he stands for the language of silence. Although the rendition of the ineffable might be one of the reasons for Celan's fame, one needs to stress that the strength of his poetry goes beyond its subjective documentation of the Holocaust as it was most prominently represented in his "Death Fugue."[8]

The intellectual dispute between Hessing and Eshel sets the parameters for a critical discussion of recent German poetry alluding to the Shoah. The emergence of a sober, almost clinical tone, the highly eloquent and educated diction, accompanied by an abundance of scientific terms are some of the features that raise questions about the relation between metaphorical and analytical language, memory and the new media. This "cool" idiom can be found in a number of poems by Marcel Beyer, Ulrike Draesner, Norbert Hummelt or Brigitte Oleschinski. Most prominently, it is represented by Durs Grünbein and Thomas Kling, the former born in 1962, the latter in 1957, who have not only been the most successful but also the more influential new talents in Germany.[9] Interestingly enough, some features of their texts can be traced back to Celan's form inventions, and some poems even refer explicitly to his biography or to the Holocaust.

Durs Grünbein slowly developed his imagery from his preoccupation with the slow-motion of everyday life and the monotony of daily traffic between workplace and home in East Germany. In *Skull Crash Course*, the thematic emphasis is on an anonymous individual in a stage of day-dreaming where everything seems to be surreal. In contrast, the only reality is the brain itself because it produces these perceptions even though it is cut off from the outside world by the skull-pan. For instance, in his poem "Cerebralis," Grünbein uses hallucinatory images to describe the innumerable masses of grey cells in the brain. Such images are not motivated by the need to actively recollect the past; instead, there is a sense of curiosity or amazement, the Greek *thaumazein*, that drives the examination of basic material conditions of thinking, speaking, and acting—in short, existence as such. Consequently, the ego's body is seen as a deep shaft or dungeon, filled with mere implants such as the human voice. In

Grünbein's imagery, the skull can also be a movie theater in which the brain serves as an apparatus to project images onto an inner screen. Hence, the outer world is an illusion, either in the present time as the "artificial fruit in the hologram" or in the past as a cinematic impression which is inextricably linked to the fascist era: "With the bunkers, the diorama of the childhood submerged."[10] Many of Grünbein's poetic modules are borrowed from sciences. They seem to objectify personal biography as media history, even though the anachronism of "diorama" is nothing more than a metaphor. In various poems memory seems to collapse. Analytical terminology, for instance such notions as a "diorama," "diencephalon" or "cerebrum," diffuses metaphorical language. One of the obsessive ideas being pursued throughout the last three volumes is the perfection of the biologically incomplete human by means of technology. Grünbein's poems suggest that our archetypical phantasms of flying and swimming cannot be explained by psychological interpretations of situations, such as dream analysis, but rather by simply recording biochemical, quasi-technical processes. Accordingly, the brain is characterized as a "holograph" that adopts superhuman capacities to compensate for biological shortcomings. One can conclude that this negative or, to use Nietzsche's term, "medi-cynical" anthropology, is responsible for the pose of general indifference to human death.

In Grünbein's much-acclaimed third volume, *Folds and Traps*, one of the poems of a cycle called "Variation without a Theme" describes a sudden horror in an everyday situation:

> And in the morning the shower spits . . . .
> Water, what else? Red and Blue
> are on the faucets to show Hot and Cold
> That the skin peels off in pieces
> Remains a silly nightmare
> No thorn in the towel, no blood
> On the tiles—the rattle of the drain
> is called hygiene, not death
> And whether soap is still made of
> bones, the foam that is drying
> on your palm, says nothing.
> Farfetched and fearfully revived,
> a brief flash of suspicion is dying[11]

The poem describes a daily habit in the unpretentious tone of the New Sensibility.[12] There is, however, a certain twist, a punch line that underscores the contrast between hallucination and reality, or more precisely, the difference between an individual enjoying the banal pleasures of a daily shower and a dehumanized victim being killed in a death chamber. Clearly, the poem does not impart the experience of somebody who is haunted by the past; instead it stages absolute despair. Similarly, in the poem "Cerebralis," the third stanza sketches a banal moment of sudden illumination:

> Funny moment, when all at once
> (was it while your skull was being x-rayed?)
> It became clear to you what it meant
>
> That in each cerebrum there are 15 billion
> Grey cells all together
> Put up, several peoples
>
> Gathered in a single control station
> and day-by-night
> the Holocaust is lying in wait for you.[13]

Given the unprecarious nature of routine medical examinations and the common knowledge on the substance of brains, the dramatization of the event leads to a metonym that seems to be highly inapposite.[14] Even if one went so far as to concede that both x-ray booth and gas chamber are manifestations of the same modern technology—a point of view that, by the way, would come close to Heidegger's[15]—one could hardly overlook the equation of chance with necessity. The identification of accidental radiation damage with meticulously planned genocide is more than just an oblique analogy. Portraying oneself as a victim, one establishes a dramatic aura, a "pathos of horror."[16] The simulation of such a scenario goes beyond the question of plausibility of analogies; instead, it touches upon the origin of such cynicism. On the one hand, the poem, in its first stanza, offers an explanation by describing the daily frenzy of the crowd in traffic jams ("most of them here are craving for a reality like second-hand"[17]); on the other hand, at no time is the disposition of the subject revealed. Is this disposition the enlightened false consciousness that "no longer feels affected by any critique of ideology," because "its falseness is already reflexively buffered," as Peter Sloterdijk defined it in his *Critique of Cynical Reason*?[18] I would maintain that it is cynical reflection in disguise, it is a pose that mirrors German necrophilia while shielding the poetic subject, making it invisible in its desire for direct experience. The poetic strategy is dissimulation by simulating the worst case.

The characteristics of Durs Grünbein's poetic approach can be shown more clearly in a comparison to the poem "Brain" (*Hirn*) by Dan Pagis, a Jewish poet, who was born in 1930 in Bukovina. After spending three years in a concentration camp he fled to Israel in 1946 where he lived as a writer until 1986. His long, narrative poem begins: "In the dark night of the skull/he suddenly discovers/he's born."[19] The third person-subject is concerned with an attempt to find orientation in his own body and the subject wonders whether there are other brains out there. In this Samuel-Becket universe the narrating voice has a suspicion, namely "that myriads of brains are imprisoned in him,/packed together,/ splitting off from him, betraying him from within, surrounding him.//And he doesn't know which evil/is the lesser."[20] The shift from loneliness to paranoia brings no relief. Finally, the discovery of a partner allows communication:

> Brain finds a companion, shut in like himself.
> A radio amateur like him.
> In their spare time
> they broadcast to each other from the attic.
> Brain asks, for example:
> Have you got syllogisms? Alarm centers?
> Six hundred million memory cells?
> And how do you feel inside your cranium, Brain?[21]

The differences between Pagis and Grünbein are a matter of degree. The prevailing impression, however, is that of a communicative act and the isolation of an individual in its prison house. Therefore, the distancing form of the third person and the dialogical principle play a decisive role in shaping the content of this poem. Dan Pagis shares Grünbein's interest in anatomy. Nevertheless, he maintains a sense of individuality that is torn between loneliness and the attempt at reaching the other, equally lost "brains."

The second poet whose work alludes more directly to Paul Celan's work is Thomas Kling. In his volume *fuel rods* (or *stinging letters*), one of the poems is dedicated to Kling's predecessor while breaking apart words and lines in an even more radical way than Celan in his late reductionist works:

> THE SALUT ("paulum, a little")
> not by antschel: pair of hearts. soft-
> haired, tall labiates
> so it goes
> on; king of wasteland, chromatics:
> strong yellow in the lion! lettuce,
> coltsmouth, dande-. So it comes close [22]

In this poem, Kling does not carry on a *dialogue* with the Jewish poet.[23] Instead he focusses on Celan as a point of departure for establishing a framework in his volume. Embedded in a complex network of allusions, Trakl, Mandelstam, and Celan serve as a counterweight to aesthetic purism (Stefan George), the academic rigor of "concrete poetry" but also to the solidity of the sound poem (Ernst Jandl). Despite Kling's offensive tone and his resistance to interpreting the situations that he evokes in his quilted forms, his denotative style manages to convey a different image of the poet from Czernowitz. Kling intentionally suppresses the ethical dimension of this poetry lest we forget Celan's aesthetic precision and his expertise in botany, which draws our attention to the odd status of "nature" in his poems. By applying an exact terminology to the disappearance of species, Celan was able to seek a linguistic identity, literally to re-root himself into an imaginary Czernowitz, and thus he surpassed the conventional "nature poems."

In his dedication to Celan, Kling uses the spin of such poems as "Todtnauberg" to direct the reader toward an exploration of botanical vocabulary and the physiognomy of a face. The provocation of "THE SALUT," a salutation as well as a salutary herb (*Heilkraut*) for the dead poet, lies in the fact that Kling concocts a multitude of references not only to Celan but also to Rilke's "Fifth Elegy" to underline the equally aesthetic qualities, that is, the "chromatics" of Celan's poetry. Without going into detail, I would assert that the main purpose of such a collage is to reconstruct historical conditions in order to write an alternative history. This becomes evident in a later poem in which Kling alludes to Celan's meeting with Heidegger by referring to the philosopher's guest book and a medicinal herb mentioned in Celan's "Todtnauberg": "Arnica, eyebright, the/draft from the well with the/starred die above it."[24] Arnica, a plant that was used to heal wounds during solstice, appears again in Kling's "rambling alpine writing" as part of a magic formula, an "arnicalitany." In the overall context of the poem, the success of mountain tourists in the Alps, in its ridiculed triviality, is contrasted with Celan's and Heidegger's failed attempt to reach the moor at a place near Freiburg. It is precisely this crucial encounter between the poet and the thinker that gives evidence for Heidegger's failed recognition of Jewish suffering. In other poems of Thomas Kling's four volumes, one finds intricate allusions to the long-term pogroms in the Rhine valley. There, the poet adopts the position of a camera in the bomber's cockpit, a location that has gained such great theoretical significance in the popular essays of Paul Virilio and the writings of Friedrich Kittler. Kling's references to media make us aware of silence-as-memory, a defect of communication that cannot be "healed," not even by omnipresent audiovisual technology. Therefore, like Celan, Kling lets the linguistic material speak for itself—but it is not linked to affective memory anymore: "extract the sentimental from languages."[25] If memories are associated images conflated with fantasies, then there is no precise recollection of the past. This is true for recent Israeli poets as well as for the younger German ones. As Harald Hartung noted with regard to Tuvia Rübner, his memory is not the reliable *mnemosyne* but has become a highly sensitive film.[26] For another contemporary from Israel, Asher Reich, the aggravating circumstance is the indifference to the present. In recent Israeli poetry, the most tectonic, poetically refined forms are developed by Reich in his collection *Works on Paper* from the 1980s.

Many situations in his volume describe an individual's isolation in a state that had to define its foundation by the Shoah. The smoke of cigarettes and the eye are recurrent motifs, evoking the passing time. And yet, memory cannot reach the past, it has to rely on camera and tape recordings, as one of his poems suggests.[77]

In conclusion, I would maintain that German poets after Adorno and Celan have come back to the "meridian" of postwar poetry by redefining the parameters. The return to more sophisticated forms of poetic language after the "New Sensitivity" of the 1970s is due to the fact that the interest has shifted to topics such as anatomy, botany, and media technology. As a consequence, a sober, analytical tone is seen as the precondition for gaining poetic strength and reactivating lost vocabularies. Writing *after* the Shoah has become a writing *about* the representation of the Shoah since experience, real biographical memory, increasingly seems to fade. In the most interesting examples of contemporary German poetry, the Holocaust, used as a metonym for death, seems to be a legitimate means to evoke the dangers of everyday life in a consumer culture. The intellectual interest in "matter" results in historical scenarios that show the conflict between personal remembrance and the "cool memories" of media. If these uncanny "holograms" of the past are meant to reconcile the sober discourse on media technology with the haunting images of the past, they can construe these scenarios only by encoding the message in cut-up poems or finding an outlet in a punch line. In such dismantled images the horror can be compensated for by a sigh of relief. Analytical detachedness is not the same as indifference; but perhaps they share a common desire for the impossible, the desire for an unencumbered experience of present and past.

NOTES

1. Amy Colin, *Paul Celan. Holograms of Darkness* (Bloomington: Indiana Univ. Press, 1991), ix.

2. Jean Baudrillard, *Cool Memories* (orig. 1987), trans. Chris Turner (New York. Verso, 1990), 230.

3. George Steiner, "Das lange Leben der Metaphorik: Ein Versuch über die *Shoah*," trans. Jörg Trobitius, *Akzente* 3 (1987): 211.

4. Cf. Steiner's statement that the "world of Auschwitz lies outside speech as it lies outside reason" (quoted in Colin, *Paul Celan,* xix).

5. Jakob Hessing, "Gedichte nach Auschwitz," *Merkur* 524 (1992): 980–992. All translations are my own.

6. Amir Eshel, "Auschwitz als Metapher. Zu Jakob Hessing's 'Gedichte nach Auschwitz'," *Merkur* 530 (1993): 463.

7. Ibid., 464.

8. Cf. Michael Hamburger's translation of *Mohn und Gedächtnis* in *Poems of Paul Celan* (New York: Persea, 1988). The poem "Todesfuge" is translated as "Death Fugue" (60–63).

9. Durs Grünbein and Thomas Kling were included as the only poets in the "Red Series/Rote Reihe," a selection of best-selling texts, accompanied by a campaign launched by the publishing house Suhrkamp in autumn 1994.

10. Durs Grünbein, *Schädelbasislektion* (Frankfurt a.M.: Suhrkamp, 1993), 42. Literally translated, the title means "Lesson on the Base of the Skull," playing on "lesion" and "lesson." For formal correspondences, see "In Tunneln der U-Bahn"/"In the Tunnels of the Subway" (p. 265), and Celan's "Give the Word," in Hamburger, *Poems of Paul Celan*, 264–265.

11. Grünbein, *Falten und Fallen* (Frankfurt a.M.: Suhrkamp, 1994), 14.

12. Cf. Rolf Dieter Brinkmann, *Westwärts 1 & 2* (Reinbek: Rowohlt, 1975), 148–150.

13. Grünbein, *Schädelbasislektion*, 135.

14. See Martin Doerry and Volker Hage, "Tausendfacher Tod im Hirn," *Der Spiegel* 41 (October 9, 1995): 228.

15. Luc Ferry and Alain Renaut, *Heidegger and Modernity* (orig. 1988), trans. Franklin Philip (Chicago: University of Chicago Press, 1992), 88; Tom Rockmore, *Heidegger's Nazism and Philosophy* (Berkeley: University of California Press, 1992), 241; Michael E. Zimmerman, *Heidegger's Confrontation With Modernity: Technology, Politics and Art* (Bloomington: Indiana University Press, 1990), 131.

16. Steiner, "Das lange Leben der Metaphorik," 201.

17. Grünbein, *Schädelbasislektion*, 134.

18. Quoted in Andreas Huyssen, *Twilight Memories. Marking Time in a Culture of Amnesia* (New York: Routledge, 1995), 160. For an excellent critical commentary on Sloterdijk's study, see Huyssen, 157–173.

19. Dan Pagis, "Hirn," in his *Erdichteter Mensch*, trans. Tuvia Rübner (Frankfurt a.M.: Jüdischer Verlag, 1993), 105.

20. Ibid., 107.

21. Ibid., 111.

22. Thomas Kling, "brennstabm," in *erprobung herzstärkender mittel. geschmacksverstärker. brennstabm. nacht. sicht. gerät. Ausgewählte Gedichte 1981–1993* (Frankfurt a.M.: Suhrkamp, 1994), 128.

23. See Celan's dialogism in poems such as "It is no longer"/"Es ist nicht mehr" (Hamburger, *Poems of Paul Celan* 184–185). The allusions to botany in Celan are of a more general nature (cf. *Poems of Paul Celan* 90, 124).

24. Kling, *erprobung herzstärkender mittel*, 293.

25. Ibid., 168.

26. Harald Hartung, "Drei Lyriker aus Israel," *Merkur* 537 (1993): 1094.

27. Asher Reich, *Arbeiten auf Papier. Gedichte*, trans. Efrat Gal-Ed et al. (Reinbek: Rowohlt, 1992), 76.

14
Claiming the Victim:
Tokenism, Mourning, and the Future of German Holocaust Poetry

KATHRIN BOWER

You onlookers
Under whose gaze murder takes place.
As one feels a gaze at one's back,
So you feel on your bodies
The gazes of the dead.—Nelly Sachs[1]

This excerpt from Nelly Sachs's poem "You Onlookers" could be read as support for the contention, reportedly made by Adolf Hitler during a table talk, that "The Jews invented conscience."[2] This statement, although fascinating in itself for what it implies about Hitler's psyche and moral sense, becomes even more provocative if read in association with Marina Zwetajewa's puzzling proclamation, made famous by its appearance as an epigram to a poem by Paul Celan, that "all poets are Jews."[3] The connection of Jews to both conscience and poetry has significant repercussions for the genre of so-called Holocaust lyric, so-called because it is necessary to distinguish, as is seldom done, between poems *from* the Holocaust and poems *about* the Holocaust. The poetry written from the midst of extremity is inscribed not only with the conditions of that context (the relentless specter of death, hunger, and suffering) but also the desire to overcome them: the combination of a longing for survival and a mission to bear witness was the most common motivation for writing. Poetry was the genre most accessible to the inmates of camps and ghettos not only because of its condensed form (a necessity in the atmosphere of lack of both time and resources in the camps) but also because of its affiliations with a set of traditions ranging from Jewish liturgical poetry, Yiddish folk song and German romantic lyric that together formed a common heritage for the majority of inmates. Poems written in the camps and ghettos between 1939 and 1945 often were made part of the group's oral lore, passing between individuals and even between camps, memorized, put to music, and transformed from a personal outburst of expression to a shared communication—the company of misery as well as encouragement to persevere by fostering a spirit of community.

Such was the nature of the Theresienstadt poems written by Ilse Weber (1903–1944), a German-speaking Czech Jew who had published Jewish children's stories and poems before the war and who continued to write both poems and songs in the camp. Her works attest to her courageous spirit but also to a strong moral sense of community and solidarity. Weber's poems were widely circulated throughout the camp and their popularity as well as the fact that they have survived while their author perished (Weber was gassed in Auschwitz together with her young son in 1944) attest to their significance for her fellow-sufferers. Alternately expressing sorrow, disillusionment, defiance, and hope, her writings speak to the complex of emotions and psychological dilemmas that grew out of the concentration camp experience. In a poem entitled "Letter to My Child," Ilse Weber reflects on the condition of loss that is both individual and collective—the atmosphere of separation and deprivation that was the context calculated by the Nazis to foment loneliness, psychological collapse, and the erasure of all that had been personal and human:

> Darkness surrounding us, life a chore
> they have taken all from us, left us nothing more.
> House, home, not a corner where we once moved,
> not a piece remained, once valued and loved.
> ....
> Not even our names have they left to us.
> Marked like animals we go through the streets
> with numbers around our necks . . . [4]

Despite this environment, or perhaps because of it, Weber persists in her faith, and in a poem entitled "Pledge" promises an allegiance to her people that is born from a mixture of oppression, despair, and conviction:

> What to my heart was dear
> gradually it from me was torn.
> And yet to me today it is clear—
> I would not of my Judaism be shorn.
> Adept with words am I not,
> and cannot use words to impart,
> what in me burns like a fire hot
> the feeling for my people in my heart.
> And if one asked me to win or lose,
> I would not think of pain or rue
> But rather new torments would I choose
> And to my people be true.[5]

Yet the spectrum is not complete, the appeal of Weber's words to her fellow inmates not fully apparent, without a reference to the touching simplicity and seemingly ingenuous tone of hope that also imbues her writing. In "Then Everything Will Be All Right," Weber indulges in fantastical conciliatory visions of salvation and brotherhood that will follow if her people manage to weather the trials of the camp experience. Most poignant and startling is the longing for reconciliation with the oppressor, and the clinging to a lost ideal of home that is somehow preserved intact and will one day be miraculously restored:

> Then ends the hate, the greed, and the enmity,
> and all suffering comes to an end;
> "my brother" says to you then your enemy
> and full of shame gives you his hand,
> . . . .
> For you the sun shines, for you the trees leaves bear,
> you again have brothers and a place;
> the evil vanishes like an awful nightmare,
> and once more life showers you with grace,
> then everything will be all right, everything will be fine
> endure the waiting and pardon,
> trust in the future, don't veer from that line:
> the world will again be a garden![6]

But how was Weber's work received after the war, after the smoke and ashes had revealed the extent of the damage to Western conceptions of humanity, morality, and conscience? The context had changed, there was a shift from the immediacy of survival to the mediation of guilt and shame and for this the simple, sometimes clumsy rhymes of much of the camp poetry seemed inappropriate or inadequate, while it nevertheless embodied the very voices whose existence had been brutally and prematurely extinguished. Not the voices of martyrs or beings made sublime by their suffering, but the voices of ordinary people—where the banality of suffering collided with the banality of evil. This was not the kind of message that post-Holocaust Germany sought or wanted, but rather one it strove to escape. It is interesting therefore to note that Weber's Theresienstadt poems, though some did appear in isolation in anthologies, were first printed as a collection in Israel in 1964 and did not find a publisher in Germany until 1991. The poetry of the camps was at best briefly celebrated as, in Ludvík Václavek's words, "documentary lament"[7]—traces of this legacy were collected in anthologies, but many manuscripts were abandoned to the archives and the majority of these writings was ultimately dismissed as a woeful failure to approximate in language the effects of unrepeatable and unspeakable experience.

This dismissive attitude toward camp and ghetto poetry was in part engendered by judgments made by the survivors themselves, here most notably H. G. Adler, whose study of the concentration camp Theresienstadt is at once sympathetic to the suffering of the inmates and contemptuous of their poetic outpourings. Referring to the lyric produced in the camp as largely symptomatic of what he termed the "Theresienstadt rhyming sickness,"[8] Adler then cites excerpts from several of Weber's poems in order to illustrate the nature and quality of Theresienstadt poetry:

> In this irritatingly helpless style, shaken by horror, empathy, fear and desperation, lay people and some writers attempted to address quotidian questions of the concentration camp experience. By writing these impressions down, they sought to console themselves and their public and to at least temporarily free themselves from the relentless onslaught of evil.[9]

Roughly contemporary with Adler's study on Theresienstadt, Hannah Arendt's book *The Human Condition* (1958) includes a section in which Arendt discusses the relevance of poetry to human history, arguing that the poem represents a kind of memory capsule, a vessel of remembrance that utilizes mnemonic strategies in its form in the service of the preservation of its content.[10] The combination of this conception of the poem as a kind of condensed archive and testimonial to history, and the fear that with the extinction of the victims' voices the public awareness of the Holocaust itself was in danger of extinction, served as the driving force behind the anthology projects of the 1960s. Pangs of conscience and the desire to atone for the immediate past may have inspired the publication of poetry by inmates and survivors in the early postwar years, but by the 1950s this remorse had been displaced by a growing complacency in part encouraged by material indulgence. Manfred Schlösser's 1960 collection, *Written to the Wind*, brings together the works of camp and ghetto poets as well as poems by exile writers. Schlösser closed the preface to his volume with a statement that reveals the dual intent of his collection, to preserve these writings both against forgetting and against the elitist judgments of the critics: "May this anthology be an initial step in the rehabilitation of this often forgotten poetry. And to the professional critics, finally, a word of warning from Karl Kraus: whoever now has something to say, let him step forward and be silent."[11] A similar collection, incorporating much of the same material but including antifascist works by contemporary German Democratic Republic poets, was published in East Germany in 1968: *What Word Called Into the Cold*, edited by Heinz Seydel. The Mitscherlichs' psychosocial study of 1967 brought the question of mourning and identity into the German public consciousness, at least in intellectual circles, but their bleak conclusions on postwar Germany's inability to mourn could not provoke the empathy necessary to achieve it. Without either a sense of loss or a sense of involvement, there is no psychic space for the work of mourning. This points to yet another complication in the reception of Holocaust poetry, where the emphasis has been on a select set of lyrical representatives chosen as mouthpieces of the Jewish fate and mascots of morally conscious memory rather than on the full spectrum of writing that was inspired by the experience and witness of extremity.

In the Germany of the 1960s and early 1970s, Nelly Sachs's poetry assumed a status as the token of German mourning—to a degree that could almost be viewed as the co-optation of her writing as a substitute for the work of mourning that was otherwise not being done in the German language. Hailed as *the* poet of Jewish fate during her lifetime and still today viewed by critics such as Gert Mattenklott as "a medium of the victims,"[12] Sachs and her poetic testimonies to the victims of the Holocaust became enmeshed in the vicissitudes of German memory politics, with reception alternating between recognition (as profoundly moving tributes to a catastrophic past) and rejection (as sentimental, mannerist, and distinctly unmodern attempts to represent the unrepresentable).

In the years immediately after the war, Nelly Sachs was unable to find a West German publisher for her first collection, *In the Residences of Death*, although she made valiant and persistent attempts. She was grateful and relieved when Aufbau in East Berlin agreed to print her collection in 1947. After this first volume met with a notable lack of popular resonance (although it did receive some critical attention), Sachs had to go outside of Germany to find a publisher for her next collection, which was printed in Amsterdam in 1949. By the latter half of the 1950s, however, Sachs's works were being printed in Germany, where her third volume of poetry, *And No One Knows Further*, was published in Hamburg in 1957. Still she complained bitterly in her letters that she despaired of ever finding a permanent home for her work in Germany. The resonance of Hans Magnus Enzensberger's *Merkur* article of 1959—in which he argued that Nelly Sachs's work refuted Adorno's dictum against poetry after Auschwitz and proclaimed her to be the "greatest poet . . . writing in German today"[13]—signaled the beginning of an upswing of interest, accolades, and awards for the poet in the 1960s culminating in the Nobel Prize of 1966.

After the time of recognition following the Nobel Prize had passed, however, and then most clearly after the poet's death in 1970, there was a shift in reception from praise to criticism, from a celebration of Sachs's verse as representative of the Jewish fate and an appeal to universal moral conscience to a derogatory attitude toward her lyric as archaic, unrealistic, and sentimental. Many critics began to insinuate that the prizes she had been awarded were more representative of German guilt than of her poetic prowess. Nor was she really regarded as a "German" poet: the label "poet of the *Jewish* fate" stuck. Sachs was in a sense both elevated and isolated as the representative of the Jewish victims *and* German-Jewish reconciliation, on the one hand acting as a balm on the German conscience, but on the other never being truly accepted as a German poet. The dubious limelight she had briefly enjoyed as a mascot of memory faded as quickly as it had once flashed, and it is only recently that Sachs's works are again beginning to be seriously addressed and reread in scholarly studies.

What the cases of Ilse Weber and Nelly Sachs illustrate is that the assessment of poetry written in response to the Holocaust must be mediated, on the one hand, by a recognition of the set of expectations we bring to these texts as post-Holocaust readers, and on the other hand, an acknowledgement of the context in which those words were written. Further, it is necessary to remain conscious of the fact that the event of the writing and the socio-historical positionality of each new reading are both embedded in an ongoing process of memory, and that our own discourse and readerly expectations exert an influence on our understanding of the past as well as our ability to determine the future. The shift in emphasis in Holocaust literary studies from documentation to representation has implications not only for the way in which we remember the past, but also threatens to further obscure the "authentic" voices of witness and their testimonies.

But where do we draw the line between canonization and preservation, between confrontation and reparation, commemoration and actual remembrance? I am referring here to the contemporary phenomenon in representations of the Holocaust, where a discursive fascination with memory has become a substitute for the work of memory itself, and assumed a degree of dominance and control over the past in the present that recalls Foucault's claims about the history of sexuality wherein loquacity and a profusion of confessionalism were in inverse relation to actual freedom and emancipation.[14] In terms of the Holocaust, many official commemorations come across as self-serving gestures of buying a place among the righteous—as substitute acts of moral conscience that do not necessarily reflect conviction, but rather grow out of externally imposed expectations for public displays of mourning and remembrance that are themselves intertwined with political motives. Ingeborg Bachmann's admonition in an unfinished essay, where she alludes to the potential for manipulation of the victims' memory and "name" in order to justify ends in the present, has become all too pertinent to the current commodification and appropriation of the Holocaust: "It is not true that the victims admonish, testify or bear witness for something. That is one of the most terrible and thoughtless, and weakest poeticizations. . . . No one can call upon the victim. It is misuse. No country and no group, and no idea is allowed to call upon its dead."[15]

Willi Brandt's fall to his knees in front of the Warsaw memorial in 1970 may have been moved by genuine sorrow and shame, but much of the ceremony that followed was carefully scripted in an ever more rehearsed and thus superficial rhetoric of mourning and remembrance. Post-Holocaust poetry has become both yet another realm in which this ritual of remembrance takes place *and* an arena in which the character of the German "work of mourning" is questioned and its underlying hypocrisy and cynicism criticized. This tone of critique comes out in the works of both Jewish and non-Jewish poets: in the sarcasm and bitter humor of Erich Fried's lyrical sound bites, in the scathing observations of Bertolt Brecht, the disturbing poetic revelations of Ingeborg Bachmann, and in the many and varied contemporary manifestations of conscience expressed via the poetic word. If indeed the Jews invented conscience, then that legacy is being carried on in the medium of so-called Holocaust poetry, although not always in reference to the Holocaust as a lived historical event. But the increasingly metaphorical quality of the Holocaust in literature and its exploitation as a trope of suffering and existential angst gives rise to questions about the future of Holocaust literature and the fate of the voices of those victims who have been doubly silenced, first by death, and then by the din of a discourse of inexpressibility and laments over the limits of language. In the contemporary effusion of words about the rupture and fracture of language there is an observable fetishization of the signifier over the signified, a fascination with tropability in an ethereal realm of aesthetic abstraction, that threatens to obscure the real victims' legacy through a new game of smoke and mirrors.

By codifying the conviction that, as Nelly Sachs once wrote, "Silence is the dwelling place of the victims,"[16] Holocaust literary scholarship has proclaimed speech an impossibility (thereby denying the victims a conventional voice) while simultaneously privileging a certain kind of language, a poetics of horror, fragmentation, and silence for which Paul Celan has been celebrated ever since Adorno's proclamation in his *Aesthetic Theory*: "Celan's poetry seeks to express the most extreme horror through silence."[17] This concentration on silence and its representations points to the increasingly self-referential nature of Holocaust literary studies. But the fixation on the opposition between language and silence is gradually being displaced by a growing concern—at times bordering on obsession—with memory. The future of Holocaust studies will be determined by whether the burgeoning discourse *about* mourning and memory vis-à-vis the Holocaust is accepted and acknowledged as a displacement of "true" *Trauerarbeit* as the discourse of mourning, and whether we regard this displacement as a natural and necessary step in the evolutionary process of remembrance. We must also continue to ask ourselves what we are talking about when we talk about Holocaust poetry: the testimonies to an event that we will never fully comprehend, or the resonances and implications this catastrophe has had for moral conscience and language, or whether there is a means of mediating this opposition. In the end, what we perhaps most need to ask ourselves is not whether there is a right or wrong way to engage with this past, but rather that no matter what form it takes, a conscious and self-reflective concern with the Holocaust as event, representation, or resonance is in any case preferable to its submersion in the amnestic wake of history.

NOTES

1. Nelly Sachs, *Fahrt ins Staublose* (Frankfurt a.M.: Suhrkamp, 1988), 20. All translations from the German are mine.

2. Quoted by George Steiner in his essay "The Long Life of Metaphor," in Berel Lang, ed., *Writing and the Holocaust* (New York: Holmes & Meier, 1988), 164.

3. Quoted in Russian in Paul Celan, *Gedichte I* (Frankfurt a.M.: Suhrkamp, 1975), 287.

4. Ilse Weber, *Theresienstadt* (Tel Aviv: Mafil, 1964), 21.

5. Ibid., 50ff.

6. Ibid., 107–108.

7. Ludvík Václavek, "Deutsche Lyrik im Ghetto Theresienstadt 1941–1945," *Weimarer Beiträge* 5 (1982): 26. Václavek applies this phrase specifically to the works of Ilse Weber, but it could be extended as a designation of the tone and form that characterizes much of the poetry written in the camps and ghettos.

8. H. G. Adler, *Theresienstadt 1941–1945: Das Antlitz einer Zwangsgemeinschaft*, orig. 1955 (Tübingen: J.C.B. Mohr, 1960), 617. Cf. also Zdenek Lederer, *Ghetto Theresienstadt*, trans. K. Weisskopf (London: Edward Goldston & Son, Ltd., 1953), 128f.

9. Ibid., 619.

10. Hannah Arendt, *The Human Condition* (Chicago: University of Chicago Press, 1958), 169-170.

11. Manfred Schlösser, ed., *An den Wind geschrieben. Lyrik der Freiheit 1933–1945* (Darmstadt: Agora, 1960), 20.

12. Gert Mattenklott, "Zur Darstellung der Shoa in deutscher Nachkriegsliteratur," *Jüdischer Almanach* (1993): 32.

13. Hans Magnus Enzensberger, "Steine der Freiheit," *Merkur* 13 (1959): 770–775.

14. Cf. Michel Foucault, *The History of Sexuality*, vol. 1, trans. Robert Hurley (New York: Vintage, 1980). Michael Geyer and Miriam Hansen offer a similar thesis that the discourse of memory was a means of controlling or appropriating memory in postwar Germany. In their essay "German-Jewish Memory and National Consciousness," they refer to "a near total usurpation of memory—every kind of memory—by the post-war state and its institutions" because, in fact, "there was no public space or

collective language for memory experience. Memory remained private or marginal . . . or it was state-sponsored and institutional." *Holocaust Remembrance: The Shapes of Memory*, ed. Geoffrey Hartman (Cambridge, MA: Basil Blackwell, 1994), 185–186.

15. Ingeborg Bachmann, "Auf das Opfer darf keiner sich berufen," *Werke* (Munich: Piper, 1978), 4: 335.

16. Nelly Sachs, *Suche nach Lebenden* (Frankfurt a.M.: Suhrkamp, 1971), 70.

17. Theodor W. Adorno, "Paralipomena," in his *Ästhetische Theorie, Gesammelte Schriften* (Frankfurt a.M.: Suhrkamp, 1990), 7: 477.

15
Hans-Jürgen Syberberg and the State of the Ghost
ROBERT SHANDLEY

"A specter haunts Europe, the specter of communism."[1] Marx's opening of the "Manifesto" is a projection into a future. The spectral field that haunts Europe in general and Germany in specific no longer confines itself to a future tense. It is no longer a question, as Jacques Derrida puts it, of a ghost that stands in front of us, but also of one that is behind us.[2] And Marx's revolution does not occupy this spectral world alone. For fifty years generations of inquirers in our fields of study have fascinated themselves and occasionally others with the ghost stories of Germany.

The metaphor of the specter is always used to summon up a particular death in order to serve as a sort of universal moral lesson to the not-yet dead. As such, ghosts are embodiments of historical memory. The ghost figure is one who while having suffered a physical death refuses the symbolic one. One particular ghost, that of the victims of the Holocaust, has haunted the field of German studies for the last fifty years. It was not always metaphoric condensation (6,000,000 : 1) nor metonymic spiritual transferal (ghost : 6,000,000 victims). Indeed, this is, in part, the product of fifty years of postwar German studies. When did we then stop dealing with the particularity of the victims of the Holocaust? Did we ever start? What is at stake in the shift? The ghost of the exterminated Jew at Auschwitz has metamorphosed from being situated firmly within the frontiers of a specific history, to a metahistorical metaphor available for the almost universal appropriation of victimhood. It sometimes calls people to remember the destruction of lives and histories wrecked by the Nazis in the name of the ghost of the Holocaust for purposes less sincere.

The metaphors placed in service of understanding and aestheticizing the German past have changed over the past fifty years. In the immediate wake of the war, sublime metaphors such as "catastrophe" and "disaster" were employed in the reconstruction of the recent past. These were metaphors connoting universal suffering and, at the same time, no agency. As that past receded and another generation of critics and artists began to address the personal history of their fathers and mothers, a new set of signifiers emerged. Among these, two metaphors of history gained currency. One was that of the angel of history. Drawing upon Walter Benjamin, the angel induces the image of the horrified, ahistorical subject who looks at history as a pile of rubble at which one can only stare in horror. This finds its most obvious manifestation in Wim Wenders's film *Wings of Desire* (*Der Himmel über Berlin,* 1987), where melancholic angels are confined only to observe the painful unfolding of human history. They can only observe, they cannot engage. And yet, the more troubling and enigmatic metaphor is that of the ghost. Unlike the angel, the ghosts of the past were actors and are now always threatening. They are a threat that forces the haunted subject to act out. Rather than merely calling one to memory of loss, this remnant of the past often attempts to regain/recoup some lost wholeness.

Perhaps the most disturbing and polemic attempt to suture the gaps of history in Germany is to be found in Hans-Jürgen Syberberg's polemical book-length, aphoristic chain, *Vom Unglück und Glück der Kunst in Deutschland nach dem letzten Kriege* (*On the Unhappiness and Happiness of Art in Germany After the Last War,* 1990), in which he makes the not-so-unsubtle argument that postwar German art has been plagued by a dogmatic adherence to the leftist, Jewish aesthetics of "the small, the dirty and the sick."[3] Many critics who had endorsed Syberberg's oeuvre in the 1980s, especially his Hitler film, as an effective theorization of imagery and the German past, saw this book as a betrayal. Syberberg's blunt anti-Semitism, Prussian provincialism, and eco-nationalism have now been met with a remarkable silence in German critical circles. Perhaps that is the most appropriate response. Yet his diatribe against what he calls the loss of German cultural identity strikes such a plethora of issues that an investigation of the stakes may well shed some light on the direction of the cultural identity that Syberberg embraces. The value in this book is not in his petty and bitter analysis as much as it is in his conjuring skills. Syberberg calls up not only the usual spectral suspects (Hitler, Wagner, or Karl May), but also a list of cultural icons ranging from Kleist to Kiefer, from Schinkel to Adorno—all of whom continue to haunt German culture.

Indeed a modern specter haunts Syberberg. Much of his text can be read as an a debate with Theodor Adorno's critical oeuvre, most specifically the *Aesthetic Theory*. More specifically, Syberberg's book can be read as, among other things, an absolute refusal to read Adorno. That fits in well with the history of anti-Semitism as a refusal to even familiarize oneself with one's Other. The reason for this, as I will attempt to explain, is that Syberberg treats Adorno as a thief, the kill-joy of postwar aesthetics who has stolen Germany's enjoyment of art.[4]

The phantomic metaphor is valuable insofar as it helps us to locate enjoyment as the object at stake. *Hamlet*, as the hegemonic spectral trope, functions as a template for my reading of Syberberg. It certainly seems to fit into his fantasy of innocent loss and loss of innocence. Let us look at Syberberg as a distraught Prince of Denmark plagued by the phantom of the *Vaterland*. In fact, this hermeneutic stretch accurately portrays the position Syberberg puts himself into in this book. As his thoughts return to his home, or *Heimat*, he discovers that the national throne has been usurped. Convinced that he must avenge the death of the *Vaterland*, our Königberger Hamlet sets out to find the killers. The dramatis personae show the evil stepfather being played by those emigrants who return to Germany after the war to impose their aesthetic *Wiedergutmachung* on a defeated Germany, while the aesthetics of feminism appear complicitous with this usurpation, filling in the role of the two-timing mother. Syberberg accuses both the emigrants and the feminists of having purloined his patriotic pleasure.

The term "haunt" is important for my reading of Syberberg because it refuses linearity that a verb such as "inform" would connote. None of these ghosts spooks Syberberg more than Adorno and, I will argue by extension, the feminists. In the case of the latter, it is conceivable that he does not recognize his own threat. Why Adorno the ghost and not the more empirical texts of the Frankfurt critical theorists? Because in both cases his fantasy depends upon a vague and unspecific threat; hence this is not a rigorous critique as much as it a phantasmagoric projection. His treatment of Adorno is bland and, by now, clichéd. While he may, at least, mention Adorno as the thief and neglect to mention feminism, ultimately his treatment of the former indicates almost as much blindness as his exclusion of the latter.

Syberberg's first nonreading of Adorno is within a few paragraphs of the beginning of the work. It does not take long for Syberberg to betray his own sentiments. Referring to Adorno, Benjamin, and the Frankfurt School crowd as the founding fathers of German postwar aesthetics, Syberberg notes: "There were those who made a career by allying themselves with the Jews or with the leftists, and it did not necessarily have to do with love or understanding, or even predisposition. How could the Jews stand this? It is as if they [the Jews] only wanted power."[5]

Syberberg's transgression here lies not so much in the claim that people made careers of identifying with leftist Jews (as if people did not also make careers in alliance with cold-warrior ex-Nazis). Syberberg asks of himself whether or not he did the same. The offense is in the rhetorical twist, which turns these observations into a conspiracy to degenerate German culture. He goes on to call it an "unholy alliance for an art without a *Volk* or even more base, a comfortable quicker disposable art such as punk, pop, or junk, that now stands in our way."[6] Read closely, the unholy alliance that blocks "us" is a refusal of the nineteenth-century German notion of *Bildung* ("self-formation"). I would not be the first critic to note that *Bildung* has served as one of the oldest anti-Semitic devices. Syberberg deploys it here *de facto* as synonymous with the "soul" of culture that has been lost. This loss of *Bildung* is the grounding of the xenophobia that pervades the text, one that hardly needs to be excavated. What I continue to find peculiar, however, is how this vilification of the banality of art in postwar Germany sounds much like Adorno himself. This mass *Volk* is being deceived by the vulgar, everyday pop culture, and is thus being kept from redemption through beauty. This is, of course, not quite Adorno himself, but a sort of uncanny ghost of Adorno; the version most proliferated in the wake of the 1960s. Syberberg admits as much, but, as Eric Santner has put it, "he seems incapable of conceiving of fantasy except in the deeply anti-Semitic terms."[7] Why is that?

Syberberg's comments reveal an obvious if unarticulated anxiety, namely the fear that an enjoyment is being or has been stolen. For fifty years, according to Syberberg, a cadre of political and cultural forces—including the "Jewish" Frankfurt School, the Allied occupational forces, and many witting and unwitting German collaborators—have combined to steal from Germany the enjoyment of its nationhood, its national consciousness, and cultural heritage. This consciousness and heritage is reduced down to the figure of Prussia, that lost eastern province that Syberberg reads as having been stolen from Germany. The contradictions in his argument are obvious and unproductive at this point. What remains interesting is the social field in which he imagines these thefts to have taken place. To whom does he imagine himself speaking? How does he imagine retrieving this lost enjoyment? Why must this field be anti-Semitic? What happens to that social field if you remove anti-Semitism? Is it possible? If so, is it possible to imagine a productive discussion and understanding of German community and cultural heritage that is *not* on loss and theft, that is, on simplified versions of lack?

Most current work on the cultural forces of the nineteenth century (that era of high Prussianism that Syberberg nostalgically reinvokes) is, at some point, attentive to the degree to which German cultures are almost always caught in a negative dialectic with varyingly violent forms of anti-Semitism. The events of the Holocaust demand of intellectuals in its wake to take note of the painful relationship between Germany (Europe) and its internal others. At the risk of being overly polemical, one would have to note in the case of Syberberg that, in his desire to recover a lost nineteenth-century culture, he would wish to have it replete with its anti-Semitic components.

The question that Syberberg poses so ineloquently is whether or not Germany will ever be allowed to enjoy itself as such, namely in its dialectically constructed *Bildungsbürgertum*-self. Maybe it is a fair question. That which he sees as standing in the way of that enjoyment is an aesthetic void. Syberberg seems unable to think outside of premodernist aesthetics. He is either paralyzed or stubborn in the face of the possibility of "the new." Whether that inability is intentional or strategic, Syberberg fails to think through the logic of the aesthetic that he sets out to oppose. For him, postwar cultures (whether popular, elitist, or fused) are merely criminal; they are culprits who have stolen the enjoyment of the national body.

More than proving an obvious and relatively uninteresting contradiction, this reading suggests the extent to which the ghosts that haunt Syberberg are so difficult to exorcise. More than Adorno (and Horkheimer) of the *Dialectic of the Enlightenment*, the Adorno of the "Cultural Criticism and Society" essay or the Adorno of *Aesthetic Theory* spooks Syberberg.[8] What is the gesture of the *Aesthetische Theorie* that is such a crime to Syberberg? As I have been suggesting, it is the void, the emptying out of the image. He opposes the beginning of an aesthetic by clearing the slate.

This is where a certain version of feminism fits in, specifically Anglo-American versions of the 1970s and early 1980s. After showing what damage prolific imagery can do, Laura Mulvey, for example, sets about removing the image from the picture, with the express purpose of disrupting enjoyment of the image. Adorno pursues the same gesture, removing enjoyment from the field until we can investigate what it is based upon. In both cases, the beginning of the new can only begin with the removal of (unnecessary) ornamentation. When he calls upon Adorno, Syberberg is eschewing the real, i.e., the textual body for the phantasmagorical one. Curiously enough, the latter body is, above all else, a Jew. Why does Syberberg need a Jew to steal his enjoyment? The answer may be found in Gertrud Koch's important work on Adorno.[9]

Were this an actual reading, Syberberg would not be the first scholar of late to read Adorno's Jewishness back into his work. Koch has performed astute observations of Adorno's modernist aesthetics within the context of the Old Testament's *Bilderverbot* ("anti-graven image commandment"). The premise of Koch's monograph on the visual representation of Judaism is that the

Bilderverbot inherent in the Second Commandment's prohibition of graven images belongs to the central ideas of Adorno's aesthetics. To be sure, Adorno refers to the *Bilderverbot* often in his own modernist aesthetic. But Syberberg takes the Jewishness well beyond its theological grounding. All of a sudden the taboo against graven images mushrooms into a list of grievances, categorized by Syberberg as a result of living in a Jewish age under the conditions of Jewish aesthetics. The blame for everything from the atom bomb (Einstein) to the obsession of modern literature with petty ugliness (Kafka) is placed squarely upon the shoulders of Jews.

Syberberg reserves most of his polemic for the loss of the aesthetic of beauty in postwar German art. In fact, he divides it more neatly (and along Adornian lines): art has been replaced by aesthetics. Art is the genuine experience of the beautiful for Syberberg, while aesthetics, specifically Adorno's modernism, is the conceptualization and advocacy of the ugly and the vulgar. Aesthetics for Syberberg is not so much the ghost of art as much as it is the exorcism of it, the spectral conjuring of a lost object.

Along with the "work of mourning" (*Trauerarbeit*) that Syberberg performs on other fronts, he is mourning what he perceives as the loss of art: "What is at stake here is an art that declines after 1945, a sacrifice of those 12 years before." Indeed, art is the ghost . . . but of what? Art as the ghost of art? In the Syberberg text, art is the ghost of Prussia: Prussia / Art, without which, according to Syberberg, the Kantian aesthetic subject (Kant as Ur-Prussian) cannot be articulated. This is the heart of Syberberg's argument; namely that the problem with art in postwar Germany is that it has not recovered from the loss of the "quarter of our provinces, the most outspoken . . . that gave us fame, sense, and the power of representation of our identity."[10]

It should be noted that the entire aphoristic diatribe is written during the fall of the Wall, known as the *Wende*. Syberberg ends it by taking issue with that overgrazed and seldom understood dictum, namely Adorno's "After Auschwitz, it is barbaric to write a poem" ("Ein Gedicht nach Auschwitz zu schreiben ist barbarisch").[11] Since Syberberg sees the postwar period as one driven by Jewish aesthetics without art, and subsequently poetry, he sees the events of 1989–1990 as a call for a "departure . . . from the grand-fathers [*Übervāter*] of emigration"—that is, from Adorno et al. Of course, in mentioning emigration he follows yet another dubious tradition of Germans who criticize and delegitimize the experiences of those who left Germany during the war, yet another accusation of the betrayal of the Fatherland. His is a call for an exorcism from that ghost that keeps him from his beloved Prussia, the missing pieces in the "total work of art" (*Gesamtkunstwerk*) of Germany.

If Syberberg is nothing but spooked, that is, if my choice of metaphors is accurate, why respond to these distasteful and ill-founded claims at all? Do we only give more currency by reacting? It is never wise, I would argue, to ignore attacks on intellectualism and cultural diversity, either in Germany or elsewhere. More importantly, Syberberg's argument contains many of the problems that confront German cultures. They are in many instances the state of the specter in Germany. Thus, they serve as much more than just a straw man against which we can prove our moral fortitude. If it were the ghost of Adorno that haunts Syberberg, the real, textual corpus of Adorno would serve as the best starting point for a response to the narrow cultural agenda Syberberg has set out for himself.

One of the best counters to the endless and often tired set of questions Syberberg dredges up is to be found in feminist scholarship. My argument is that a genealogy of thought leads from Adorno's emptying out of the image to Laura Mulvey's call in the 1970s for an end to the baroque treatment of image of woman in film. In her 1974 essay "Visual Pleasure and Narrative Cinema"[12] (still canonical reading in film studies), Mulvey traces the necessary sadism of cinema and proposes that the only solution is the removal of the image of woman from cinema. That is, like Adorno, this invocation of a *Bilderverbot* (or, for the former, a *Poesieverbot* as well) is a polemic from which they later will retreat. The more radical gesture is that which, in both cases, sticks, in part because it is itself a response to excessive representation.

So, where do Mulvey and Adorno confront the Syberberg text? Feminism is absent from Syberberg's polemic attacks. Given that he has taken pot shots from the Prussian woods at nearly every other political and intellectual force in Germany, this absence is curious, even more so given Syberberg's cultural position as, among other things, a film maker. For it is really in feminist film making in Germany that much of what Syberberg decries has been done, and done quite well. The cultural forces of feminist film making both informed by and contributing to the theoretical constructs articulated by Mulvey and others counters the cultural pessimism and nostalgic sense of loss invoked by Syberberg. Retrograde cultural preservationists like Syberberg tend to call upon the rhetorical strategy of myopia, that is, he chooses the easier and less traumatic ghost. It is significant that anti-Semitism is less of a risk for Syberberg than would be the blatant misogyny that would necessarily follow from his naming his other true enemy.

In closing, let me suggest the possibility of Syberberg's rhetoric being merely provocative, for I find it is that much, to say the least. Indeed, it would be nice for it to be no more than that. It would then make some of his conjuring more productive. And, I would not want to make of the Frankfurt School a sacred cow, untouchable by contemporary criticism. But Syberberg's book comes off merely as a virulent diatribe against the "Jewishness" of the Frankfurt School and not an honest exchange with the work. In the historical context in which it was written, namely the tumultuous events of 1989–1990, a much more serious, levelheaded discussion of the ramifications of the ongoing *Wende* would have been more effective. His work is an unfortunate noncontribution. For new ways of articulating a German culture, both its past and future continue to be necessary. Working with the Syberberg text has also led me to the realization of how much of what we do in the field of contemporary German studies is so intimately tied to the same ghosts that haunt him. But demonizing and ignoring the most ethical voices in the culture is no way to find our way out of the haunted house.

NOTES

1. Karl Marx, "Manifesto of the Communist Party," in Robert C. Tucker, ed., *The Marx-Engels Reader* (New York: Norton, 1972), 473.

2. Jacques Derrida, *Specters of Marx: Mourning, The New International and the State of the Debt* (New York: Routledge, 1994).

3. Hans-Jürgen Syberberg, *Vom Unglück und Glück der Kunst in Deutschland nach dem letzten Kriege* (Munich: Matthes & Seitz, 1990), 38. Referring to Grass's *The Tin Drum*, Syberberg states, "The fact that the central figure of the best known postwar novel in Germany is a dwarf characterizes this observation" (39). All translations are my own unless otherwise noted.

4. For a lucid articulation of the notion of enjoyment employed here, see Slavoj Zizek's "Eastern Europe's Republics of Gilead," *New Left Review* 183 (1990): 50–62.

5. Syberberg, *Vom Unglück und Glück*, 14.

6. Ibid.

7. Eric L. Santer, "Postwar Aesthetics and the Legacy of Fascism," *New German Critique* 57 (1992).

8. Theodor W. Adorno, "Kulturkritik und Gesellschaft," in his *Prismen* (Frankfurt a.M.: Suhrkamp, 1955), 7–31.

9. Gertrud Koch, *Die Einstellung ist die Einstellung: Visuelle Konstruktion des Judentums* (Frankfurt a.M.: Suhrkamp, 1992).

10. Syberberg, *Vom Unglück und Glück*, 127 and 161.

11. Theodor W. Adorno, "Ein Gedicht nach Auschwitz zu schreiben ist barbarisch," in his *Prismen*, 31.

12. Laura Mulvey, "Visual Pleasure and Narrative Cinema," in her *Visual and Other Pleasures* (Bloomington: Indiana University Press, 1989), 14–26.

16
Restaging Riefenstahl: The Lure of Nazi Iconography
JANET WARD

There has been much critical ink spilled—and rightly so—over the ethical question of the inimitability of the Holocaust in artistic representation. This chapter addresses the rival system of representation that has been with us over the last half-century: that of Nazism itself. The lure of Nazi iconography consists in its being a sign-system of cinematic desire. We have to admit, if we are honest with ourselves, that the filmic iconography of fascism has been winning the day over the *Bilderverbot*, or "anti-graven image commandment," of the Shoah. My regrets to Susan Sontag's or Saul Friedländer's edicts, but "fascinating fascism," like "kitsch and death,"[1] have not decreased in filmic terms; rather, the exact opposite has occurred. I do not wish to sound a pessimistic note here: it is just that fascism in film has proven so much longer-lived and more widely distributed a product than well-intentioned enterprises in bearing witness to the Holocaust. Nor is the spectacle of fascism, namely its circus-show quality,[2] particularly "fascist" anymore, in the political sense of the word: it has become molded into our expectations of what cinema is, because it first molded itself on the strategies and effects of cinema, located as the latter has always been within the modern culture industry.[3] The lure of Nazi iconography, the hyping of its own symbols, began as an integral part of the Nazi credo. It was based on cinematic success and hence on our approval as viewers, as well as on an intimate relation to American-style marketing, advertising, and consumer culture.[4] Iconography forms a major part of the semiotic film criticism of this same culture, and Nazi imagery functions like the *mise-en-abyme* of this visual style.

It is time that we academics admit to the obvious defeat of the *Bilderverbot* in terms of fascism and cinema.[5] In this sense, then, *Schindler's List* marks the shift, even in a Holocaust film, from Shoah-witnessing to Nazi iconography, which explains its commercial success. To extend the logic of pictorial censorship and repression, as practiced by policies of the Federal Republic of Germany (and first imposed by the attitude of the Allies) as well as by theories of the Frankfurt School, would only continue the potentially explosive fetishization of this legacy in Germany. We are not going to be able to get rid of Nazi nostalgia, because in so doing we would be ridding Western society of its major historical dream: World War II as the metanarrative of the late twentieth and now early twenty-first century for a populace living in an age that has purportedly, according to Jean-François Lyotard, buried metanarrative—thus, the re-creation of Nazism on screen serves as a substitute for (or simulacrum of) the unattainable or lost "real" history; it is, states Jean Baudrillard, a symptom of our "desperate historical search for a posthumous truth,"[6] of our collective state of *post-histoire*.[7] Small wonder, then, that cinema audiences are not letting go of it, and have, where necessary, updated the uniforms into contemporary fantasies of sex and death, massification and cyborg-armor.

I am not excusing unlimited restagings of Nazism in films that aim to reincite fascist responses. Nor is this a plaidoyer for a blame-equation of Hollywood with Hitler, or of left-wing German political correctness vis-à-vis the war with Jewish influence, as Hans-Jürgen Syberberg has so problematically depicted.[8] But let's stop bemoaning the masses' (our own) fascination with screenic Nazism, and stop being the cultural pessimists of cinema's relation to history. Instead, let's lift the taboo by acknowledging the relationship of Nazi iconography to the experience of cinema per se; analyze how it functions in society; and further see how it can, upon happy occasion, be subsumed within ironic engagement until it is aestheticized (i.e., anaesthetized) out of meaningful (i.e., political) existence.[9]

Ray Müller's[10] 1993 bio-documentary of the former Nazi propaganda filmmaker Leni Riefenstahl may give us a clue about this last strategy. *The Wonderful, Horrible Life of Leni Riefenstahl* is a recent example of *Bilderverbot*-bashing, of admitting that the Nazi "emperor" is not wearing any clothes—and yet it does not make fascists of its viewers who are nonetheless subjected to its serial projection of National Socialist imagery. Müller would appear to throw ethical caution to the wind in letting the Nazi "Other" speak in her own language. He dares to refilm and restage the iconography of Nazism without apologizing for the "aestheticization of politics" or our visual pleasure ensuing therefrom. He does this via the life of the filmmaker Riefenstahl, whose very understanding and practice of filmmaking has been the epitomy (Sontag would say even the very founding) of cinematic-cum-Nazi iconic desire. Riefenstahl's films have been the most convincing example in the history of cinema of "the power of images" (*Die Macht der Bilder* being Müller's original German title).

The Wonderful, Horrible Life of Leni Riefenstahl stages itself as a series of interviews that will objectively endeavor to let the subject tell her own life. Müller presents his documentary as one that will let this ex-director control her own self-image. As a German reviewer stated, Müller allows Riefenstahl to "represent herself."[11] The most striking feature of this film is indeed the free rein apparently yielded to Riefenstahl as she uses Müller quite ruthlessly as a mirror for the staging of her own life story within another director's film, most specifically as Junta, the self-protagonist in her first feature film, *The Blue Light* (1932): a figure of natural, apolitical womanhood, an exotic-erotic outcast "much loved and much hated" by her own people, as Riefenstahl comments, an innocent icon of cinematic desire, living far above the snares of civilization and politics in a pure realm of mountain crystal. She packages herself as sympathetic spectacle in every frame, ensuring the pro-filmic is to her liking, just as she had always done as director. Evidently her intent was to help create a film in which she appears as similar as possible to the Leni of her own 1987 autobiography.[12]

Indeed, if Müller's efforts had stopped at the above, then his product would have been likely to fall prey to the recent German controversy: that is, of a documentary film on a Nazi topic (*Profession Neonazi*, 1994, directed by Winfried Bonengel), a film which listens to and frames its subject—the neo-Nazi Ewald Althans—too obsequiously, thereby inviting neo-Nazi spectatorial reaction (and governmental banning) in Germany.[13] Germany's fuss over Bonengel's *Profession Neonazi* almost obliterated the impact of Müller's film there, but in the United States Müller received a TV Emmy Award in December 1993.

Most telling in the Bonengel case is not so much that cinema's "power of images" makes too disengaged a restaging of fascism into highly flammable material; it is that our society reacts more to the power of media-related images than to the power of an actual event; only when it is transferred into media-imagery does the event assume a mimesis-inspiring position. Television reporting for the Gulf War was a case of this "virtual reality": Baudrillard has termed this situation our "necroperspective" on history and culture, where the simulacrum takes over from the real.[14] Paul Virilio, likewise, warns of the "impending mutation of the movie or video-recording camera into a computerized vision machine."[15]

As with the Bonengel controversy, Riefenstahl was blamed in 1945 more than many other fellow travellers because of her role as filmmaker in coproducing the simulacrum of Nazism, rather than in coauthoring Nazism itself. The voice-over narration in Müller's film asks of the postwar scapegoating of Riefenstahl: "How dangerous can images be?" As Hitler himself stated in his hierarchical ordering of propagandistic means of representation in *Mein Kampf*, the best way to convert people is at a staged mass event with himself as spectacle, but the next best substitute is the cinematic medium of the same event.[16] Riefenstahl's *Triumph of the Will* is, then, to the memory of Nazism what all film is to the actual happening.

Thankfully, the self-proclaimed auteurial passivity of Müller is a front for a more multifaceted agonistic exchange between interviewee and interviewer. Müller not only satisfies both the audience's and Leni's need for the Riefenstahl aesthetic to be regurgitated as our voyeuristic, cinematic pleasure; through sceptical voice-over narration, jump-cutting, parallel editing, and candid camera shots, Müller ensures that there is always an alternative subcommentary on his subject's versions of events. We can term this a dialectical restaging of Riefenstahl. In this dialectical interaction we have an exercise in ironic reconnoitering of the lure of Nazi iconography.

The dialectic is geographical as well as temporal: Müller accompanies Leni to the major (dis)locations in the stages of her life: her home today, the Nollendorf underground train station in Berlin where she first saw a poster for a mountain film by Dr. Fanck in 1923, the Babelsberg studios where she argued with Marlene Dietrich, the Nuremberg arena, the Berlin Olympic stadium, her Kitzbühel house where she lived out the war, her scuba-diving expeditions in the Red Sea. At each location, images of today are intercut with photographic or filmic images of yesterday: her films as actress or as director, or both; Weimar scenes, Nazi scenes, war scenes, Holocaust scenes, Nuremberg trial scenes. And the relationship between these intercuts provides the film with its dramatic tension, irony, and distancing effects. These intercuts, and the occasional narratorial voice-over, lend an alternative, questioning opinion to those tiresomely non-self-questioning ones of Riefenstahl herself.

This dialectic is apparent as early as the opening sequence of the film, and extends beyond the images. The film commences with a series of shots of the underwater Riefenstahl, beyond time and place in a vibrantly colored sea world with the sound only of water and air, violently intercut with excerpts from her Nazi films shown to the beat of a threatening (Nazi) drum, hence very much located in a specific time and place. Even her Nuba days, with obviously a rather different context of drumming, are intercut as a continuation of the Nazi clips. The drum roll echoes as the film title is shown with Riefenstahl at the "helm" of the camera, in an implied position of mastery over her images. Then the film's theme music begins, and the camera approaches Riefenstahl in her home today, apparently just a harmless old lady in her nineties, but even the music introduced here is a clear rhythmic reference to the "Horst Wessel Song" (and during a subsequent *Triumph of the Will* clip, it becomes an exact melodic inversion of the same). The English narrator's opening comments about how the film should go about re-representing Riefenstahl announce the film's agenda of "deconstruct[ing] her myth and look[ing] at it afresh," while the language of the German original here indicates that this antimythic work will revise blind prejudice (*die Demontage des Mythos oder Revision des Vorurteils*).

Müller thus carefully reconstructs that which Riefenstahl gives him in the form of carefully practiced spoken memory. While German reviewers noticed the video-recorded "film within the film"—candid-camera scenes wherein Riefenstahl dictatorially rules how Müller is to film certain scenes (lighting, lens, etc.)—these same reviewers failed to see that the seemingly so accommodating, mild Müller simply did not carry them out (he made Leni walk and talk to the camera at the same time in the Babelsberg studios; he used just one shot, not several, of the Alpine backdrop for Riefenstahl's description of her mountain films).[17] The very inclusion of these viewfinder shots showing Leni at her most temperamental, to be then immediately juxtaposed with Leni on her best behavior (i.e., in the official filmed interview segments), constitutes a humorous doubling and demythologizing of the subject.

Undermining Riefenstahl's obsessive and lifelong self-staging (*Selbstinszenierung*) is thus the covert topic of the film. The ultimate "power" of these "images" is Müller's (and, by ethical implication, ours)—not hers.[18] So when Riefenstahl arrogantly refuses to analyze her own films under the rubric of fascist aesthetics ("I cannot imagine anything by the term fascist aesthetics," she claims: "I don't even know what that is supposed to mean"), it is the turn of the audience to benefit from Müller's sustained dialectic. We know, from the editing skills of this film, how to read her films even if she does (or will) not. As the film's narrator states, Hitler can be seen as an imitator staging himself in the image of Riefenstahl of her Juntaesque mountain film days: an unreachable myth far above the people. Her insistence that she only filmed beauty that the subject matter first created (i.e., mountains, herself, Nazis, Olympic athletes, the Nuba, sea life) runs contrary to her own trademark auteurial skills, which do not simply record the beautiful, rather they *create* the beautiful—via shots of rhythmic-musical montage, fluid camera, rapid contrasts of the individual with the masses, and juxtapositions of extreme camera perspectives (low angle with high angle, close-ups with long shots). She sees *all* life in terms of images: it is the 1945 image of Hitler and the images of the Holocaust that shocked her, not the events themselves, according to her own wording in the Müller film. Above all, she creates the beautiful in her obsession with filming the body—be this the male armored body or female iconic archtetype—the body (and soul) in extremis:

in short, the physical sublime, the ultimate dictate of (post)modern consumerist display.[19]

It is to Müller's credit that he manages to ironize this, the most sacred of all Nazi and culture-industry icons. For one of the inevitable voycurisms in this film, one that rivals all the Nazi images, is of course the body of Riefenstahl herself. The body of Leni (alias Junta) is the icon, the source of fascination in most every frame; this is what distinguishes Müller's film. Certainly, it seems as though Riefenstahl, as rival director for her restaging, has preempted Müller as much as she can. Her own home, for example, is a photo-filled museum of her previous physical incarnations. And one cannot help but notice her brightly colored outfits, all carefully chosen anew for each moment of the interview according to the lighting and the locale: brown draped velvet for the intimacy of her library; white tight pants, scarf, and jacket for the Alpine snow scene; blue silk blouse to describe *The Blue Light*; aqua-turquoise coat for the swimming pool used in *Olympia*, and so on.

But Müller retaliates in the editing process. Just after Riefenstahl's plaintive self-dramatization in front of a poster of Junta, we are given an extreme close-up shot of Junta, which is then dissolved into a photo of Hitler in exactly the same size and facial proportion and the same positioning of the eyes. Or again, just after Riefenstahl has recounted how Goebbels once threatened to have her thrown down the stairs if she had been a man, we are shown a photo of Goebbels, Leni, and Hitler in ascending height order, from which it is easy to infer that her physical strength far outweighed Goebbels's own.

Müller repeatedly shows us clips to demystify the body in extremis of Nazi iconography, which takes its origins in the prewar German culture) of the body (*Körperkultur*) and is today a sine qua non of dominant cinema. The viewer is bombarded with contrasts of the decaying old Leni (no matter how uncannily well preserved) with the eternally young Junta type. Müller uncovers scenes from Riefenstahl's rather nonbeautiful first National Socialist party rally film, *Victory of Faith* (1933), which show comic disorder rather than mass ornament, and which serve as the best possible introduction to the technique of *Triumph of the Will*, much to Riefenstahl's chagrin. Or again, Müller shows us a clip of the moment of the Olympic javelin-thrower stepping on something sharp: a taboo-image for Riefenstahl's vision of the body as immaculate, "primal torso."[20] These strategies undermine the emblematic positioning of the body in Riefenstahl's films, as well in her self-staging in this documentary. How else are we to explain Müller's choice of closure for his film on this woman's role in fascist and filmic aesthetics? As dramatic climax prior to his last brief interview with Riefenstahl, we are shown a scene from her unreleased oceanic footage, an encounter of two bodies: a stingray endangering Leni, who seeks it out and calmly strokes it. This example of the power of images is thus how Müller chooses to end his deconstruction (but not destruction) of the same.[21]

By way of conclusion, I would like to suggest that we should not be quite so hard on the Germans' (or Overwoman Leni's) documented "inability to mourn," and by this I am *not* suggesting that we fall in line unquestioningly with the most recent German (and American) post-Wall attempts at normalization, nor that we dilute Germany's special responsibility in maintainiing the memory of the Holocaust for all time. Rather, I suggest that we realize the inevitable difficulty of this nation's coming to terms which what Eric L. Santer terms the "symbolic debts" and "ideological phantasms" of National Socialism,[22] when the entire shared system of filmic-commercial fantasy in the Western world is dependent on the very same debts and phantasms. Perhaps the most obvious confimation of this image-parallelism, at the millennium, is the planned Hollywood film about Riefenstahl's life: a tale of both National Socialism's and Leni's lure, in which the character of Riefenstahl is to function as a sexy Amazonian, a veritable "adventurer-type like Lawrence of Arabia."[23]

It is hence imperative to remain alert to the differences between a film such as Müller's and other examples of the (now Berlin) Republic's normalization process that are reintroducing the aesthetics of Nazism in a somewhat less questioning manner. In this way, recluse Leni is being reinstated nowadays as a German (as opposed to a Nazi) artist in Germany; she held press conferences at both the Potsdam Film Museum's 1999 retrospective of her films and the "Camera Work" Berlin art gallery's display and sale, in 2000, of a limited edition of her handheld photographs of the 1936 Nazi Olympics in Berlin. Reinstatement acts such as these are not restricted to Germany: in 1997, the Hollywood-based Cinecon group awarded Riefenstahl for her film artistry. These are all markers of a new acceptability of the Riefenstahl icon, and of a less than self-aware admittance of her work's (and her myth's) confluence with what makes the cinematic and photographic image tick.

Until recently, any creative artist in Germany who dared re-treat these myths was immediately blamed as a sympathizer, as happened not just to Syberberg or Bonengel, but also to artist Anselm Kiefer—not when the latter depicted the Holocaust but when he touched upon the myths of Nazism such as his depictions of the Hitler salute in *Occupations* (1969), fascist architecture in *The Stairs* (1982–1983), Wagner, Heidegger, the Nazi book burnings, or Nuremberg, as Andreas Huyssen has pointed out.[24] But it is to be hoped that we are now witnessing shifts in German cultural production, as instanced by Müller's film, that indicate a new therapeutic ability to de-auratize these images and thereby help create an engaged, narrative-oriented environment—one that will be better equipped to deal with real-life instances of neofascistic vandalism and violence among the disaffected German youth, predominantly in states of the former GDR. Müller thus deserves full credit for letting the Riefenstahl aesthetic "speak" its pictorial self, for letting it run its seductive course in his film, in order to ironize it, not censor it or be overly astounded by it.[25] His is an updated filmic version of the necessary creative obsession with restaging the multiple lures of Nazi iconography.

I would like to thank Thomas A. Kovach and Walter H. Sokel for their advice in reading and discussing earlier versions of this essay.

NOTES

1. See Susan Sontag, "Fascinating Fascism," in Susan Sontag, *Under the Sign of Saturn* (New York: Farrar, Straus, Giroux, 1972), 73–105; and Saul Friedländer, *Reflections of Nazism: An Essay on Kitsch and Death* (New York: Harper & Row, 1984). See also Jean Baudrillard's response to the *Bilderverbot* in his *Simulacra and Simulations*, trans. Sheila Faria Glaser (Ann Arbor: University of Michigan Press, 1994), 4.

2. Cf. Hans-Jürgen Syberberg's figure of the circus barker, who introduces the Brechtian-Wagnerian, taboo reincarnations of Hitlerism in the film *Hitler, A Film From Germany* (1977) as "the greatest show of the century, big business, the show of shows."

3. These cinematic strategies of fascism were themselves virtual versions of the three-dimensional architectural "real," i.e., the aesthetics of neoclassical monumentality (*architecture parlante*), as George L. Mosse has indicated. See Mosse, "National Monuments," *The Nationalization of the Masses: Political Symbolism and Mass Movements in Germany from the Napoleonic Wars Through the Third Reich* (New York: Howard Fertig, 1975), 47–72. I would like to thank Steven E. Aschheim for noting this genealogy.

4. See Eric Rentschler's study of the common roots of the popular-commercial and the political in films of the Nazi era, in Rentschler, *The Ministry of Illusion: Nazi Cinema and Its Afterlife* (Cambridge, MA: Harvard University Press, 1996). For a study of the ways in which the Nazi visual aesthetic utilized advertising techniques, see Peter Labanyi, "Images of Fascism: Visualization and Aestheticization in the Third Reich," in *The Burden of German History 1919–1945*, ed. Michael Laffan (London: Methuen, 1988). See also Lutz Koepnick's related interpretation of Benjamin's *Arcades Project* as an exploratory site of how fascist aesthetics operates within the modern culture industry. Koepnick, "Fascist Aesthetics Revisited," *Modernism/Modernity* 6.1 (1999): 51–73.

5. Examples of the wave of Nazi iconographic films include Ingmar Bergman's *The Serpent's Egg* (1977), Luchino Visconti's *The Damned* (1969), or Joseph Losey's *Mr. Klein* (1976). Foucault's complaint against this kind of film was that it engendered a defeatist fatalism about fascism's powers: cf. the *mode rétro* debate in *Edinburgh Magazine* 2 (1977), cited by Anton Kaes, *From Hitler to Heimat: The Return of History as Film* (Cambridge, MA: Harvard University Press, 1989), 219.

6. Jean Baudrillard, *The Transparency of Evil* (New York: Verso [Routledge], 1993), 90–91.

7. For an analysis of *post-histoire*, see Kaes, *From Hitler to Heimat*, 47–49. Cf. also Thomas Elsaesser: "Baudrillard detected in the general retro-fashion a distinct 'retro-scenario': the peoples of Western Europe, locked into political stasis, nostalgically imagine through the cinema a time where their country's history still meant individual villains and victims, causes that mattered, and decisions of life and death. One attraction of such a history was the excuse for still telling stories with a beginning, middle and end, which would give the illusion of a personal or national destiny: a need fascism had tried to gratify on a collective scale. The return to history in the cinema was therefore for Baudrillard not a move towards coming to terms with the past, but the fetishisation of another trauma altogether, located in the present." Elsaesser, "Filming Fascism: Is History Just an Old Movie?" *Sight and Sound* 2.5 (1992): 19.

8. Cf. Syberberg's film, *Hitler, A Film From Germany*, and his more recent commentary, *Vom Unglück und Glück der Kunst in Deutschland nach dem letzten Kriege* (Munich: Matthes & Seitz, 1990). The latter is discussed by Robert Shandley in his essay for this volume.

9. Justin J. Lorentzen's essay on the visual culture of Nazism focuses exclusively on the legacy of horror, technology, and death, and underplays the coexisting Nazi iconography of beauty, mass ornamentation, and *Körperkultur*, all of which are most pertinent to Leni Riefenstahl's film aesthetics. As a result, Lorentzen's conclusions are far more somber than mine. See Lorentzen, "Reich Dreams: Ritual Horror and Armoured Bodies," in Chris Jenks, ed., *Visual Culture* (New York: Routledge, 1995), 161–169.

10. Ray Müller is a known television filmmaker of documentaries in Germany. He was, however, the nineteenth person approached by the producer to direct this film (sponsored by Zweites Deutsches Fernshen [ZDF]), and the first to agree to do so. See Ruth Starkman's discussion of Müller's approach to Riefenstahl in her article "Mother of All Spectacles: Ray Müller's *The Wonderful, Horrible Life of Leni Riefenstahl*," *Film Quarterly* 51.2 (1997-1998): 21–31.

11. Thomas Koebner, "Triumph des Wollens," *Kölner Stadt-Anzeiger* (Feb. 26, 1994).

12. Leni Riefenstahl, *Leni Riefenstahl. A Memoir* (New York: St. Martin's Press, 1992). In a review of this book, bell hooks attacks Riefenstahl's "mask of femininity" as one of "symbolic drag," enabling her to adopt a false "state of purity and innocence" regarding the Nazi patriarchy and the Holocaust. See hooks, "The Feminazi Mytique," *Transition* 7.1-7.3 (1998): 160, 159.

13. As Ralf Schenk stated in "Die Nazis, Das Kino, die Hilflosigkeit" (*Neues Deutschland* [Feb. 17, 1994]), the irony in the nationwide condemnation of Bonengel and his film was that this reaction was not focussed on his actual subject matter, namely Althans and his neo-Nazi group. Schenk bemoans the lack of governmental measures taken against neofascist activities in today's Germany, and contrasts this with the fuss made over Bonengel's documentary, which, in showing the free rein Althans enjoyed, points up this very lack of governmental initiative. Tellingly, Bonengel's film certainly contributed to Althans's subsequent, if short-lived, jail term. See David Bathrick, "Anti-Neonazism as Cinematic Practice: Bonengel's *Beruf Neonazi*," *New German Critique* 67 (1996): 133–146.

14. Baudrillard, *The Transparency of Evil*, 91. Cited in Lorentzen, "Reich Dreams," 166.

15. Paul Virilio, *The Vision Machine* (Bloomington: Indiana University Press, 1994), 60.

16. Hitler posits an ascending hierarchy in the various media of propaganda according to the Platonic principle of iconic immediacy: a text is the least effective (furthest removed) in convincing masses, while "a leaflet or a poster can, by its brevity, count on getting a moment's attention from someone who thinks differently. The picture in all its forms up to the film has greater possibilities. Here a man needs to use his brains even less." Adolf Hitler, *Mein Kampf*, trans. Ralph Manheim (Boston: Houghton Mifflin, 1971), 470.

17. In the *Stuttgarter Zeitung* (March 24, 1994), the reviewer Thomas Klingenmaier only grudgingly admits how Müller is also showing "the other Riefenstahl"; for the most part he does not pick up on Müller's irony. Klingenmaier appears uncomfortable with cinema's relationship to the beautiful, which he terms always already fascistic in Riefenstahl's hands, including her forays into deep-sea filming. Schenk's review is also hard on Müller for not being tough enough with his subject matter (as a way of defending Bonengel). Schenk wants Müller to blame Riefenstahl more directly (i.e., vocally) for the rise of Nazism, which depended on her stylization of the Hitler-image. He does not appreciate Müller's level of engagement with Riefenstahl's images.

18. Precisely the lack of this filmic strategy (as used by Müller) was bemoaned by the reviewer of a ZDF six-part series on Hitler in December 1995: "The film was always more effective and successful when something of the contradictoriness of the Hitler regime was transmitted via the contrast of images, when posture and reality were put opposite each other, when Hitler was exposed by Hitler himself. But that happened only occasionally." Hans-Ulrich Thamer, "Hitler, ein Film. Bilanz der ZDF-Reihe," *Frankfurter Allgemeine Zeitung* (Dec. 13, 1995): 35.

19. Koebner's review comments on Riefenstahl's body-obsession as a "will toward a visual over-formation." Koebner, "Triumph des Wollens."

20. Koebner, "Triumph des Wollens."

21. One reviewer, Mariam Niroumand, following the Sontag anti-image edict, found that this ending repeated the fascist aesthetic of worshipping monumentality (*Die Tageszeitung* [December 30, 1993]).

22. Eric L. Santer, "The Trouble With Hitler: Postwar German Aesthetics and the Legacy of Fascism," *New German Critique* 57 (1992): 11.

23. These words are from Munich film producer Thomas Schühly, who is currently rumored to be seeking either Sharon Stone or Jodie Foster for the Riefenstahl role in his film. Quoted in Peter von Becker, "Der lebende Mythos," *Der Tagesspiegel* (May 5, 2000): 27. For more on Riefenstahl's comeback, see Rainer Rother's new book, *Leni Riefenstahl: Die Verführung des Talents* (Berlin, Henschel Verlag, 2000).

24. Cf. Andreas Huyssen: "[T]he issue is not whether Kiefer intentionally identifies with or glorifies the fascist iconography he chooses for his paintings. I think it is clear he does not. But that does not let him off the hook. The problem is in the very usage of those icons, in the fact that Kiefer's images violate a taboo, trangress a boundary that had been carefully guarded, and not for bad reasons, by the postwar cultural consensus in West Germany: abstention from the image-world of fascism, condemnation of any cultural iconography even remotely reminiscent of those barbaric years. This self-imposed abstention, after all, was at the heart of Germany's

postwar reemergence as a relatively stable democratic culture in the Western mode." *Twilight Memories: Marking Time in a Culture of Amnesia* (New York: Routledge, 1995), 214.

25. In this way, Müller's film project with Riefenstahl echoes the art of Kiefer. As Huyssen reflects, "What if Kiefer . . . intended to confront us with our own repressions of the fascist image-sphere? Perhaps his project was precisely to counter the by now often hallow litany about the fascist aestheticization of politics, to counter the merely rational explanations of fascist terror by recreating the aesthetic lure of fascism for the present and thus forcing us to confront the possibility that we ourselves are not immune to what we so rationally condemn and dismiss." *Twilight Memories*, 222.

Section IV: Sites of Meta-German Multiplicity

17
Nazi Germany and the Holocaust in Norwegian Literature

ANN SCHMIESING

Norway was treated rather differently under the Nazis than were the other continental Scandinavian countries. For although Norway was invaded by the Nazis on the same day as Denmark (April 9, 1940), the Norwegians offered more formal resistance to occupation than did the Danes. The Norwegians were thus subjected, at least initially, to more brutality than were their neighbors to the south. Because Finland was a co-belligerent with Nazi Germany from 1941 to 1944 and Sweden remained neutral throughout the war, the Norwegians' struggle was also more pronounced than that of their eastern neighbors.[1]

This struggle is recorded not only in the numerous historical studies of occupied Norway, but in much of Norwegian wartime and postwar literature as well. Scholars of Norwegian literature have drawn considerable attention to authors such as Nordahl Grieg, Sigurd Hoel, Kåre Holt, Dag Solstad, and Tarjei Vesaas, many of whose works explore the problems faced by Norwegians during the Occupation. Although much of Norwegian literature on World War II is thus set in Norway and concerns non-Jews, several Norwegian writers have also written about Nazi Germany and the Holocaust, as it is my purpose to show in this chapter. Because I shall survey the works of only a handful of authors—and focus for the most part on the novelist, essayist, and dramatist Jens Bjørneboe—my comments are not intended to be exhaustive; instead, I hope simply to provide an overview.[2]

Many of the Norwegian writers who are primarily known for their writings on occupation and resistance themes also wrote about the Nazis' persecution of the Jews. The poet Nordahl Grieg, for example, decries Nazi anti-Semitism in "The Sprinters" ("Sprinterne"), a poem written in 1936 which consists of eight short, very regular lines. The first half of "The Sprinters" describes the German spectators' reaction to Jesse Owens at the 1936 Olympics; in the second half of the poem, the speaker addresses the Germans directly, advising them that, although their runners failed to overtake Owens at the Olympics, they should "cheer up, thinking of many/ Jewish women and men/ who ran for their lives in the streets—/ *them* you could catch again!"[3] Sigurd Hoel is another writer who is known in large part for his writings on Norwegian resistance themes, yet who also wrote about the plight of the Jews in World War II. In an essay titled "The Jews" ("Jødene"), which appeared in the December 6, 1944, edition of the Norwegian paper *Norges-Nytt*,[4] Hoel expresses worry that anti-Semitism might linger in Norway long after the departure of the Germans:

> If Nazi Germany is beaten on every front, if all of the highest-ranking Nazi leaders commit suicide or are hanged, if Germany is occupied, and her wartime industries destroyed, if all the occupied countries become free again, etc. etc., *but* anti-Semitism is still rampant . . . , *Nazism will still have won*. If we accept anti-Semitism, we also accept the Nazi race theories."[5]

The efforts of writers such as Grieg and Hoel to condemn anti-Semitism are particularly riveting when one considers that, although a strong resistance movement flourished in Norway, this movement allegedly did little to help the Jews. Leaders of the resistance movement commonly issued directives alerting the population to protest against various encroachments of civil or political freedoms, such as the attempted Nazification of Norwegian organizations or the deportation or arrest of a particular individual or group. But, according to Samuel Abrahamsen, "No nationwide directive . . . was ever issued to alert the population not to assist or cooperate with quislings or Nazi authorities in any aspect of Jewish persecution."[6] As a result, 49 percent of the Jewish population residing in Norway at the start of the war later died in the Holocaust—a percentage that, as Abrahamsen notes, is considerably higher than that of France, Bulgaria, or Italy.[7]

Norwegian writers of the 1960s and 1970s who write on Nazi Germany and the Holocaust include Georg Johannesen, who composed his poem "Jewish Partisan Song" ("Jødisk partisansang" [1966]) in memory of the uprising in the Warsaw ghetto in the spring of 1943. Writers of this period often write about Nazi Germany and the Holocaust in a context similar to that in which they address twentieth-century events such as Hiroshima and Vietnam, in that these events are all treated as unforgettable examples of man's inhumanity to man. Indeed, it is with the intention of depicting the Holocaust primarily as an example of man's evil that the Norwegian writer Jens Bjørneboe incorporated Holocaust themes into his works. Bjørneboe was fascinated by the problem of good and evil, and rejected the social and political explanations commonly given for the rise of the Nazis. In an essay on Nazism from 1949, he insists that the only true explanation that can be given for Nazism and its consequences is the "inherent bestiality of the human being."[8] Bjørneboe, it must be noted, was greatly influenced by German literature, and chose as the mottos for his novels *Moment of Freedom* (*Frihetens øyeblikk* [1966]), *The Powder Magazine* (*Kruttårnet* [1969]), and *The Silence* (*Stillheten* [1973]) verses taken respectively from the poetry of Rainer Maria Rilke, Conrad Ferdinand Meyer, and Goethe.[9] But he seems never to have come to terms with the fact that *das Land der Dichter und Denker* was also the country of concentration camps. It is perhaps as a result of his love-hate relationship with Germany that, in exploring the theme of good and evil in his works, Germany (both Nazi and postwar) is almost without exception among his main subjects.

And indeed, although he aims in many of his works to reveal the general in the particular—that is, to portray the Holocaust as a particular example of man's general evil—the unparalleled horrors of the Holocaust actually become, more often than not, the focus of his works. This is especially true of his early novel *Before the Cock Crows* (*Før hanen galer* [1952]). *Before the Cock Crows* begins as a documentary novel narrated by a Norwegian journalist who visits Germany after the war, with the purpose of finding out more about the medical experiments that the Nazis conducted on concentration camp prisoners. This portion of the novel is highly autobiographical, since Bjørneboe had himself come into contact in Germany with the family of Sigmund Rascher, one of the doctors involved in the Nazi experiments. Like the narrator, moreover, Bjørneboe had spent one whole summer as a teenager reading a book about the medical experiments carried out at Oranienburg. According to the narrator:

> [The book] . . . was written by someone who had been a prisoner there, and who had managed to escape . . . While I read it, it became clear to me that I would never be able to forget the things which were recorded there.—And that I would never be able to undo the changes that occurred in me while I sat there and read in the still, sunny afternoon hours. But throughout the entire summer, the others went about their business, and thought that the sunshine and the sea and the wind—that everything was the same as before. I was the only one who knew better.[10]

Bjørneboe would later speak of the book to which he refers in *Before the Cock Crows* as "perhaps the most important . . . I have ever read, and on reading it, my childhood ended."[11]

The largely autobiographical, first-person narration of *Before the Cock Crows* is soon replaced by omniscient narration, and the postwar setting reverts to Nazi Germany, where several characters are involved in performing the horrific medical experiments carried out in the concentration camps. In this section of the novel, Bjørneboe focuses on the SS officials who devise the plan to perform experiments on the prisoners, and a doctor, Heinrich Reynhardt, whom they convince to take part in it. Implicitly criticized for failing to take a stand against the moral atrocities, Reynhardt attempts to convince himself that he is conducting experiments for the good of humanity; after the war, he insists, the results of his experiments will be shared with the rest of the world. He further attempts to excuse his actions, and those of his colleagues, by claiming that there are two sides to every human being, as well as two sides to every issue. By contrast, Reynhardt's wife Gerda does not believe in a grey area of morality, and thus disagrees with her husband on the subject of collaboration with the SS: "Such an issue has but one side. . . . Anyone who works with them has sold himself."[12]

Attempting to remind his reader that his aim is to explore the general problem of evil, and not, specifically, to write a novel about the concentration camps, Bjørneboe writes in a note at the beginning of *Before the Cock Crows*: "The action [in this novel] is possible also in other countries and under other forms of government than the ones depicted here."[13] Nevertheless, as the narration and setting change in the novel, the general problem of evil as depicted in *Before the Cock Crows* is overshadowed by the particular horror of the Holocaust. As Janet Garton remarks: "What had begun as the investigation of the problem of evil on a broad scale dwindles into the study of a pathological case."[14] Indeed, because of its structural problems, the novel has always been regarded as rather poor. In this context, it is interesting that Bjørneboe had first written the material as a play, albeit with even less success. For the play was rejected by the Studioteater in Oslo on the grounds that "the public will flee from such a subject,"[15] at which point Bjørneboe rewrote his material as a novel.

By contrast, among Bjørneboe's best-received novels that address Holocaust or Nazi themes are those which form the trilogy titled *The History of Bestiality* (*Bestialitetens historie*), written between 1966 and 1973. In the trilogy, which is written partly in the form of narrative fiction and partly as personal memoir, Bjørneboe again discusses Nazi anti-Semitism and the medical experiments conducted by the Nazis. Yet Nazi Germany is not the only subject of study in the trilogy; fascism in Italy, the wrongs committed by early explorers of the New World, colonial injustices in Africa, and the torturing of innocent Vietnamese during the Vietnam War are among the subjects that are discussed at length. Bjørneboe's decision to examine the Holocaust alongside other atrocities has been used to account for the enthusiastic critical and popular reception of the trilogy both in Scandinavia and abroad. As Sigurd Aarnes observes: "Bjørneboe is not primarily interested in Nazism as material for his writing, but in the large, basic philosophical and religious questions which National Socialism revives:

the problem of pain and suffering, the problem of evil. Paradoxically one could say that Nazism is most effective as a motif in Bjørneboe's works *after* he has stopped using it as his only or central subject!"[16]

Bjørneboe's philosophical interest in both Nazi and postwar Germany is evident in his drama *The Bird Lovers* (*Fugleelskerne*), which is not only his best-known dramatic work, but also the work that has, of late, been the subject of the most controversy. *The Bird Lovers* was written in 1966 and takes place in a fictional Italian village several years after the war. It portrays a group of Italians who have survived the concentration camps, only to find that their former torturers have arrived to turn the village and its surroundings into a bird sanctuary. The villagers react with horror, not only because, on recognizing their former SS guards, they relive in their minds the inhuman treatment that they received from the Nazis, but also because the favorite food of the villagers just happens to be small birds. Thus, the villagers initially refuse to cooperate with the wishes of the bird lovers to ban the shooting and eating of birds, although they later give in to their former captors. Bjørneboe implicitly criticizes the villagers for selling themselves to their captors, and condemns the Germans not only for the Nazi attempt at world military domination, but for their postwar economic domination of Europe as well (a theme that also appears in his trilogy). Indeed, the back cover of the original edition of *The Bird Lovers* announced that the play has to do with "Germany's next and imminent occupation of Europe."[17]

As many critics have pointed out, the drama also reveals Bjørneboe's immense fascination with Brecht, although there is no consensus among scholars as to whether *The Bird Lovers* is the most Brechtian of Bjørneboe's plays.[18] Brecht's influence can be seen, for example, in Bjørneboe's incorporation of songs—many of them quite bawdy—into the text. However, there are frequent flashbacks to the Nazi concentration camps, where the Italian villagers are being tortured by the same SS guards who are now zealous bird lovers. These scenes are hardly Brechtian, and, in addition to the abundant use of Nazi symbols and imagery, it has been alleged that they make *The Bird Lovers* too much a play about the concentration camps in particular, and not, as Bjørneboe intends, a play about the problem of evil and blind submission to authority. Rejecting this criticism, Bjørneboe maintained in a letter to Peter Palitzsch that it is only coincidental that he chose to use Nazi and postwar Germany as a vehicle for his message. He stresses that all human beings, regardless of nationality, have the sinister potential to commit atrocities—as all human beings, not just the Italian villagers whom he portrays, might, in a moment of weakness, sell themselves to their former oppressors. As in many of his earlier works, he thus attempts to remind his readers that he is merely portraying generality in particularity.[19]

Recent controversy concerning *The Bird Lovers* has concerned not only the play itself, but also a filmed version that was broadcast to Norwegian television viewers in March 1989.[20] Edvard Hoem has suggested that Terje Mærli, the director of the film, has, in attempting to politicize Bjørneboe's play, misunderstood its message. Hoem further maintains that the play itself fails precisely because "whereas Brecht used a general plot to convey a concrete meaning, Bjørneboe attempts [in *The Bird Lovers*] to convey a philosophical idea." [21]

It is interesting that, while Bjørneboe expressly endeavored to emphasize the generality of his message in *The Bird Lovers* and other works, critics have continued to question whether his works that address Holocaust and Nazi Germany themes are indeed general or rather too particular. The reason for this ongoing discussion may well be twofold: while Bjørneboe's attempts to write about the Holocaust primarily as an example of man's inhumanity to man are not entirely successful, the reader might likewise find it difficult to read a work that attempts to treat the Holocaust in this manner. That is, perhaps we are justifiably reluctant to view the Holocaust as an atrocity that is simply illustrative of man's inhumanity to man, given that we are aware of the particular horrors of the Holocaust. Viewed in this light, it is not surprising that Bjørneboe's works that deal with Nazi Germany and the Holocaust are often problematic, and that readers find it difficult to read even his more successful works as he expressly expects them to.

Despite—or indeed because of—the considerable controversy that his works have aroused, Bjørneboe has been the subject of much study in the 1980s and 1990s. Indeed, *The Bird Lovers* is today the only play by Bjørneboe that has been performed at more than one theater in Norway. And Bjørneboe himself, after Ibsen and Bjørnstjerne Bjørnson, is the most known Norwegian dramatist abroad.[22] One other sign of the heightened interest in Bjørneboe was the Danish Odin Theatre's announcement of the "Jens Bjørneboe Prize" in 1984; in the light of Bjørneboe's love-hate relationship with Germany, it seems fitting, if a touch ironic, that the prize was awarded to Heinrich Böll.

The growing interest in Bjørneboe's work might be attributed in part to his death by suicide in 1976, although, as Leif Longum observes, even in the late 1970s his reception in Norway was "still very modest." [23] Yet regardless of its motivation, today's interest in Bjørneboe—and in other Norwegian authors who examine Nazi Germany and the Holocaust in their works—seems particularly fitting in the light both of Norway's recent efforts to combat its own neo-Nazi movement and, indeed, of the fiftieth anniversary of the end of World War II; within academia, I would suggest in closing, it seems also to reflect the changing face of German—and Scandinavian—studies.[24]

NOTES

1. For the information in this paragraph, I have relied heavily on Samuel Abrahamsen's insightful article "The Holocaust in Norway," in Randolph L. Braham, ed., *Contemporary Views on the Holocaust* (Boston: Kluwer-Nijhoff, 1983), 109.

2. Because my audience at the Symposium was composed of scholars of German—rather than Scandinavian—studies, I must stress that I have endeavored in this essay to provide a very general overview. The essay is by no means intended to afford an in-depth look at the subject of Norwegian literature on Nazi Germany and the Holocaust.

3. This translation by Martin Allwood and John Hollander appears in Martin Allwood, ed., *Modern Scandinavian Poetry: The Panorama of Poetry 1900–1975* (Mullsjö, Sweden: Anglo-American Center, 1982), 189. Unless noted, all translations in this essay are my own.

4. The essay can also be found in Sigurd Hoel, *Sigurd Hoel: Litterære Essays*, ed. Helge Nordahl (Oslo: Dreyer, 1990), 148–154.

5. Ibid., 150.

6. Braham, *Contemporary Views on the Holocaust*, 112.

7. Ibid., 109.

8. Jens Bjørneboe, "Det utrolige" ("The Incredible Truth"), *Spektrum* (1949): 103.

9. The novels form the trilogy titled *The History of Bestiality* (*Bestialitetens historie*), to which I refer later in the essay.

10. Jens Bjørneboe, *Før hanen galer* (Oslo: Aschehoug, 1952), 55. Abbreviated in the main text as BCC.

11. Bjørneboe, *Stillheten* (Oslo: Gyldendal, 1969), 163. Bjørneboe did not identify the title or author of the book to which he refers; however, Sigurd Aarnes concludes in note 4 of his essay "'Det ondes problem'—nazismen i Jens Bjørneboes diktning" (*Nazismen og norsk litteratur*, ed. Bjarte Birkeland & Stein Ugelvik Larsen [Oslo: Universitetsforlaget, 1975]: 73-98), that the book was most probably *Myrsoldater* by Wolfgang Langhoff (trans. Hans Heiberg).

12. Bjørneboe, *Før hanen galer*, 168.

13. The translation is that of Janet Garton, *Jens Bjørneboe: Prophet Without Honour*, Contributions to the Study of World Literature IX (Westport, CT: Greenwood Press, 1986), 37.

14. Garton, *Jens Bjørneboe*, 40.

15. This citation can be found in the postscript to the Pax edition of *Før hanen galer* (Oslo, 1967), 186–187.

16. Sigurd Aarnes, " 'Det ondes problem'—nazismen i Jens Bjørneboes diktning," 187. Cited in Garton, *Jens Bjørneboe*, 46, n. 29.

17. Cf. Leif Longum, *Drama-analyser fra Holberg til Hoem* (Bergen: Bergen University Press, 1977), 119f.

18. Garton, for example, regards *Congratulations* (*Til lykke med dagen*) as the most Brechtian of Bjørneboe's plays (*Jens Bjørneboe*, 79).

19. The letter, dated September 27, 1967, is reproduced in Jens Bjørneboe, *Om teater*, ed. Tone Bjørneboe (Oslo: Pax, 1978), 35. Bjørneboe's comments to Palitzsch concern the production of *The Bird Lovers* at the National Theatre in Oslo; Bjørneboe

maintained that the production had wrongly transformed the play's message into a political one.

20. It is significant that when *The Bird Lovers* was first written, Norwegian television refused to produce a filmed version, to Bjørneboe's deep disappointment.

21. *Dagbladet* (March 29, 1989), 33.

22. Cf. Longum, "Jens Bjørneboes 'Fugleelskerne'," 114.

23. Ibid.

24. While this essay has examined the representation of Nazi Germany and the Holocaust in Norwegian literature, the existence of personal memoirs written by Norwegians who resided in Germany or were held in concentration camps during World War II should also be noted. One such memoir is *Hver fredag foran porten* (1984), in which the author, Wanda Heger, relates how she and her family struggled to save the lives of numerous Norwegian concentration camp prisoners between 1942 and 1945. In 1989, a German translation of Heger's memoir was published under the title *Jeden Freitag vor dem Tor* by Schneekluth Verlag in Munich.

18
One Language—Two Literatures Again? Swiss Literature Since the *Wende*
MARTIN R. DEAN
Translated from the German by Axel Reitzig

The evening before I began writing this chapter, Günter Grass's new novel, *A Wide Field* (*Ein weites Feld*),[1] was discussed on the German TV show *Literary Quartets*. It was already clear from the introduction that one of the themes of this Fontane-esque novel was that of coming to terms with German reunification. Interestingly enough, the discussion not only focused on the novel's lack of quality, but also on the question of why an attempt was being made, once again, to transcribe an event full of historical importance into a literary one. The critic Sigrid Loeffler asked whether perhaps the incessant anticipation and calls for *the* big novel of the German *Wende* ("turning") wasn't just a figment of the big critics' imaginations. The vehemence with which, for example, Marcel Reich-Ranicki countered this suspicion strengthened it even more. It should be pointed out that the TV show also discussed the novel of the Italian author Antonio Tabuchi, *Pereira Explains*,[2] deemed it to be of a far higher literary quality, and yet gave it a mere fraction of the air time dedicated to Grass.

I would like to quickly sketch a personal background for my argument in this chapter. While I have studied German literature, philosophy, and ethnology, I write here not so much as a scholar but as an author. I have two reasons for having chosen this point of view. First of all, it has become a habit for me, since the completion of my studies, to speak, think, and live only as an author. Therefore, I would like to contribute a few subjective sentences from personal experience with the theme of Swiss literature since the *Wende*. Secondly, the topic itself exists on the edge of scholarly investigation. It demands, I believe, a spontaneous, unprotected, and speculative manner of speaking. In order, however, to protect you from the concentrated capriciousness of my subjective speculations, I carried out a survey among my fellow authors and critics, friends and acquaintances alike. Due to its relatively small size and selection, this survey is not a representative one as such.

"Swiss (by which is always meant German-speaking) literature after the *Wende*?—Can we consider the fall of the Wall and German reunification as a literary-historical event?" The literary critic Andreas Isenschmid rejects this possibility by pointing out the open selection of topics that is available to each author. He goes on to make the restrictive remark that the German intellectual discursive climate has undoubtedly been preoccupied with this theme. Not only has *the* German novel about reunification been desired for years, but also any novel with even the least to do with Germany is closely judged and evaluated by this standard.

The predominant opinion among the majority of the participants in my survey was overwhelmingly as follows: that since the *Wende*—or radicalized through this event—a drifting-apart has occurred in the German-speaking arena between German and Swiss literatures. (The relationship between German literature and other German-speaking literatures—such as in Austria, Hungary, and Siebenbürgen (in Rumania)—must be left out of the discussion, although interesting enough in their own right.) Allow me to summarize several personal experiences. My first novel, *The Concealed Gardens* (*Die verborgenen Gärten*),[3] appeared in 1982, that is, in the middle of the "hot" phase of the passion for Swiss literary reception in Germany. The years shortly before that, and above all after 1988, have established this relationship as an uninterrupted love story, with all the accompanying misunderstandings and projections. Determined by a sweepingly idyllic image of intact nature, unsoiled by war and guilt, and a strong currency, Switzerland was viewed for a long time by West Germans as a model country (*Musterländle*), including her ideological self-understanding. West German self-criticism, as it intensified especially in the wake of the 1968 movement, came as a relief from the Federal Republic of German's own difficult discourse with East Germany. The Swiss authors Hermann Burger, Erica Pedretti, Gerold Späth, Peter Bichsel, and Otto F. Walter were read as popular exotics, precisely because of their bulkiness, their quaintness, as well as their country charm—all as stylistic promises of authenticity.

My second book, a collection of short stories entitled *The Feathered Woman* (*Die gefiederte Frau*),[4] had a positive echo in Germany and brought me a three-week reading tour through German cities, both small and large. But by 1994, when my fifth book, *The Guiana Knot* (*Der Guaynaknoten*),[5] appeared, the landscape had fundamentally changed. While the book was approvingly discussed, I was, however, already the exotic among the exotics, and the themes that it addressed, such as migration and hostility toward foreigners, were neglected by Germans. The Germans had their horrible xenophobic outgrowths in the new eastern states and paid attention only to domestic signs of trouble, if at all. And not one sentence of my book had mentioned reunification.

Jürg Laederach writes that "Germany has become more provincial since reunification, more introspective."⁶ Jürg Amann states in the same vein:

> Due to their self-obsession, German feuilletons and the entire German market have presently no room and no interest for us [Swiss]. The German overcoming of the past (*Vergangenheitsbewältigung*) is now entering the third generation. And because of this overcoming the past, the Germans are always missing the mastery of the present (which would be, in contrast to the past, something to master.)⁷

And the literary critic Elsbeth Pulver notices in addition a "regression of the reception of Swiss-German literature in Germany—as if we were still that little country from the nineteenth century."⁸ This federal contrition is only further verified by my German colleague Alban Nikolai Herbst, whom I also included in the survey. Herbst states: "From the German standpoint, I have the clear impression that the literary focus here has turned itself very much towards inner-German themes."⁹

The *Wende* is to be used in this context only as a buzzword for a development that has already been under way for a long time. Zsuzsanna Gahse, a German author living in Switzerland, has this to say: "In the time since these changes, the question is more obscured than clarified by the term *Wende*. The changes had already begun—approximately in the middle of the 1980s—and it was they that brought about the so-called *Wende*."¹⁰

Not only political hopes were engendered by the fall of the Berlin Wall, but literary-political hopes as well: aspirations for a new pan-German linguistic arena to transcend all borders and, without hegemonic claims, spring from the European center and open up as well as intensify the exchange of discourses between countries. Instead of this large arena of literature in the German language, a hegemonic Germany (*Grossraum Deutschland*) has emerged, with satellite areas around it. From the Swiss point of view, the economic power has always belonged to Germany. Today, this predominance has increased vis-à-vis the press and the publishing industry. Even if one is published by a German press, as I am, one's reception in Germany itself has only become more difficult. This satiation with "exotic" Swiss literature, however, was prepared by the Swiss political scene itself, in its mistaking foreign policy for domestic, as well as in its isolation from the European Union and in its hostility towards foreigners (the process of Swiss self-provincialization).

As unanimous as the results of these divergently developing German literatures are, the reasons for them are varied. Like Klaus Merz,¹¹ I consider this intensified nationalization process as a reaction, in a negative sense, to a prior receptivity to other literatures. In the trail of the oversaturation of the German market (above all through international best sellers), the tendency toward the "national" followed as a futile attempt at self-preservation. Claudia Storz[12] links this drifting apart with the beginning of the postmodern, that is to say with the emergence of a noncommittal as well as playful literary perspective. The predicate "European author," an astounding concept, has indicatively never been granted to a Swiss author. Authors such as Jorge Semprun or Cees Noteboom vouch for this type of postmodern literature, whose thematic soil is so poor that they can effortlessly cross borders, and whose range stretches from the playful to the noncommittal.

Christopher Geiser points out that the only reason his novel *Prison of Desire* (*Das Gefängnis der Wünsche*)[13] received a broad resonance in Germany was that it included a confrontation with the fall of the Wall. Laederach, the most cosmopolitan of Swiss writers, goes a step further: for him, the provincialization of Europe is not a result of German unification, but rather of the collapse of the Soviet Union. "Not only is the enemy missing now, it is no longer even necessary to expend energy in polishing one's own system." Laederach continues: were the Germans not obsessed by reunification, the "energies thus freed would find a comparable opportunity to be self-entertained."[14] What happens here on the literary *niveau* can be thoroughly understood as a mirror image of the political one: in contrast to the European efforts toward unification, a nationalism is now on the move in Europe that finds its horrible apex in the ethnic cleansing taking place in the former Yugoslavia.

The literary relationship between Germany and Switzerland was never exclusively an *amour fou*. As Pulver points out, in the last twenty years, the Swiss authors who found themselves on the renowned "best authors" list of the Southwest Radio were those who promoted a particular picture of Switzerland for German critics. This includes the literary bloodline that leads from Frisch through Bichsel, rather than through Dürrenmatt, to Otto F. Walter, even when the opinion has gradually grown that the much-valued Swiss realism has since been dissolved by a sophisticated literary creativity that is playful with language and fiction. The opposite has definitely happened, with the reception of German literature in Switzerland having decreased.

Above and beyond borders and social-political differences (which are only further solidified through the clichés of national stereotypes) there are also authors whose writing styles are oriented toward Anglo-Saxon or romance fields of interest. Whoever has, in addition to German literature, included—as I have— Anglo-Saxon, Latin-American, and French literature in their intellectual fabric, has had to reckon with the very frustrating attempts of being compartmentalized on the German market. Indicative is this statement of Paul Nizon's, published in May of 1994:

> I have more than often thought that a significantly large misfortune of my life as an author stems from the fact that I was born into a German-speaking culture. Firstly, I noticed very early on that my literary tendencies did not fit into the new German literature. Secondly, that which I seek out on a literary niveau obviously does not interest the Germans that much. I define myself now mostly as a German-writing Parisian author with a Swiss passport. I am apparently something like a special enterprise.[15]

Swiss literature—insofar as it allowed itself to be called such (and therein lies Helvetic self-criticism as well)—was able to be released of its "relief" function for the Germans after the end of the German Democratic Republic (GDR). German Swiss literature offered perspectives and criticisms of dissenting authors who did not have to be read through the lens of the East-West conflict. It is in relation to the varying degree of medial penetration that Hans-Peter Ecker directs his comment: "The literature of such a relatively less industrialized literary system comes across to contemporary [German] readers as individual and 'cumbersome': in short, as 'authentic'."[16] As a further source of relief, it was also experienced that Switzerland, as Max Frisch once polemically remarked, is a nation without history, and at the very least, without a monstrous one.

On the other hand, a loss has occurred of the specific interests of German studies in the GDR—a field that grew out of self-definition against the West, and benefited from the recognition of their critique of capitalism by leftist Swiss authors. If an interest had attached itself for a long time to Swiss literature (which had been the sole German-language literature that could protect its continuity throughout the wars), this interest falls away now with the incorporation of East Germany and the undoubtedly problematic "normalization" of the Germans. It strikes me as a fact that many non-Germans, foreigners, and outsiders have been created through this incorporation of all Germans into the German national body. In contrast with France, where a Frenchman is someone who speaks French—whether a Martinican, a Senegalese, or a Quebecois—the German concept of identity is still tied to bloodlines. As a member of the extended German family, a Swiss can at best achieve the status of an adopted son or daughter. As such, he or she is involved neither in the Stasi debate nor in identity reconstruction, which uses mythology and a patchwork of historicization for resuscitating a hybrid German national feeling: his/her problems are quite different ones.

On the other hand, it is precisely the younger generation of Swiss authors who appear to be most offended by this retreat into the "national." Geiser writes: "I believe it would help us to rid ourselves of the etiquette of Swiss literature.

The national is politically devastating, and for literature simply untenable and uninteresting."[17] Hansjörg Schertenleib adds: "No, I have never viewed myself as a 'Swiss author'."[18]

The younger generation is abandoning the tradition in which writers act as social-political guardians who see themselves, like Frish and Otto F. Walter, as the "conscience of the nation." As Kurt Aebli remarks: "I have never considered myself as a representative of a so-called Swiss literature."[19] In the same spirit, only perhaps more decidedly so, Switzerland is becoming for the younger generation just one theme among others. Extensive travel and a certain hunger for the world are letting this former duty of national conscience-raising, once so obligatory for our critical dissidents, fade away. The link to the "national" weakens the use of personal experience, which has a more heterogeneous relationship to political discourse and does not respect national borders.

Whether the nationalization-tendencies I have described today are just a passing wave, as Jörg Steiner believes,[20] remains to be seen. Or is Swiss literature facing a hard winter ahead? The special case, I believe, is not Switzerland anymore, but Germany. I would like to conclude with a personal comment that could be understood as the quintessence of my last novel, *The Guiana Knot*: everything national, everything pure, everything exclusively provincial, all purified ethnicity carries within itself the seed of the inhuman. There is no other home than that of language, that is, the home of mixture, of the heterogeneous, of overcoming borders. Sooner or later, this will have to be of importance to German readers again.

NOTES

1. Günther Grass, *Ein weites Feld. Roman* (Göttingen: Steidl Verlag, 1995).
2. Antonio Tabucchi, *Erklärt Pereira* (Munich: Carl Hanser Verlag, 1995).
3. Martin R. Dean, *Die Verborgenen Gärten. Roman* (Munich: Carl Hanser Verlag, 1995).
4. Martin R. Dean, *Die gefiederte Frau. Erzählungen* (Munich: Carl Hanser Verlag, 1982).
5. Martin R. Dean, *Der Guayanaknoten. Roman* (Munich: Carl Hanser Verlag, 1994).
6. Jürg Laederach, letter to the author (August 1995).
7. Jürg Amann, letter to the author (August 1995).
8. Elsbeth Pulver, letter to the author (August 1995).
9. Alban Nicolai Herbst, letter to the author (August 1995).
10. Zsusanna Ghase, letter to the author (August 1995).
11. Klaus Merz, telephone call to the author (September 1995).
12. Claudia Storz, letter to the author (August 1995).
13. Christoph Geiser, *Das Gefängnis der Wünsche. Roman* (Zurich: Nagel & Kimche, 1992).

14. Jürg Laederach, letter to the author (August 1995).
15. Paul Nizon, "Ich bin ein Hund meiner Zeit. Im Gespräch mit Peter Henning und Horst Sumerauer," *Akzente* 41.2 (April 1994): 203–204.
16. Hans-Peter Ecker, "Blick über den Rhein. Das alte und neue Interesse an Schweizer Literatur," *Passauer Pegasus* 11:21–22 (1993).
17. Christof Geiser, letter to the author (August 1995).
18. Hansjörg Schertenleib, letter to the author (August 1995).
19. Kurt Aebli, letter to the author (August 1995).
20. Jörg Steiner, telephone call to the author (August 1995).

19
"Not Everything Written in the German Language Is German Literature": Austrian Literature—A Special Case?

KARLHEINZ AUCKENTHALER
Translated by the author, with Lori Medley

I

"Not everything written in the German language is German literature" was the main theme of the 1995 Frankfurt Book Fair where the central idea was an autonomous Austrian literature. This assertion is the outcome of an ongoing discussion that authors, publishers, researchers, newspaper editors, and literary critics in Austria and other countries began in the winter of 1993–1994. Such a discussion implies an uncertainty as to whether an independent Austrian literature really exists, by virtue of the fact that such a motto is necessary. In a similar vein, this is implied in the anthology *Literatur über Literatur*,[1] commissioned by the Federal Ministry for Science, Research, and Culture and the Central Association for Austrian Book Trade. Throughout, the question is addressed as to whether an Austrian literature exists and how its characteristics may be defined.

During the 1960s and 1970s a lively debate surrounding this issue took place. The rhetorical questions of *what* and *since when* dominated the field of discussion. After the reunification of the two German nations, a dispute over the notion of two independent German literatures emerged, which led to a variety of symposiums in Bonn, Palo Alto, Angers, and Szeged. If we look at a selection of them, we find a great deal of uncertainty about these questions. Despite a suspicion or rejection of cultural imperialism, a mild dose of them is detectable in Wilfried Barner's *Geschichte der deutschen Literatur von 1945 bis zur Gegenwart* (*History of German Literature from 1945 to the Present*),[2] which treats the three western literatures of the German language as a single entity and devotes a separate section to East German literature because of "differences in the system." A similar presentation is to be found in the four-volume collective work *Die deutsche Literatur von 1945–1960* (*German Literature 1945–1960*), edited by Heinz Ludwig Arnold.[3] Here Austrian and Swiss authors are taken into consideration in terms of their significance for West German authors. In *Epochen der deutschen Literatur* (*Epochs in German Literature*),[4] differences between West German and East German literatures are distinguished in the nearly 200-page chapter "From 1945 to the Present," in a format that otherwise organizes itself according to genre: the novel, documentary literature, the new folk play, women's literature.

The literary scene in West Germany dominates the discussion, which simply absorbs a selection of Swiss and Austrian writers. In *Hansers Sozialgeschichte der deutschen Literatur vom 16. Jahrhundert bis zur Gegenwart* (*Hanser's Social History of German Literature from the 16th Century to the Present*),[5] developments in Austrian and Swiss-German literature are treated only superficially and in a one-sided manner. In Viktor Zmegac's *Geschichte der deutschen Literatur vom 18. Jahrhundert bis zur Gegenwart* (*History of German Literature from the 18th Century to the Present*),[6] Austrian literature is more predominant due to the collaboration of Germanists from Graz. Nonetheless, here German-speaking Switzerland is absorbed by West German literature.

With facts like these, it is no small wonder that numerous projects are now underway in France, Austria, and Russia in an attempt to create an Austrian literary history. At a Soviet-Austrian symposium in 1981, "Historical Depiction of National Literature," Walter Weiss reported on a project in Salzburg with the goal of writing an Austrian literary history that never came to fruition.[7] He outlined the concept of an "open" Austrian literary history, but immediately pointed out its specific problems. The same intention of creating an Austrian literary history is also the goal of the Institute for Research and Promotion of Austrian and International Literary Processes.[8] To date, the project that has come the furthest with such an effort is led by Herbert Zeman. Together with Fritz Peter Knapp, Werner M. Bauer, and Joseph P. Strelka, Zeman seeks to replace the *Deutsch-Österreichische Literaturgeschichte* (*German-Austrian Literary History*)[9] with simply *Eine Geschichte der Literatur in Österreich* (*A History of Literature in Austria*). In December 1994, the first of seven planned volumes was published, *Die Literatur des Früh- und Hochmittelalters* (*Literature of the Early and High Middle Ages*)[10] by Knapp.

II

If we look back on literary history, many Austrian writers have stressed the autonomy of their literature on the basis of the political ambitions of the Habsburgs. Franz Grillparzer underlines the distinct qualities of the Austrian character and literature, differences of modesty, healthy common sense, and honest emotion.[11]

These qualities must also be seen in contrast to the German nation and its literature. The "unconditional" Austrian Hugo von Hofmannsthal refers to Grillparzer in particular and adds another three specifically Austrian characteristics: the "Baroque heritage,"[12] Austria's position in the middle of Central Europe,[13] and the influence of landscape in the notion of a homeland.[14]

Hermann Broch's analysis of Hofmannsthal's oeuvre displays a future-oriented attitude in the question of what characterizes an Austrian literature. Only later when he was asked to write a preface to one of Hofmannsthal's books did Broch start to deal with the problematic of the existence of an Austrian literature. Broch did not proclaim an Austrian literature like his colleague, but rather analyzed the notion. He states the following thesis as his point of departure:

> Each genuine work of art is at the same time new and bound to tradition: later generations recognize its relationship to tradition (as they become increasingly blind to revolution), while contemporaries (for their part blind to tradition) see only the unusual and new in it.[15]

In this way Broch approaches Hofmannsthal's work and comes to the conclusion that it does indeed contain unmistakably Austrian characteristics, notably the significance of the theatrical tradition (the Baroque theater) and a tendency toward ritual derived from the Jesuit dramas. He examines the function of order, namely its social aspects and the notion of a divine order and creation, which have shaped the Austrian myth. In this context, it is important to consider that in his portrait "Robert Musil—ein österreichischer Dichter?" ("Robert Musil—An Austrian Author?"),[16] Broch intentionally makes no effort to distinguish between Austrian and German literature above and beyond the usual arguments. Like his predecessors Gottsched and Nicholai, Broch presumes a distinct and unmistakably quality in Austrian literature and integrates it into a supranational European literature.

From the turn of the century up until this time, many philologists have attempted to overcome the problem of how to distinguish what characterizes Austrian literature.[17] When one approaches the problem of the differentiation between an Austrian literature and Swiss-German literature, several presumptions must be made, for any attempt at delimitation is accompanied by a host of complexities.[18] Similarities between authors and the styles of a certain period may be emphasized, tasks that become increasingly difficult as a larger spectrum of writers are taken into consideration. This becomes most difficult in the identification of the typical structures of a national literature or the literature of a given state as the basis of induction broadens. It is possible to include a large number of works, but exceptions to the rules must also be identified, namely works that typify only a few of the given criteria or even stand in contrast to them. In such an effort, a certain sensitivity to social and cultural-historical conditions is essential.

Based on years of research, I have identified Austria as a territorial-political concept in an attempt to specify an Austrian literature in all its complexity.[19] This concept views all developments as reflections of the state and incorporates all intellectual developments. It is a concept of nationality, birthplace, residency, subject matter, theme, linguistic peculiarities, spirit, and character. Moreover, I identify the underlying essence of Austrian literature as a search for identity and a critical analysis of it. Eugen Thurnher correctly asserts that "the most decisive breaks in the development of Austrian literature coincide with the great political decisions. The years 1156, 1438, 1618, 1740, 1866 and 1918 are not only milestones in the history of the state, but definite turning points in intellectual developments as well." In contrast to Germany, "the state's glories and historical tragedies" constitute "intellectual periods" that lead to increased self-contemplation, "in which work and achievement may often be seen as confirmation of an incomprehensible doubt."[20] Furthermore, a tendency toward the extreme or an aversion to the extreme may be detected in German literature and Austrian literature respectively. This is apparent in Josef Franz Ratschky´s rather weak comedy *Der Theaterkize,* which is a mockery of the *Sturm und Drang* movement; or one can compare Gerhart Hauptmann´s early dramas to those of Arthur Schnitzler. The poems of Georg Trakl with all their melancholic resignation to fate and decay may be contrasted to those of August Stramm. Likewise, the women found in Austrian literature appear more warm-hearted than their counterparts in Germany. One need only compare Grillparzer's Hero, Eschenbach's Lotti, Werfel's Barbara, or Broch's Mother Gisson to Goethe's Iphigenie, who stands as the epitome of the cool nobility of Weimar classicism.

III

Identification of typical characteristics such as these presents us with fewer difficulties when we look back on the literary canon of the past. Contemporary literature, that is to say, post-1945 literature, presents us with new challenges, although we have already identified certain "postwar classics." A demarcation between literary studies and literary criticism is made, the first relevant for literary history, the second for contemporary discussion. Moreover, with no established canon, one is faced with the problem of reading and assessing a large number of works. This proves itself to be an almost impossible task when one considers the sheer number of books published: in the 1980s, 800–900 titles were printed by the larger and smaller publishing houses. Nonetheless, it must be asked whether contemporary literature shows similar typical characteristics and structures as distinctive and unmistakable as the Austrian literature from the twelfth century on, in order to concretely differentiate between the "unique direction" of Austrian literature from the equally unclear "unique direction" of German literature. How does this manifest itself in the aesthetic realm, that is to say in the literary works of Austrian writers?

A typical characteristic reflected in the subject matter, themes, spirit, and nature of these works is the coming to terms with Austrian identity and thus with Austrians themselves. Here I differentiate between two major periods: the time between 1945 and 1970, and 1970 to the present. In the early part of the first period, one strove to invest a faith in the Second Republic for better or for worse, and at the same time the Austrians tried to see themselves as Hitler's victims, although a larger percentage of the Austrian population were members of the National Socialist Party than in Germany. For these reasons, continuity and cultural heritage were stressed in an attempt to build a national identity. One need only think of Heimito von Doderer's novels *Die Strudelhofstiege* (*The Strudelhof Steps*) and *Die Dämonen* (*The Demons*) in which the years 1918 and 1945 are *not* depicted as watersheds, or one can recall the journal *Forum* supported by the U.S. Central Intelligence Agency and edited by Friedrich Torberg, with its anecdotes "Die Tante Jolesch" ("Aunt Jolesch") and "Die Erben der Tante Jolesch" ("Aunt Jolesch's Heirs"). After the departure of the occupational forces and the State Treaty in 1955, Austria took on the identity of neutral mediator between east and west. Although the media (radio and publishing houses) and the older influential generation of writers rejected the new directions taken by more innovative writers such as the *Wiener Gruppe*, these younger writers gained significance for the next generation of writers in the 1980s. Almost twenty years later than in Germany, a new wave of authors began to establish itself, for example the writers of the *Forum Stadtpark* in Graz. With the victory of the socialists under the leadership of Bruno Kreisky, new possibilities opened up for the younger generation with a more liberal cultural policy. This marks the beginning for the second main phase of postwar literature in Austria. Representative of this change is Oswald Wiener's *die verbesserung von mitteleuropa, roman* (*the improvement of central europe: a novel*), an expression of the loss of orientation and helplessness of this time in its most explicit and crass form, and as such, it may be labelled as a political novel. From the early 1970s on, it was acceptable to engage in a more critical search for identity in the homeland Austria. The result is the typically Austrian "anti-homeland" novel as seen in Gert Jonke's *Geometrischer Heimatroman* (*Geometric Homeland Novel*), Michael Scharang's *Der Sohn eines Landarbeiters* (*The Son of a*

Farm Worker), Elfriede Jelinek's *Die Liebhaberinnen* (*The Female Lovers*), Franz Innerhofer's *Schöne Tage* (*Beautiful Days*), *Schattenseile* (*Shadow Ropes*), and *Die großen Wörter* (*Big Words*), and Gernot Wolfgruber's *Herrenjahre* (*Gentlemen's Years*), among others. The works of other Austrian authors (for example, Peter Roesi, Gerhard Roth, Walter Kappacher, and Bernhard Hüttenegger) stand as expressions of a lack of social connection, a rejection of language and human communication. Isolation of the individual is the central experience of Roesi's characters, beginning with the early narratives up until his project of five novels and short stories and an essay that together present an overall picture in the style of a winged altar. With *Wunschloses Unglück* (*A Sorrow Beyond Dreams*), Peter Handke begins his journey into himself, a voyage that reaches its climax in *Versuche* (*Essays*) and in his latest novel, *Mein Jahr in der Niemandsbucht* (*My Year in the No Man's Bay*). These developments of the 1970s were critically received as the "New Subjectivity"[21] in West Germany. Since the mid-1980s, Austrian authors have begun to react more strongly to the political situation (the Vienna General Hospital scandal, Waldheim, Groer) and thus made a significant contribution to the analysis of the questions of identity and Austria's and the Austrians' past. According to Magris's *Habsburger Mythos* (*Hapsburger Myths*) and Greiner's *Der Tod des Nachsommers* (*The Death of the Indian Summer*), the significance of myth for recent modern literature (Christoph Ransmayr, Inge Merkel, Lilian Faschinger, Klaus Hoffer) must be taken into consideration as part of a search for identity. When a writer no longer can tell a story with contemporary fables, old myths are revived and depicted in a new way to provide an answer to the questions of the time. Ransmayr's Mazzini refers to this type of poetic strategy as "a game with reality,"[22] as newly retold stories are tested in respect to the far-removed past and the most recent present. The territorial-political development in Austria, which has uniquely shaped Austrian belles-lettres with a variety of approaches and themes, may also be seen in light of the identity question. Some authors may write about the daily political scene, while others deal with coming to terms with the past, or occupy themselves with the cultural and literary landscape, while yet others examine their own autobiographical experiences in relationship to their homeland and the mentality of Austria and the Austrians. In his essay "The Destruction of That Which Is Austrian," Josef Haslinger explains the reason for the often sullenly accepted absorption of Austrian artists, and refers to a "strategy of Germanization for Austrians,"[23] undertaken in an effort to transfer Austrian criminals of the likes of Hitler, Eichmann, or Seyss-Inquart to Germany. Gerhard Roth analyzes the Austria of today and refers to it as the living proof for the theory of relativity:

Nothing is real, nothing is tangible—every insight, every promise, every pledge dissolves into nothing, turns into its opposite. The country finds itself in a perpetual state of suspense. If the Hanging Gardens of Semiramis are one of the Seven Wonders of the World, then Austria is the eighth: a land of pending decisions, . . . pending opinions, judgements, resolutions, and above all, pending actions.[24]

The influence of day-to-day political events is reflected in Gerhard Roth's novel *Der See* (*The Lake*), in which the leader of the far-right Austrian Freedom Party (FPÖ), Jörg Haider, may be recognized by a call for his assassination, and in Elfriede Jelinek's ghost story *Die Kinder der Toten* (*The Children of the Dead*). According to Jelinek in this 666-page novel, Austrian identity is based on death. Among other things, she calls the attempt at self-disinfection during the so-called Year of Commemoration (1995) into account:

Commemorate! Commemorate! We'll certainly not have any doubts about ourselves. Nevertheless, nevertheless, for once we're going to do it for a year, at least. The Chancellor certainly wants to go to that much promised land and, after that, personally return to civilization. Men weep with pain at their memorial stones. They always cast them first, always on others, not belonging to the few holy ones back in those days. For that reason, everyone today can call them hangers-on, who nevertheless amounted to a few million back then. Now we would rather entrust the entire matter to the rustling tissue paper in the Chancellor's throat, stretch it over the rack of a comb, blow on it, and listen to it again on a highly accelerated soundtrack. We can look at ourselves in the mirror in his Cabinet room as we, as if innocent, wash our hands.[25]

Ransmayr's recent novel *Morbus Kithara*[26] concerns itself with the National Socialist past and tells of the power of memory: the continual effect of the past as well as memory's fraudulent lie. He tells the story of three strikingly exceptional people from Moor, a hole in the mountains: Ambras, the dog king and earlier prisoner in a Moor quarry; Lily, a Brazilian whose guilt-laden father wanted to emigrate to Brazil; and Bering, the son of Moor's smithy and the bodyguard of Amras. A similar thematic is also taken up by the author Gerald Szyszkowitz in *Die Badenweiler oder Nichts wird bleiben von Österreich* (*The Badenweilers, or Nothing Will be Left of Austria*).[27] In the novel *Hexeneinmaleins* (*Witches' Spell*),[28] Hans Heinz Hahnl tries to decipher what takes place in the Austrian book market, specifically the Viennese literary scene, and at the same time questions what Wendelin Schmidt-Dengler has termed the "good literature" of the past fifteen years.[29] In this satirical novel, three perfidious professional critics create the literary genius Tomassonj, who in reality does not exist, and by means of rumor accredit him with things the nonexistent writer cannot have written. Their invention becomes the glorious discovery of their entire branch of work. Everyone writes about the indescribable one. The most notoriously loud schoolmaster gives a scientifically concrete analysis of the originality of the fantasy that has been placed into the literary world, and this fantasy receives academic recognition and even a state prize. Norbert Gestrein critically examines his native region in his account *Der Kommerzialrat* (*The Industrialist*),[30] a satire on tourism and an "anti-homeland novel." He tells the story of the distinguished businessman Marsoner and his model village in the Tyrol that has been destroyed by tourism. Robert Menasse's latest novel, *Schubumkehr* (*Thrust Reversal*),[31] constitutes an attempt to deal with Austria's recent history from the perspective of a middle-aged man who has just returned from an extended stay abroad. He depicts the difficulties of overcoming one's own inner boundaries despite open political borders. In *Magdalena Sünderin* (*Magdalena the Sinner*), the young Carinthian author Lilian Faschinger concerns herself with the Austrian mentality and her critical attachment to her country. Young Magdalena Leitner from Carinthia kidnaps a priest from East Tyrol during a church service and confesses her life story to him, telling of her sexual adventures and how she has murdered her lovers. She explains why she has abducted an Austrian priest:

> I sought out an Austrian priest to listen to my general confession, because it is clear to me that only an Austrian priest would be capable of completely relating to this general confession. Only an Austrian priest can transplant himself into the wounded passages of an Austrian brain, in which the meanders of the cerebrum are different than in the brains of people from other countries. Only he can really force his way into the grey and white substance of an Austrian person. Only an Austrian priest can push his way forward to the right and left vestibules of the heart of an Austrian person. Only he will be able to keep his composure in the face of what he will see in the chambers of this person's heart. The blood in his veins will not freeze when he sees the fiend, the monster dwelling in the chambers of the Austrian heart, because in all probability, the conditions in which these monsters creep into the chambers of Austrian hearts are not unknown to him.[32]

These few examples from the past several years demonstrate how closely the Austrian authors are tied to a territorial-political Austria and how this manifests itself in the various themes, motifs, and the spirit and character of their works. Based on these facts, Roger Willemsen made the following observation after the Frankfurt Book Fair: "It seems to me that Austrian literature is more lively, daring, witty, and abrupt than German literature. As such, I perceive it as more vital, original, and experimental than the incommensurate, more commercial German literature."[33] Seen like this, Austrian literature is a special case in the German-speaking literatures with its distinctive characteristics, not in the sense of a negative contrast, but rather as a complementary and enriching development.

NOTES

1. Petra Nachbaur and Sigurd Paul, eds., *Literatur über Literatur. Eine österreichische Anthologie* (Graz: Scheichl, 1995).
2. Wilfried Barner, ed., *Geschichte der deutschen Literatur von 1945 bis zur Gegenwart*, vol. 18 (Munich: Beck, 1994).
3. Heinz Ludwig Arnold, ed., *Die deutsche Literatur von 1945–1960* (Munich: dtv, 1995).
4. Joachim Bark, Dietrich Steinbach, and Hildegard Wittenberg, eds., *Epochen der deutschen Literatur* (Stuttgart: Klett, 1989).
5. Klaus Briegleb and Sigrid Wiegel, eds. *Gegenwartsliteratur seit 1968*, vol. 12, *Hansers Sozialgeschichte der deutschen Literatur vom 16. Jahrhundert bis zur Gegenwart* (Munich: dtv, 1992).
6. Viktor Zmegac, ed., *Geschichte der deutschen Literatur vom 18. Jahrhundert bis zur Gegenwart*, vol. 3.2 (Weinheim: Betz, 1994).
7. Walter Weiss, "Das Salzburger Projekt einer österreichischen Literaturgeschichte. Konzept und Probleme," *Sprachkunst* 14.2 (1983): 56–66.
8. Herbert Arlt and Donald G. Daviau, eds., *Geschichte der österreichischen Literatur*, 2 vols. (St. Ingbert: Röhrig Universitätsverlag, 1996).
9. Johann Willibald Nagl, Jakob Zeidler, and Eduard Castle, eds., *Deutsch-Österreichische Literaturgeschichte. Ein Handbuch zur Geschichte der deutschen Dichtung in Österreich in vier Bänden* (Vienna: Verlagsbuchhandlung Carl Fromme, 1899–1938).
10. Fritz Peter Knapp, ed., *Die Literatur des Früh- und Hochmittelalters in den Bistümern Passau, Salzburg, Brixen und Trient von den Anfängen bis zum Jahre 1273. Geschichte der Literatur in Österreich von den Anfängen bis zur Gegenwart*, ed. Herbert Zeman, vol. 1 (Graz: Bundesverlag, 1994).
11. Franz Grillparzer, *Sämtliche Werke*, ed. August Sauer (Vienna: Schroll, 1925), 14: 26.
12. Hugo von Hofmannsthal, *Reden und Aufsätze II. 1914–1924, Gesammelte Werke*, ed. Bernd Schoeller and Rudolf Hirsch (Frankfurt a.M.: Fischer, 1979), 258–263, 325–328.
13. Ibid., 43–54, 454–458.
14. Ibid., 13–25.
15. Hermann Broch, "Hofmannsthal und seine Zeit," in Paul Michael Lützeler, ed., *Schriften zur Literatur/Kritik 1*, vol. 9:1 (Frankfurt a.M.: Suhrkamp, 1975), 120. All translations are my own.
16. Ibid., 95.
17. Cf. Karlheinz Auckenthaler, "Anmerkungen zur österreichischen Literatur," in Karlheinz Auckenthaler, ed., *Lauter Einzelfälle. Beiträge zur moderneren österreichischen Literatur* (Bern: Lang, 1995), 11–55, 23–27.
18. See Karlheinz Auckenthaler: "Ich sah, daß die Österreicher eine ganz andere, fremde Nation sind. Die gemeinsame Sprache täuscht ... Sie sind viel älter, erfahrener, viel weiser im Umgang mit anderen Völkern." In "Überlegungen zum österreichischen Literaturbegriff," *ÖGL* 38 (1994): 149–151.
19. Karlheinz Auckenthaler, "Die Dichtung des Biedermeier—Die erste Geniezeit der österreichischen Literatur? Zum österreichischen Literaturbegriff," *Neohelicon* 14:1 (1992): 78f.

20. Eugen Thurnher, "Das Problem der Periodenbildung in der österreichischen Literaturgeschichtsschreibung," in Johann Holzner, Michael Klein, and Wolfgang Wiesmüller, eds., *Studien zur Literatur des 19. und 20. Jahrhundets in Österreich. Festschrift für Alfred Doppler zum 60. Geburtstag* (Innsbruck: Universität Innsbruck [Germanistik], 1981), 273.

21. Cf. Klaus Zeyringer, *Innerlichkeit und Öffentlichkeit. Österreichische Literatur der achtziger Jahre* (Tübingen: Francke, 1992), 90–94.

22. Christoph Ransmayr, *Die Schrecken des Eises und der Finsternis* (Frankfurt a.M.: Fischer, 1987), 18.

23. Josef Haslinger, "Die Vernichtung des Österreichischen," *Standard Album. Buchmesse Spezial* (Oct. 6, 1995): 1f.

24. Gerhard Roth, "Das doppelköpfige Österreich," *Das doppelköpfige Österreich* (Frankfurt a.M.: Fischer, 1995), 56.

25. Elfriede Jelinek, *Die Kinder der Toten* (Reinbek: Rowohlt, 1995).

26. Christoph Ransmayr, *Morbus Kithara* (Frankfurt a.M.: Fischer, 1995).

27. Gerald Szyszkowitz, *Die Badenweiler oder Nichts wird bleiben von Österreich* (Vienna: Boesskraut & Bernardi, 1995).

28. Hans Heinz Hahnl, *Hexeneinmaleins* (Vienna: Österreichische Staatsbücherei, 1993).

29. Wendelin Schmidt-Dengler, "Haltbar bis zur nächsten Ernte?" *Die Presse. Spectrum* 7.8 (Oct. 1995): 1f.

30. Norbert Gestrein, *Der Kommerzialrat* (Frankfurt a.M.: Suhrkamp, 1995).

31. Robert Menasse, *Schubumkehr* (Salzburg: Residenz, 1995).

32. Lilian Faschinger, *Magdalena Sünderin* (Cologne: Kiepenhauer, 1995), 36.

33. C. Hirschmann, O. Lehmann, "Die österreichische Literatur ist mutiger und vitaler. John Irving, Siegfried Unseld, Hellmuth Karasek und Dacia Maraini über ihre Präferenzen," *News* 42 (Oct. 19, 1995): 176.

20
The Role of Literature in German Studies Programs (1945–1995): A Canadian Case Study

KARI GRIMSTAD

Recently a friend's mother, who was moving from a large apartment to a senior citizens' residence, presented me with a box of German books that she had read in her courses as a student in the modern languages and literatures program at the University of Toronto from 1928 to 1932. Twenty-seven years later, from 1955 to 1959, I was a student in the same program at the same university. And after one Great Depression, one world war, and one *Wirtschaftswunder*, not much had changed in the prescription of German texts at the University of Toronto. Although in the 1950s undergraduates might not have heard of a "literary canon," such a creature certainly existed. German honors students spent two years studying the Enlightenment, *Sturm und Drang*, and classicism, with a heavy emphasis placed on Goethe and a much lighter one on Lessing and Schiller, and another two years principally on the nineteenth century. Twentieth-century writers were hardly dealt with; of these, the majority was represented by works written before 1933. The two or three authors writing in the postwar period made no mention of the war: even Wolfgang Borchert would be remembered by a "cheerful tale," "Schischyphusch, oder der Kellner meines Onkels" ("Sisyphus, or My Uncle's Waiter").[1] Furthermore, at the other end of the scale, although we spent a year on middle-high German literature, we could not tell from our program whether *any* German literature existed between the end of the medieval period and the mid-eighteenth century. As for women writers, from our prescribed list we would assume there was only one: Annette von Droste-Hülshoff. Finally, texts were read as belles-lettres, which were part of literary history, but very little attempt was made by most instructors to relate them to social or political history. I do not mean to imply that this undergraduate training in German literature was bad. On the contrary, for reasons I will go into shortly, I believe some aspects of that experience were seminal and many have positively affected how I teach. But the relatively immutable quality of the list of prescribed literary texts, as evidenced by that gift of books from the late 1920s, and the awareness from my present-day perspective of what was emphasized and what was excluded, made me want to explore the role of literature in German studies as I have experienced it in Canada. However, first we should take a brief look at the history of *Germanistik* in Canada. I will take the province of Ontario as my paradigm.

The Canadian university with the longest tradition in the teaching of German is the University of Toronto.[2] As early as 1840, German was listed as one of the modern languages offered; in 1866, the first German department was established. Students arrived at university with three or four years of high-school German. From the *Prüfungsordnung* ("exam ruling") of 1886–1887 for fourth-year honors students, we can see what was stressed: (1) philology courses (gothic, old, and middle-high German), (2) practical exercises in grammar, composition and translation, which then aided (3) the study of literature. In this year it was Goethe and the *Goethezeit*, Schiller being represented only by *Maria Stuart*.[3]

Anti-German sentiment as well as the drain on manpower during World War I contributed to a decline in German programs—at the University of Toronto there were 319 first-year course registrations in 1911 and only 194 in 1916. An advertisement for a new German course for beginners in the 1919 calendar of one university (*not* the University of Toronto) shows that Germanophobia did not end with the war: "It is easier to compete with a man you understand than with a mystery. The German department imparts knowledge of German and the Germans. The subject is not compulsory, and any student who finds he is in danger of learning to admire the Germans can at once change to another subject."[4]

Although the number of students increased only slowly, German was able to hold its own in the 1920s and 1930s. As had been the case previously, the goal of German honors programs was an introduction to literature, and language courses were to prepare students primarily for reading and writing.[5] Following the model of British universities, the language of instruction was English and written assignments were in English. This was still the case in the 1950s. As for graduate programs, until 1955 the University of Toronto was the only Canadian university granting Ph.D.s in German, with a mere five doctorates conferred before 1950.[6] Consequently, along with Canada's political colonial status (she was a colony of Great Britain until 1867 and did not have her own constitution until the 1980s), her universities also experienced a degree of colonization. Although a Ph.D. was not a prerequisite for teaching at a university, insofar as professors of German had doctorates, these were from Germany: at the University of Toronto, Barker Fairley came from Britain with a degree from Jena (1910), Hermann Boeschenstein from Switzerland with a degree from Rostock (1924), to name only two. From the 1920s until just after World War II, Canadian doctoral students increasingly went to the United States. However, between the two world wars, the groundwork for a Canadian *Germanistik* in the sense of "homegrown" graduate studies and research was being laid, as several universities established German M.A. programs.[7]

The great upswing in Canadian German studies began after World War II. At the University of Toronto, not only did the number of undergraduate students increase, but new faculty were added to the prewar base of Fairley and Boeschenstein. These were Canadians and Americans with Ph.D.s, as well as European émigrés from immediately after the war who completed graduate degrees at the University of Toronto. However, as we saw earlier, they did not create a radical change in the curriculum, schooled as they were by professors who for the most part had completed *their* graduate work in Germany in the 1920s or earlier and who had followed the path laid down by nineteenth- and early twentieth-century literary historians from Gervinus on.

The major change did not occur until the mid-1960s, when the baby boomers reached university age and swelled the ranks of all programs. To accommodate this flood, new universities were founded; in Ontario alone five were added. And of course new faculty had to be hired. In Canada between 1956 and 1971, the number of full-time faculty in German increased by 500 percent.[8] Canadian graduate departments could in no way provide the necessary candidates. As a result, large numbers of faculty were imported—from the United States, Britain and, increasingly, from Germany. As a consequence of the latter, German became the language of instruction in many literature courses. Also, more and more graduate students at Canadian universities were immigrants from Germany. The explosion in graduate studies in German is stunningly illustrated by the following figures: in all of Canada in the five years from 1956 to 1960, five Ph.D.s were awarded; fifteen years later, in the five years from 1971 to 1975, seventy new Canadian Ph.D.s entered the job market.[9]

Ironically, by the mid-1970s that job market was starting to shrink. The abolition of the foreign-language requirement at most universities drained first-year language courses, the bread-and-butter courses that gave employment to teaching assistants and junior faculty. Changes in the high-school curricula downgraded traditional foreign languages, meaning fewer potential candidates for university honors programs and fewer teaching career prospects for German honors graduates. With the economic recession in the 1970s and the shrinking of university funds, deans cast withering looks at tiny course enrollments in upper-level classes. Tenured faculty were not replaced after retirement—at the University of Toronto, the number of tenured positions in German shrank from 26 in 1966 to 18 in 1986 and to 11.5 in 1998. And new Ph.D.s did not find positions in postsecondary teaching. Although theoretically the job market should open up by the year 2005 when those hired in the late 1960s reach mandatory retirement age, prospects for a turnaround do not look good. The economic climate in Canada is conservative, with balancing of the budget and cutting back on a huge financial debt taking precedence over funding for social programs and education. Furthermore, the thinking behind cuts that have been made to cultural and educational institutions very often demonstrates a distinctly anti-intellectual bias. This in turn is often reflected—perversely—in the attitude of university administrators, who, for all their talk of academic excellence, look on the student as the consumer who must be satisfied. In their view, if German programs with a traditional emphasis on literature do not sell, then they must either be repackaged or dropped.[10]

But let us go back to the mid-1960s, when a mood of optimism prevailed and the world seemed to be one's oyster. At that time I started working on my Ph.D. at the University of Toronto and began teaching as a lecturer in German at the University of Guelph, one of those five new Ontario universities. In my first year at Guelph, *I* was the German section; one year later, we were five full-time faculty: a British full professor imported to head the section, a German with a German Ph.D., a German with a Canadian Ph.D., an American, and myself, the only "native-born" Canadian. The German literature program that was initiated was highly conventional: the divisions were by century or period or genre, and these were "covered." Old notes from undergraduate and graduate courses were revived, the canon was never challenged. Many still teach literature this way. There is always a text in this class, to paraphrase Stanley Fish, and that text usually exists without any reference to a historical or social context or to the experience of the students. Its prime raison d'être, on the course at any rate, is apparently to illustrate the definition of a genre or a literary movement: naturalism or expressionism or classicism or romanticism equals the following ten points, and this text proves points three to seven.

At the opposite pole, with the "direct method" of language teaching on the rise in the 1960s, literature was being pressed into the service of language acquisition, particularly at the intermediate level. Anthologies of short stories, laden with paraphernalia—vocabulary exercises, margin glosses, drill sentences, synthetic exercises, content questions to be answered in German—appeared in the mail as examination copies, "free gifts" from American publishers. What is remarkable is that (1) few of the exercises engaged the students on a truly intellectual level by posing questions either about the relevance or significance of the stories or about how they worked as literature; (2) with the exception of a requisite work by Borchert or by Böll, stories that would remind students that there had been a Second World War—yet alone the Holocaust—and that Germans were having problems coping with questions of guilt and individual responsibility, were (what now seems conspicuously) missing—in fact the selections were often of a blinding triviality; (3) if you picked up the 1960s editions of readers such as *Der Weg zum Lesen* or *Die Mittelstufe*, you would assume German women never wrote, at least not to be published [11]; and (4) in keeping with cold-war policy, with the exception of Brecht, East German writers were not represented.

How does an instructor break away from that double bind of the strictures of the accepted canon and of language acquisition, and go on to teach literature in a meaningful way? My first attempt was in the late 1960s in a course on German history and civilization that I created, in other words in a course that was not strictly a literature course. Along with an introduction to German political and cultural history, I included shorter literary texts that introduced the problems of guilt and individual responsibility, and the attraction and danger of fascism, to underscore the part of the course dealing with the rise of National Socialism, the Third Reich, and the *Wirtschaftswunder* ("economic miracle") of the 1950s. We read works such as Frisch's *Biedermann und die Brandstifter* (*Biedermann and the Arsonists*), Brecht's *Der kaukasische Kreidekreis* (*The Caucasian Chalk Circle*), Borchert's *Draußen vor der Tür* (*Man Outside*), Dürrenmatt's *Die Panne* (*A Dangerous Game*), and Thomas Mann's *Mario und der Zauberer* (*Mario and the Magician*).[12] This was also one way of broaching the social or historical significance of texts, of reminding students that literature cannot exist in a vacuum.

But the teaching of undergraduate literature courses still remained a challenge. In the 1960s and 1970s, there was a broadening of the spectrum of literary works that could easily be made available to students, whether in inexpensive German paperbacks or in American or British annotated editions. This enrichment affected not only those teaching contemporary literature. Authors were rediscovered. A new interest in Karl Kraus, for example, focused attention on one of his seminal essays, "Nestroy und die Nachwelt" ("Nestroy and Posterity"), which in turn helped kindle an interest in Nestroy as a satirist. The centennial of the birth or death of a writer often occasioned the republishing of his or her works and their subsequent reevaluation by scholars and critics. In the 1950s, I had never heard of Arthur Schnitzler. By the 1970s, not only was he *unterrichtsfähig* ("teachable"), but fin-de-siècle Vienna had become a literary industry. However, the possibility of enriching literature programs, of offering students an in-depth picture of a writer or a period that they might not have had under the old canon, also entailed problems, principally of evaluation. For example, in trying to right the balance so as to include in a literature course works by members of groups that have been underrepresented, whether these be women or immigrants to Germany or Afro-Germans or writers of *Volksstücke* ("folk plays"), what criteria do we apply: those of literary excellence or those of cultural relevance, or both? Can we even agree on criteria of literary excellence? If we include poems by Sophie Mereau in a *Goethezeit* course, do we disregard the question of whether Goethe was a better poet than she, or do we face it? Or, as another possibility, should we play devil's advocate and purposely include texts that are flawed, so as to develop our students' critical judgment and challenge the assumption by many students that, if a work appears in print, it must be good? A case in point might be Hebbel's *Agnes Bernauer*, in which the sacrifice of the individual for the state, a sacrifice that is rationalized, even glorified, betrays a blatant proto-fascism.

In his book *The Defeat of the Mind*, Alain Finkielkraut laments the tendency of postmodernist thought "to apply the label 'cultural' to any form of distraction that may come along."[13] Although technology (television and computers) can "introduce all forms of knowledge into every home, the logic of consumption destroys culture. The word lives on, but emptied of any idea of education.... From now on in, the pleasure principle—self-interest in its postmodern form—dominates the individual's spiritual life.... Adolescent culture ... [has become] the lifestyle of everyone in society."[14] We can see this trend in education in general and, by extension, in German studies. The new, the contemporary, or the modish can crowd out the traditional; youth culture dictates that it is cooler—and easier—to read a modern text dealing with situations with which one can more immediately identify, or even better to watch a video based on this, than to tackle an eighteenth- or nineteenth-century work that may be linguistically more difficult and topically more remote. The result is that courses on the Enlightenment, classicism, and romanticism risk falling by the wayside because students—the consumers—will avoid them. Even at a large university such as the University of Toronto, "Deutsche Klassik" is now offered in alternate years instead of every year, which it had been for about a century. There are those Germans who would reply that in several of the German states an acquaintance with Goethe's works is not required of high-school graduates, therefore why make such a fuss? Is this not just another case of the conservatism of the diaspora? I cannot answer for the Germans. If you live in Germany you may be able to take Goethe for granted, but at least you probably know *whom* you are taking for granted, and Faust and Werther are more than just names. If you are a North American student studying German, however, this is not likely the case.

But perhaps Goethe can advise us how to provide primary access to literature through the word, rather than through entertainment. Struck by the similarities between a Chinese novel he was reading and his own epic, *Hermann und Dorothea*, he remarked to Eckermann that this novel proved to him further that "spirit transcended society and history." [15] In eschewing national literature and looking forward to an ideal of world literature, Goethe placed a great deal of importance on translation in order to further the exchange of ideas. In my opinion, I would rather that students at the undergraduate level read *Faust* in translation than not at all. And where texts are read in German, I would prefer that undergraduates used translations as a backup rather than pore over a work that is linguistically too difficult for someone with only two or three semesters of language training. I would also propose that by using translations we can broaden the range of students whom literature courses in German studies can reach. In doing so, we can hope to foster intellectual curiosity and critical inquiry.

Having said this, I do not want to give the impression that I am against using contemporary texts. On the contrary. While I certainly do not think that contemporary texts should make up 90 percent of the literature that German studies students read, which seems to be the current trend, I am well aware that modern short prose can form an ideal basis for an introductory literature course. In fact, there is a need for anthologies such as Brigitte Turneaure's *Im Spiegel der Literatur* (*In the Mirror of Literature*), which are geared to this kind of a course. In her introduction to this text, Turneaure writes: "While much of the literature of the Federal Republic and the former German Democratic Republic necessarily draws students into the dark themes of this century and the German trauma of remembering—or trying to forget—the past, the texts, by virtue of their aesthetic richness, their compelling descriptions, and the provocative ideas they raise, engage and excite the students." [16] Ideally, this is what the mandate of a literature course should be: the exploration of texts whose aesthetic qualities underscore or illuminate ethical or moral problems, creating resonance beyond the course itself and opening up new perspectives in other disciplines. Last but not least, they should foster a love of reading.

I will conclude on the positive note of "fostering a love of reading," by recalling the scholar and teacher who exemplified for me the best in German culture, who was himself a voracious reader, and who engendered a love of reading in many of his students, including myself. The Swiss-Canadian Germanist Hermann Boeschenstein combined breadth of knowledge with tolerant understanding, critical insight, and a commitment to humanistic principles.[17] His contributions as a scholar aside, his influence on Canadian *Germanistik* as a teacher and as *Doktorvater* to scores of students was tremendous. If I look back on my notes from his graduate courses, I find not only what one would expect in a course on the German novel or German romanticism, but also countless references to a world of reading far beyond any established canon. It was Boeschenstein who unwittingly caused a scandal with his open-mindedness when, in 1973 and 1974, he gave a graduate course on East German literature at McGill University in Montreal, a course that was welcomed by the students because no one else was teaching this in eastern Canadian graduate schools, but which did not make him popular with the representatives of official West German cultural policy.[18] Rodney Symington states in his afterword to Boeschenstein's *History of Modern German Literature*: "In the post-modern age of literary criticism Boeschenstein's approach and interests might be thought old-fashioned, for his view of literature is avowedly traditional.... He saw... literature, as a continuum, within which that which has been found to be valuable should be conserved and absorbed into new forms and new themes."[19] Old-fashioned? Perhaps. And yet the significance of that continuum is something I would like my own students to grasp.

If I have ended this essay by paying homage to a great teacher, I have done so because I am still trying to practice what I have learnt from him: we must not jettison what is best in German literature for the sake of "relevance" or ease of consumption; there really is a canon; but this canon must always be subject to change, and it must always be open-ended.

NOTES

1. Leonard Forster, ed., *German Tales of Our Time* (Toronto: Harrap, 1953).

2. For information on the history of German studies in Canada, I am indebted to Michael Batts's pamphlet, "Germanistik in Kanada," presented to the Canadian Association of University Teachers of German on the occasion of the twenty-fifth anniversary of that association in Hamilton, Ontario, Canada in May 1987 (typescript, 34 pp.). See also his *A Brief History of Germanic Studies at Canadian Universities From the Beginnings to 1995* (New York: Peter Lang, 1998).

3. Batts, "Germanistik in Kanada," 9.

4. Ibid., 26.

5. Ibid., 15.

6. Ibid., 34. The first Ph.D. in German was conferred in 1912, the second not until twenty-one years later.

7. Ibid., 16. A slow "Canadianization" of German textbooks was also beginning, as an increasing number of German readers and composition and grammar texts for high schools were written and edited by Canadian professors (p. 17).

8. Ibid., 19.

9. Ibid., 34.

10. Since the writing of this paragraph, the situation has deteriorated further. It is more than a straw in the wind that Carleton University in Ottawa is shutting down its foreign language departments (except, of course, French, which is not a "foreign language" in Canada).

11. In *Die Mittelstufe*, this bias was not corrected until the fourth edition in 1981, with the inclusion of stories by Gabriele Wohmann and Helga Novak.

12. To reach a broader audience, I now use the English translations of these works.

13. Alain Finkielkraut, *The Defeat of the Mind*, trans. Judith Friedlander (New York: Columbia University Press, 1995), 117.

14. Ibid., 123–124, 129.

15. Ibid., 34.

16. Brigitte M. Turneaure, *Im Spiegel der Literatur. Kurzprosa aus dem 20. Jahrhundert* (New York: Norton, 1992), xii.

17. The genuineness of this commitment was demonstrated when, from 1943 to 1946, Boeschenstein obtained leave from his teaching duties at the University of Toronto to assume the position of secretary of the War Prisoners' Aid of the Y.M.C.A., a job that took him all over Canada, seeing what German prisoners of war needed and then trying to get it for them.

18. See Ernst Gallati, *Hermann Boeschenstein. Eine Biographie* (Bern: Lang, 1995), 118ff.

19. Hermann Boeschenstein, *A History of Modern German Literature*, ed. Rodney Symington (Bern: Lang, 1990), 271.

21
Literature as Peace Research: Re-Vision in Heinrich von Kleist and Christa Wolf

JEAN WILSON

Toward the end of her Büchner Prize acceptance speech (1980), Christa Wolf urges that literature today be "peace research." Writing under the threat of nuclear annihilation ("the land on both sides of the Elbe River would be among the first to suffer extinction"), Wolf posits the existence of maps charting the course of this extinction and proposes "that literature should be allowed to draw its own map, to counteract those maps of death." The plea is for a powerful social and political engagement: ". . . for once, the literature of the Germans should not remain ineffectual . . . and should be applied to help ensure that the things of this earth endure." The brief but striking mention of Cassandra's love for Troy in this context ("Cassandra, I think, must have loved Troy more than herself when she dared to prophesy to her countrymen the ruinous end of their city")[1] anticipates Wolf's own contribution to peace research, her Cassandra project (1983), a narrative and four essays originally presented as the Frankfurt "Lectures on Poetics" in 1982.

Critics have by no means neglected what Wolf calls "the most utopian of [her] books,"[2] a feminist attempt to "scrape the overlay of male mythology" from "the first [female] voice to be handed down to us."[3] Much has been made, and rightly so, of Wolf's act of "re-vision," in Adrienne Rich's sense of the term[4]:

> Re-vision—the act of looking back, of seeing with fresh eyes, of entering an old text from a new critical direction—is for women more than a chapter in cultural history: it is an act of survival . . . [and] part of our refusal of the self-destructiveness of male-dominated society. A radical critique of literature, feminist in its impulse, would take the work first of all as a clue to how we live, how we have been living, how we have been led to imagine ourselves, how our language has trapped as well as liberated us, how the very act of naming has been till now a male prerogative, and how we can begin to see and name—and therefore live— afresh. . . . We need to know the writing of the past, and know it differently

than we have ever known it; not to pass on a tradition but to break its hold over us.⁵

To read some of Wolf's pronouncements, however, one might be forgiven for wondering just what the fuss is all about. What kind of hold can a work like the *Iliad*, for example, exert, if, indeed, as Wolf admits, it "bores" her?⁶ How powerful need an aesthetic of resistance to such a tradition be, and what is the nature of the author's "confrontation with the patriarchal mythological and poetic canon" if—as one, certainly reliable, critic puts it—she "has no interest in the Homeric epic, based on conquest and violence. . . . Conceived around the rage of Achilles, dealing with battle and slaughter, focused on male experience, the epic can evoke no response in Wolf as a woman"?⁷

I have no wish to be disingenuous or to detract from Wolf's remarkable achievement in *Cassandra*. It is not difficult to share her frustration with the exclusion of "everyday life, the world of women," which in the ancient text "shines through only in the gaps between the descriptions of battle."⁸ Against the tradition of producing "stories of heroes, or [even] of antiheroes," Wolf imagines something she calls the subversive, "living word," which, viewing its material through a different lens, "might reveal hitherto unrecognized possibilities."⁹ Studies have illuminated many of the ways in which Wolf's project of demythologization¹⁰ exposes the blind spots of our culture and challenges firmly established patriarchal structures of thought. Less satisfactory, however, is the critical treatment of the specifically intertextual aspects of *Cassandra*, which, following the lead of certain of Wolf's comments, is in danger of constructing more of those "false alternatives" against which the author continually writes.¹¹ The question "Who was Cassandra before anyone wrote about her?", for example, suggests a dichotomy between the "real" and the ideal, the literary and the historical, which is too easily perpetuated in discussions of Wolf's feminist rejection of the exclusionary and objectifying Homeric focus on a "line . . . of male action."¹² As a start in developing a more precise understanding of the intertextuality of *Cassandra*, I propose a closer look first at that "boring" Homeric poem and then at a re-visionary work that very much engaged Wolf, but is, surprisingly, rarely considered in discussions of her Cassandra project: Kleist's *Penthesilea* (1808).

"Doesn't even Homer contain a utopian element?" asks Wolf in the third of the *Cassandra* lectures.¹³ An astonishing question, given that the utopian aspects of the *Iliad* are rather hard to miss. How else does one read all those highly significant gaps, to borrow Wolf's formulation, between the descriptions of battle, such as the encounter between Hector and Andromache in book 6 or Sarpedon's speech in book 12, both of which movingly, if fleetingly, evoke a life beyond that governed by the heroic code? The shield of Achilles described in book 18, that Wolf, in an inexplicably one-sided view, links to the glorification of war and the "expulsion of utopia,"[14] must surely also be recognized as a work of art within a work of art that puts war in its place— contains it, so to speak—and maps various alternative scenes of life, once again opening up a perspective beyond that of the battlefield, which to the characters in the poem has come to seem like the whole world. Greeks and Trojans alike find themselves caught in designs they have forgotten are at least partly of their own making, constrained by forces now seemingly beyond their control. Hector, in book 22, about to face certain death at the hands of Achilles, suddenly comes up with the incredible idea of simply giving Helen back, "and all her treasures with her, all those riches / Paris once hauled home to Troy in the hollow ships— / and they were the cause of all our endless fighting."[15] But he breaks off: "Why debate, my friend? . . . No way to parley with that man—not now." At this point it really is too late, but the discourse of inevitability, of fate, has been undermined throughout the poem by clear indications of the all-too-human failure to imagine any viable alternative to a life of, as Hector puts it in book 6, "winning my father great glory, glory for myself." "I would die of shame," he says, "if I would shrink from battle now, a coward. / Nor does the spirit urge me on that way. / I've learned it all too well."[16]

Confused and speaking a language of utter contradiction—Hector, for instance, imagines the day people will speak of the enslaved, widowed Andromache as having been "robbed of the one man strong enough / to fight off [her] day of slavery"—the mortal characters, like the goddess Hera in book 1, at times rebel against the hierarchical sociopolitical order, only, like Hera, to fall back into line when confronted with the question that Zeus puts to his wife in order to silence her: "Ah but tell me, Hera, / just what can you *do* about all this? Nothing."[17] Most important is Achilles, of course, who questions the reasons for the war in the first place as well as his own part in it, but cannot issue his challenge in terms other than those of the heroic code, terms of honor and glory, shame and disgrace. The disaffected hero advises his fellow Greeks simply to leave the shores of Troy—"sail home now!"—only to fail to act on his own advice, refusing to fight but refusing to go home either. Achilles ultimately rejoins the battle because of the death of Patroclus, not in response to Agamemnon's appeal, the latter's offer of gifts being only a thinly disguised version of Zeus' silencing of Hera: "All this—/ I would extend to him if he will end his anger," proclaims Agamemnon, and then the all-important stipulation: "Let him submit to me!"[18] Achilles's reaction—"His gifts, I loathe his gifts"—is purely oppositional, and his profound disillusionment with heroic society, because he "has no language" in which to express it, cannot be heard by the other characters, who persist in reading his rebellious stance as evidence of simple pride.[19] Unable to articulate an alternative vision, Achilles remains caught in an impossible position: he cannot stay and yet he cannot leave; he cannot be the hero he is expected to be and yet he cannot be anything else.

When Achilles rejoins the war after the death of Patroclus, it is not as a conventional hero—we cannot speak of a simple "return" to battle—but as a force beyond anything his society has known. This is indeed a tragic account of what it means not to have a chance, to have run out of options. In her *Cassandra* essays, Wolf asks with regard to the nuclear threat, "Do we have a chance?" and "Was this course of events inevitable?"[20] The Homeric poem speaks powerfully to these issues, itself arguably a subversive, "living word" rather than an obstructive discursive overlay that needs to be scraped away. With the death of Patroclus, Achilles loses "the will to live, / to take [his] stand in the world of men." The real fight, as it were, has gone out of him, is beaten "down by force," a force that causes him to flaunt heroic conventions so outrageously, to engage in such extreme behaviour, to practice such slaughter, that even nature, in the form of the great river Scamander, rebels.[21] The perversity of Achilles's behavior, culminating in his killing of Hector and his shameful treatment of the corpse, is something the gods cannot ignore. They agree that, all evidence to the contrary, this man "is no madman, no reckless fool," and the scene of reconciliation, the utopian vision of book 24, shows that Achilles has, after all, at some level been heard.[22] The beginning of book 24 finds Achilles not eating, sleeping, or making love, but fixated on the horrifying ritual of dragging Hector's corpse around the tomb of Patroclus; he is more radically estranged here than he was in book 9 when Agamemnon's embassy sought to bring him back. His oppositional stance at that time proved ineffectual, and only when he assumes the role of hero, indeed, plays it for all it is worth, does the urgency of his eccentric position become clear.

In the last book of the *Iliad*, Priam "touches" Achilles (to evoke one of Wolf's concepts[23]) with the sheer madness of his own approach. In contrast to Agamemnon and his conventional embassy in book 9, the old king amazingly goes in person, alone, straight to Achilles, kneels down beside him, clasps his knees and kisses his hands, "those terrible, man-killing hands / that had slaughtered Priam's many sons in battle."[24] The epic simile that describes Achilles's reaction—it is one of utter marvel—emphasizes the "madness" that characterizes Priam's appeal, which is the only match, after all, for Achilles' own extraordinary, unprecedented behavior. Although in his offer of gifts Priam uses the same conventional language of reconciliation as Agamemnon had, the gifts no longer signify a return to the established, hierarchical order, but suggest instead a breakthrough, becoming an outward sign of something as yet impossible to articulate. Similarly, Priam, like Agamemnon's emissaries, asks Achilles to "remember [his] own father,"[25] but his is an intensely personal appeal, rather than a formulaic reminder of filial duty, and it leads to a coming together of Greek and Trojan in mutual acknowledgment. Beyond anything that is realistically conceivable, this moment of "touching" represents exactly what has been called for: an imaginative response, a daring, alternative vision, the charting of an opening into peace.

The *Iliad* may have been pronounced "boring" by Wolf, but for one of her most cherished authors, Heinrich von Kleist, it was anything but.[26] Elsewhere, I have treated in some detail Kleist's bold reworking of the Homeric epic in his play *Penthesilea*.[27] His reappropriation both of the *Iliad* and of Euripides's *Bacchae* in this work might be understood in terms of Harold Bloom's theory of "creative correction,"[28] with Kleist answering not just the ancient texts, but also more immediate literary influences, such as Goethe's *Iphigenie*. Indeed, in her afterword to an edition of *Penthesilea*, published the same year as *Cassandra*, Wolf regards Kleist's imitation of the ancients in the context of the path to inimitability prescribed by Winckelmann, yet perceives to what degree it was at odds with the harmonious ideals of Weimar classicism. Kleist's choice of a female protagonist in this play that expresses his "innermost being"[29] fascinates Wolf, as does his acute sense of a "lack of alternatives" (*Alternativlosigkeit*),[30] his insight into human entanglements in irreconcilable necessities and desires. Wolf writes of how Kleist suffered from the alienating structures of an androcentric society, his depiction of Penthesilea's impossible position constituting a cry for a life of viable options. Kleist's power derives from his refusal to adopt an aesthetic of false alternatives, his resolute nonalignment, his ability to make us see what it means to have "no way out, no chance, no hope."[31] And rather than leading to the pessimism one might expect, his work sustains, nourishes, gives hope especially to women, for it gives voice to the experience of living without alternatives in a patriarchal culture, while suggesting at the same time ways beyond—"sorties," to quote Hélène Cixous in *The Newly Born Woman*.[32]

In that study, Cixous writes: "One gets beyond everything with Kleist. . . . I said I owed my life to [him]. For a long time I lived on the knowledge that he had existed. I owed him not only the will to live but the will to live several lives. . . . [To grasp Penthesilea] Kleist goes 'to places where no human being ever goes'."[33] It is remarkable that a play so bleak, and which Kleist advised was "made less for women than for men,"[34] should strike such a utopian chord in feminist writers such as Wolf and Cixous. If, however, their admiration—particularly Cixous's—sounds excessive, this should come as no surprise, given Kleist's own hyperbolic tendencies. Nowhere do we see this more clearly than in *Penthesilea*, where the protagonist, who has baffled readers ever since Goethe, recalls parodically the Homeric Achilles. Like him, she challenges the conventions of her society without anything to put in their place, and, like him, she cannot find a way to leave the society from which she has become alienated. Just as Achilles's estrangement manifests itself in his outrageous slaughter of the Trojans, so Penthesilea's mad attack on the Greek hero in Kleist's play takes Amazon custom to its most horrifying extreme. Moreover, in her killing and dismemberment of Achilles, which borrow from Euripides's *Bacchae*, she outperforms even the Iliadic hero, whose slaying of Hector is so horrific. In the end, Penthesilea breaks with the Amazon law that effectively confuses "love and bites [war]" (*Küsse und Bisse*), not by ignoring it, but by taking it literally, and thus she ultimately resists assimilation into Greek society, at the same time as she "talks back," as it were, to the voice of her own predecessors, before which, as she indicates earlier to Achilles, she was to have remained silent.[35] Unlike a figure such as Goethe's Iphigenie, who redeems the race of Tantalus, Penthesilea can only undo what her ancestors have done; she can only expose what Amazon culture has become. But precisely this nonalignment, evident in Penthesilea's flaunting of the strictures of both Amazon and Greek society, is what makes Kleist's work such fertile ground for feminist re-vision.

Cixous's focus is a transvaluation of Penthesilea's transgressive, "frenzied desire"; she celebrates "the unsettling transformation of Achilles" in the play, his getting "mixed up" with the Amazon queen.[36] While Wolf's response appears rather sober in comparison with Cixous's ecstatic mediations, both writers are stimulated to answer Kleist's call for the imagining of "a livable existence."[37] Wolf appears to have missed a comparable challenge in that early example of peace research, the *Iliad*, although she does, significantly, discuss the poem in the context of storytelling, which "is humane and achieves humane effects, memory, sympathy, understanding—even when the story is in part a lament for . . . the loss of memory, the breakdown of sympathy, the lack of understanding." [38] But Kleist's re-vision of the Homeric text focuses the problem of *Alternativlosigkeit* ("lack of alternatives") too urgently to ignore. Even though his play has twenty-four scenes, in imitation of the twenty-four books of the *Iliad*, there is no equivalent utopian conclusion. Like the Homeric hero, at her moment of greatest estrangement—"woman no more, how should I name thee?" (*Mensch nicht mehr, wie nenn ich dich?*)[39]—Penthesilea is reconciled, even symbolically born into new life, but the typically difficult Kleistian ending raises a whole series of questions that, I submit, are among those that "constitute the internal 'plot' " of Wolf's own re-visionary work, *Cassandra*.[40]

Unlike the problematic "Who was Cassandra before anyone wrote about her?", a question embedded within the narrative, a more intertextual question this time, takes us and Wolf much further: "Who was Penthesilea?"[41]. Still the Kleistian figure of extraordinary, uncompromising strength and stature, Penthesilea becomes in Wolf's narrative a "man-killing warrior woman," who does not look for allies among the Trojans because "[s]he [is] not merely fighting the Greeks; she [is] fighting all men."[42] She succumbs to male mimicry, to the acceptance of "butchery," to the desire for "everything to come to a stop," because she does not know "any other way to make the men stop."[43] Persisting in what Wolf calls "the masculine way," "the way of carrying all inventions, circumstances, and conflicts to extremes until they have reached their maximum negative point: the point at which no alternatives are left," Penthesilea, whose ultimate triumph is that she forces Achilles to take her seriously,[44] functions to expose the urgent need for "new ways to live" beyond the false alternatives of "killing and dying."[45] Cassandra recognizes that the Amazon queen "offered herself, her life, her body, to carry the wrong too far in the sight of us all."[46] When Achilles rapes the dead woman, Penthesilea,[47] she does not feel it, but all of the other women do, and what this feeling does to them—leading them to "mass counter-violence" so that they "become exactly the thing they claim to hate"[48]—reveals the necessity of an alternative existence, such as can be found in the caves along the Scamander.

A site of destabilized identity, which holds out the possibility for transformation, the cave community brings together Greeks, Trojans, and Amazons, women and men, slaves and members of the ruling class, its utopian constitution confounding the "clear-cut distinctions" that both "[hold] together and [tear] apart" patriarchal culture.[49] The narrative traces Cassandra's journey into this community, where she does, for a time, align herself,[50] and into visionary power, which Wolf illuminates as simply the courage to see: the present, the past, and hence the future.[51] Cassandra's experience of life beyond the walls of the citadel, which includes her deeply disturbing encounter with Penthesilea, helps her acquire this visionary power, by forcing her to ask how many "realities" there are in Troy besides hers, which she "had thought was the only one."[52] The way that Wolf imagines beyond the impossible situation of the Homeric Achilles, the Kleistian Penthesilea, is a vision of community that necessitates the rethinking of alliances, of what it means to say "I," to say "they," to say "we." (C 94, 124).[53]

As we know, Wolf's political engagement, like that of Kleist,[54] has had very mixed results. By 1990, even literature may have come to seem, in Wolf's words, a "theatre of war,"[55] but it also remains a site of peace research, a place of resistance and a place of hope, where we are "able to play with the possibilities left open."[56] Wolf's own radically interrogative work does not present itself as the last word, and ultimately resists being read according to any linear scheme.[57] In contrast to the closing words of Cassandra in another modern reworking of the myth, which convey a sense of definitive correction ("Perhaps one day those who come after us will know the *truth* of Troy and its fall"[58]), Wolf's character's imagining of her story as a "tiny rivulet," a subversive alternative "alongside the river of heroic songs," claims only a heightened complexity.[59] The author of *Cassandra* uses a number of different images to describe her re-visionary project. We might think of it as part of a larger fabric,[60] or as something that enters into an elaborate discursive "network."[61] Asking questions that ultimately can be approached only "by asking further questions,"[62] *Cassandra* draws from many sources and becomes a "reservoir" from which others can draw.[63] The main aim of her work in recent years, says Wolf, "has been to tackle the question of what it is that has brought our civilization to the brink of self-destruction."[64] *Cassandra* maps several responses to this. As for the matter of whether or not we have a chance, it is left to readers to engage in their own peace research, in the spirit of British writer Jeanette Winterson's call to "start another drawing" and "identify, if you can, the places you have not found yet on those other maps, the connections obvious only to you." "The earth is round and flat at the same time," maintains Winterson. "That it is round appears indisputable; that it is flat is our common experience, also indisputable." However, "round and flat, only a very little has been discovered."[65]

NOTES

1. Christa Wolf, *The Author's Dimension: Selected Essays*, ed. Alexander Stephan, trans. Jan van Heurck (New York: Farrar, Straus & Giroux, 1993), 185–186.

2. Ibid., 275.

3. Christa Wolf, *The Fourth Dimension: Interviews With Christa Wolf*, trans. Hilary Pilkington (London: Verso, 1988), 109.

4. For the connection between Rich and Wolf, see Linda Schelbitzki Pickle, "Christa Wolf's *Cassandra*: Parallels to Feminism in the West," *Critique* 28 (1987): 154; Anna K. Kuhn, *Christa Wolf's Utopian Vision: From Marxism to Feminism* (Cambridge: Cambridge University Press, 1988), 178; Edith Waldstein, "Christa Wolf's *Kein Ort. Nirgends*: A Dialogic Re-Vision," in Sara Friedrichsmeyer and Barbara Becker-Cantarino, eds., *The Enlightenment and Its Legacy: Studies in German Literature in Honor of Helga Slessarev* (Bonn: Bouvier, 1991), 184; Kathleeen L. Komar, "The Communal Self: Re-Membering Female Identity in the Works of Christa Wolf and Monique Wittig," *Comparative Literature* 44 (1992): 52.

5. Adrienne Rich, "When We Dead Awaken: Writing as Re-Vision (1971)," in her *On Lies, Secrets, and Silence: Selected Prose 1966–1978* (New York: Norton, 1979), 35.

6. Christa Wolf, *Cassandra: A Novel and Four Essays*, trans. Jan van Heurck (New York: Farrar, Straus & Giroux, 1984), 236.
7. Kuhn, *Christa Wolf's Utopian Vision*, 186.
8. Wolf, *Cassandra*, 233.
9. Ibid., 270–271.
10. Wolf, *The Fourth Dimension*, 109.
11. Wolf, *Cassandra*, 267; *The Fourth Dimension*, 124.
12. Wolf, *Cassandra*, 273, 233. I would agree, however, with Judith Ryan's contention that even as Wolf asks this question, "she knows that there is, in fact, no other accessible reality than the Cassandra of fiction." Judith Ryan, "Twilight Zones: Myth, Fairy Tale, and Utopia in *No Place on Earth* and *Cassandra*," in Marilyn Sibley Fries, ed., *Responses to Christa Wolf: Critical Essays* (Detroit: Wayne State University Press, 1989), 314.
13. Wolf, *Cassandra*, 232.
14. Wolf, *The Author's Dimension*, 268. Cf. *Cassandra*, 155, where Wolf also, however, admits that she would not want Homer "changed into a historiographer who stuck to the facts."
15. Homer, *The Iliad*, trans. Robert Fagles (New York: Penguin, 1990), 545.
16. Ibid., 210.
17. Ibid., 211, 96.
18. Ibid., 265, 256.
19. Ibid., 264, 275. See Adam Parry's illuminating essay, "The Language of Achilles," *Transactions of the American Philological Association* 87 (1956): 6.
20. Wolf, *Cassandra*, 229, 251.
21. Homer, *The Iliad*, 470, 471.
22. Ibid., 593, 594. In Wolf's novel, both Penthesilea and Cassandra also ultimately succeed in being taken seriously. See note 44.
23. Christa Wolf, "In Touch," in Edith Hoshino Altbach et al., eds., *German Feminism: Readings in Politics and Literature*, trans. Jeanette Clausen (Albany: State University of New York Press, 1984), 161–169.
24. Homer, *The Iliad*, 604.
25. Ibid., 604, cf. 260.
26. Wolf, *The Fourth Dimension*, 132.
27. Jean Wilson, *The Challenge of Belatedness: Goethe, Kleist, Hofmannsthal* (Lanham, MD: University Press of America, 1991), 128–161.
28. Harold Bloom, *The Anxiety of Influence: A Theory of Poetry* (New York: Oxford University Press, 1973), 30.
29. Heinrich von Kleist, *Sämtliche Werke und Briefe in vier Bänden*, ed. Helmut Sembdner (München: Hanser, 1982), 4:797.
30. Christa Wolf, *Die Dimension des Autors: Essays und Aufsätze, Reden und Gespräche 1959–1985*. 2 vols. (Frankfurt am Main: Luchterhand, 1990), 2:670.
31. Ibid., 2:674.
32. Hélène Cixous and Catherine Clément, *The Newly Born Woman*, trans. Betsy Wing (Minneapolis: University of Minnesota Press, 1986), 63ff.
33. Ibid., 98, 112, 115.
34. Kleist, *Sämtliche Werke*, 4: 796.
35. Heinrich von Kleist, *Penthesilea*, trans. Humphry Trevelyan, in *Plays*, ed. Walter Hinderer (New York: Continuum, 1982), 229.

36. Cixous and Clément, *The Newly Born Woman*, 117, 115.
37. Wolf, *Die Dimension des Autors*, 2:676.
38. Wolf, *Cassandra*, 173. Cf. Northrop Frye's estimation of the importance of the *Iliad* in his *Anatomy of Criticism: Four Essays* (Princeton, NJ: Princeton University Press, 1957), 319.
39. Kleist, *Penthesilea*, 256; *Sämtliche Werke*, 1:416.
40. Wolf, *The Fourth Dimension*, 109.
41. Wolf, *Cassandra*, 117.
42. Ibid., 7, 117.
43. Ibid., 118. Cf. Wolf's interpretation of "the Penthesilea position" (Wolf, *The Fourth Dimension*, 125).
44. Ibid., 244, 120. This relates to Cassandra's belated recognition that her mother, Hecuba, took her seriously (*Cassandra*, 37). Both passages suggest what finally separates these women from the legendary Cassandra, whose prophecies were never given any credence.
45. Wolf, "In Touch," 168; *Cassandra*, 118.
46. Wolf, *Cassandra*, 107.
47. Unlike Kleist's play, in which Penthesilea kills Achilles, Wolf's *Cassandra* follows the ancient story of the Amazon queen's death at the hands of the Greek hero. However, whereas Achilles is traditionally said to have wept at the sight of the slain Penthesilea and "mourned her for her beauty" (Paul Harvey, *The Oxford Companion to Classical Literature* [Oxford: Oxford University Press, 1984], 4), in Wolf's novel he brutally "hurls himself on the dead victim so that he can go on killing her" (*Cassandra*, 120).
48. Elise Marks, "The Alienation of `I': Christa Wolf and Militarism," *Mosaic* 23 (1990): 82.
49. Wolf, *Cassandra*, 106, 301.
50. Current feminist theory relates the notion of provisional affiliation to alternative constructions of subjectivity. See Gisela Brinker-Gabler, "Alterity—Marginality—Difference: On Inventing Places for Women," *Women in German Yearbook* 8 (1993): 235–245.
51. Wolf, *Cassandra*, 238.
52. Ibid., 20.
53. Ibid., 94, 124. See also Myra Love, "Christa Wolf and Feminism: Breaking the Patriarchal Connection," *New German Critique* 16 (1979): 52–53; Komar, "The Communal Self," 42–58; Karin Eysel, "Christa Wolf's *Kassandra*: Refashioning National Imagination Beyond the Nation," *Women in German Yearbook* 9 (1994): 163–181.
54. See Gordon A. Craig, "German Intellectuals and Politics, 1789–1815: The Case of Heinrich von Kleist," *Central European History* 2 (1969): 3–21.
55. Quoted in Thomas Anz, ed., *"Es geht nicht um Christa Wolf": Der Literaturstreit im vereinten Deutschland* (München: Spangenberg, 1991), 238.
56. Wolf, *The Author's Dimension*, 31.
57. Ibid., 186; cf. Wolf, *The Fourth Dimension*, 113.
58. Marion Zimmer Bradley, *The Firebrand* (New York: Simon & Schuster, 1987), 612. Emphasis mine. Wolf writes of "truth" rather differently; on this issue too she holds views similar to those of Adrienne Rich. See Love, "Christa Wolf and Feminism," 43–44.
59. Wolf, *Cassandra*, 81.

60. Ibid., 142; Wolf, *The Author's Dimension*, 275; *The Fourth Dimension*, 117.
61. Wolf, *Cassandra*, 262.
62. Ibid., 305.
63. Christa Wolf, "Documentation: Christa Wolf," *German Quarterly* 57 (1984): 110.
64. Wolf, *The Fourth Dimension*, 111.
65. Jeanette Winterson, *Sexing the Cherry* (London: Vintage, 1989), 81. I am indebted to Lisa Hicks for suggesting this passage to me.

22
Working on German Memory: Peter Weiss and Uwe Johnson

ALEXANDER HONOLD

This chapter discusses two German writers and their most important works, two bulky novels, each composed of more than a thousand pages. Nonetheless, I would like to start this reflection on the ways in which literature deals with memory with a third author, who very recently set out to treat contemporary German politics from a historical perspective. I am of course referring to Günter Grass and his novel *Ein weites Feld*, published in August 1995.

This book met with a critical response in Germany that, considering its author's standing, was not exactly flattering. I would suggest that there are two main reasons for this. First, *Ein weites Feld* is a kind of a synthetical late Fontane novel, with its hero, Fonty, being a twentieth-century Fontane living in Berlin, who observes and comments on the process of German reunification with a good deal of Fontanian scepticism; and this leads us to the second reason for the widespread damnation of this novel: East Germany after 1989. For Grass it is not only "ein weites Feld" (as this famous quotation from *Effi Briest* would suggest), it also appears to be a "waste land" due to the rigid privatization policies implemented by the Kohl administration, leading to the closing of over 60 percent of the factories and industrial complexes in what used to be the German Democratic Republic. Indeed, the novel does sound exceedingly bad-tempered, not so much stylistically but by virtue of its moralizing stance. Grass violently disturbs the cheering around Brandenburg Gate with drastic dissonances, proving that Germans now have to listen to tunes they never expected to be confronted with again. To put Fonty's disenchantment in a nutshell, it was a quick step from "We are the people" (*Wir sind das Volk*), the slogan of the democratic revolution in the East, to "We are one people" (*Wir sind ein Volk*) and the renaissance of an aggressive patriotism.

In addition to its symptomatic value for the state of cultural life in present-day Germany, this novel is a useful introduction to some of the topics I want to point out in Peter Weiss and Uwe Johnson as well. First, Grass is now facing a Europe that has been totally "remapped," while Johnson and Weiss always had to take into account the situation of the "two Germanies" in a divided world. Second, he stresses that any critique of the political present demands an understanding of the historical past, and that at the same time any understanding of the present generates a retrospective critique of the past. In short, he formulates a "work of memory" (*Erinnerungsarbeit*) as a kind of historical view that is charged and made responsible by the present, as Walter Benjamin has put it. Third, and this seems to be the most ironical point of the whole debate, the construction of Grass's novel itself implies a kind of *Wiedervereinigung* by reunifying the voices of the past and the present, of the old Fontane and of Grass himself. Finally, it is the beginning of a whole series of personal references connecting our three authors. Grass's novel contains an episode in which he pays tribute to his friend Uwe Johnson, who died in 1984. Two years previously, Uwe Johnson had been the only writer associated with West German literature to attend the funeral of Peter Weiss in Stockholm. Though Grass, Weiss, and Johnson were of different ages, they belonged to a group in German literature that in the early 1960s came to public attention as the "new generation." Names such as Enzensberger, Walser, and Bachmann emerged on the scene.

When his first novel was published in Germany in 1960, the 44-year-old Peter Weiss did not of course belong to this young generation in any literal sense. But the fact that he was "discovered" at last after about twenty years of writing and publishing in Sweden was symptomatic of a cultural change in those days, when postwar Germany opened up to traditions that had been disrupted by the Nazis: the modernist literary avant-garde, psychoanalysis, and the sociological criticism of the Frankfurt School, to name but a few. And some of these influences could be found in Weiss, this late surrealist inspired by Breton and Buñuel. Until the early sixties, Weiss did not consider himself primarily a novelist. He put much more emphasis on his experiments as a film director and dramatist, especially in the 1950s. And again, it took a long time to discover that Weiss had actually started his career as a painter while living in Prague and Switzerland.

Peter Weiss was forced to leave Germany in 1934 with his parents, and after a few years in London and in Czechoslovakia he finally went to Sweden in 1939. He did not return after the war, except for short visits—his rigid critique of all forms of oppression imposed by the cold war confrontations made an identification with either part of Germany impossible. Hence he wrote *The Aesthetics of Resistance* [1] under the political auspices of a dissident socialism, a position unlocated and unlocatable in the territorial patterns of East-West-antagonism; the book continued to recall the voices of exile and the names of those who had fought against Nazi barbarism—in Germany itself, in Spain, and in the exile's host countries.

How did Weiss manage to evoke those correspondences between the past and the present that, according to Benjamin, are fundamental to any real historical knowledge? As there was no party for him to belong to, Weiss accepted his lifelong exile as a precondition for a committed but nonaligned standpoint, and both his political statements as well as his aesthetics are shaped by this decision. In his plays of the sixties, this tension was acted out by antagonistic couples such as Marat and Sade, or Marx and Hölderlin.

In his *Aesthetics of Resistance*, published in three volumes between 1975 and 1981, Weiss describes the political and personal education of a young German worker between 1937 and 1945, his odyssey through different countries, the formative experiences of the Nazi dictatorship and the Spanish civil war, and his difficult life as an exile in Czechoslovakia and Sweden—a life remarkably close to Weiss's own biography. There is a permanent, unsolvable tension between the protagonist's efforts to join political action in favor of the Communist International and an opposing tendency, his scrupulous, hesitating scepticism. What can you do when the means of violent resistance undeniably lead to collaboration with repression and dictatorship? As a volunteer during the civil war in Spain, the young, nameless protagonist cannot ignore the executions of anarchists commanded by communist leaders, and when it comes to the Hitler-Stalin Agreement in the summer of 1939, his political orientation is seriously disturbed. Which way of resistance is left for him to pursue?

Behind these conflicts, as Weiss shows, there is a fundamental split between political rationality and personal imagination, a rift that goes right through the history he set out to recollect and to describe. While the protagonist's father resorts to economic explanations for Nazism and war, so that Hitler is regarded as an incarnation of a final and most terrifying stage within the logic of capitalism, his mother faces all that remains inconceivable in the strict terms of this interpretation. The unthinkable dimensions of the Holocaust, in 1943 only known by hearsay, were so hard to imagine that emigrants simply could not believe what was happening and therefore did not react. The protagonist's mother, rather than striving for exact knowledge, is lead by emotion and imagination. During her endless flight through occupied Czechoslovakia and Poland, she sees trenches filled with corpses and hears rumors about the extermination camps. Her way of solidarity with the victims is to succumb to a silent melancholic isolation that amounts to a slow self-sacrifice. While the name "Auschwitz" is never uttered directly in the text, her death seems to tell us that if Auschwitz was possible, no rescue or salvation can be imagined and hoped for. Weiss himself knew that his name was on the list of those destined for deportation; though he escaped, he never lost the impression that this was the place he really belonged to, and after his visit to Auschwitz in 1964 he called it "my place."

So the end of war is not perceived as a sign of victory and hope, but of an everlasting guilt; and from the perspective of the weak powers of resistance and liberation, 1945 is seen as a reason for deception and even resignation. Once more the logic of military solutions proved decisive in the founding of a new order. The cold war and the division of Europe, as Weiss saw them, eliminated any prospects of a third way, that of a socialist democracy. Thus far, the *The Aesthetics of Resistance* can be considered a work of retrospective explanation: looking back from the postwar situation of two antagonistic blocs, the novel shows the historical developments that have lead to this confrontation. But let us return to our question of where the correspondences between past and present are to be found: Is there a direct, immediate line connecting history to the reader's reality of today? I think there is, and it can be found in the way this novel incorporates reflections on aesthetics and art itself.

While political history, treated with all the accuracy and documentary detail resulting from years of investigation, leads the protagonist (and even the readers) into to a jungle of disparate facts and unsteadiness, the Archimedean point or, as it were, the only refuge of reliability is discerned in works of art. Beginning with a fascinating description of Berlin's Pergamon Museum on the very first pages, there is a continuous and intense bias toward museums and artists, and thus the whole novel can be read as a new kind of exploration of art history. There is an obvious emphasis on French paintings of the nineteenth century, with their "classical" themes of revolution, of course, but also of disaster and pain—and, most of all, of violence. One of the most impressive reflections is devoted to Géricault's study of two decapitated heads, which reminds the hero of his own parents; another one is on Géricault's large painting *The Raft of the "Medusa,"* which shows a group of shipwrecked sailors drifting on the ocean, obviously in the moment of their greatest despair. Museum visits, books, even vague allusions and recollections about art are not heterogeneous elements in this novel, since they are taken as "action" itself, an encounter with the experience of seeing.[2] The reader is faced with those pictures and imaginings in the most direct and brutal way possible within the limits of language. Concluding these brief remarks on Peter Weiss, I would like to stress that this mode of interpreting art is key to an understanding of the novel and its approach to history: just as the protagonist recognizes that the paintings and sculptures he sees are concrete memories of past struggles, past violence, and past victims, so, too, does the reader relate with the novel itself.

When the first volume of *The Aesthetics of Resistance* was published in 1975, Uwe Johnson's great project of novelizing the German past had already grown to three large volumes and was expected to be concluded soon by a fourth. Both novels operated on the cyclical scale of a Balzac or Zola, rarely encountered in contemporary literature and difficult to swallow for the general reader. Both were enterprises with an uncertain outcome; one need only think of how much of their writers' lifetimes they absorbed. But in the case of Johnson's novel, the end of the story was at least as determined as in the case of Weiss. For Weiss, the final point had to be the failure of resistance and the execution of a young group of antifascist fighters in the prisons of Berlin. In Johnson's novel, the ending to be reached was doubly fixed, by its composition and by history itself. Nevertheless, he could not, for personal reasons, finish the last volume until 1983—not, as he made his audience believe, due uniquely to the mysterious writer's block he suffered in 1975, but also to the story he had to tell.

If one regards German culture of the postwar decades as a topographic formation, Johnson was dislocated in quite a similar way to Weiss. In the German Democratic Republic, he belonged to the first generation of students, defining himself as a skeptical socialist. Though he was engaged in political organizations, he did not accept the official damnation of all Western (especially American) literature as hostile and decadent, and his first novel, inspired by Faulkner, could only be published in the West, which meant that he had to leave East Germany immediately. After a few years in West Berlin he moved to New York and later to England, were he died in 1984.

His last novel, and surely his most important one, was named *Jahrestage*, which means both "anniversaries" as well as simply "days of the year" (his English translator, Leila Vennevitz, opted for the former). This ambiguous sense of *Jahrestage* gives an idea of the novel's basic structure. Like the author himself, his main protagonist, Gesine Cresspahl, a young woman born in Pomerania, a German province to come under Soviet control after the war, moves first to West Germany and then to New York in the 1960s. The novel simply consists of one year in the life of Gesine Cresspahl in Manhattan, told day by day as in a diary, though not with the means of an ordinary diary: 365 days, starting with August 21, 1967, the very day when Uwe Johnson commenced writing. He had been invited to New York by his American publisher, Helen Wolff, and was provided with a job in a publishing house for exactly one year. An odd contract was stipulated between the writer and his female hero Gesine, introduced ten years earlier in another novel: now she would share the narrator's task, and he would share her life. "Who's telling this story, Gesine?" he once interrupts the narration, and her answer is: "We both are. Surely that's obvious, Johnson." [3] Similar contracts can be found in the literary tradition, such as that between Faust and Mephisto, or the sabbatical year granted to Robert Musil's Man Without Qualities. One year of writing (though Johnson of course could not accomplish all this within his own time limit), a fiction that provided one year of lifetime for Gesine Cresspahl in New York, for her ten-year-old daughter Marie and, first and foremost, for her memories of the German past, evoked by the never-ending chats with her daughter. This task of recollecting and remembering that the author had assigned to his female hero was to form the other dimension of the word *Jahrestage*: anniversaries, days of remembrance, or memorial days. Her daughter keeps asking questions about her dead father, about Gesine's parents, about the small village called Jerichow they had lived in, and about the conditions of everyday life in Germany before and after 1945.

The whole puzzle full of biographical and historical details, broken into pieces by spatial displacement and by time itself, is put together again day by day. Gesine's recollections of her childhood and youth are a way of reflecting herself in her daughter's childhood, and at the same time serve as a transfer of individual and collective knowledge from one generation to the next. With few exceptions, this work of memory generally sticks to the chronological order of events, so that the German past comes closer and closer to the New York present. Moreover, the kind of questions little Marie asks changes in the course of that year. She grows up with memory, and that stimulates two processes: her memory grows, and she comes of age by passing the threshold that history imputes to survivors, realizing that it is a world of the dead, and that narration has to compromise with the victims of violence.

In Johnson's novel, anti-Semitism and the Nazi pogroms of 1938 are touched on in a highly emotional part of the story, and again there is a symbolic act attributed to the role of a mother. In the night of November 9, Gesine's mother is deeply shocked when she sees that a little Jewish child is killed by the Nazi thugs; the child wilfully dies in the flames in a form of martyred self-sacrifice. Too much and too far away for a ten-year-old American schoolgirl? There are indications that this knowledge could be linked with present circumstances: for instance, little Marie's confrontation with American racism at school; or the biography of Mrs. Ferwalter, the mother of her best friend. Mrs. Ferwalter is forty-five years of age but looks sixty; her whole body is conserving the memory of the concentration camp. "As we are talking here, you can't imagine," she says, "that once Dr. Mengele was talking to me" (on the novel's date of August

11, 1968).⁴ Although her testimony is lively and powerful, it signals that her experience cannot be shared by others. Gesine Cresspahl did not understand what had happened when her mother died; she did not grasp it until she was confronted with the evidence, until British soldiers forced her to look at a photograph of a concentration camp. Her awakening is symptomatic of the state of the collective mind in 1945; Gesine's biography corresponds allegorically to German history, as she was born in March 1933, exactly when the Nazi regime was established (while Uwe Johnson's year of birth was 1934).⁵

New York City seems a place of historical discontinuity, distant enough from the German past. But in fact it is not, and when Gesine enters the process of deliberate recollection she is haunted by remembrance again. She realizes that the past cannot be controlled or represented by recollection; memory is "like a cat" (February 2, 1968), free and independent, always ready to jump but not willing to obey. Only when Gesine is talking to her daughter is there an apparent chance to ban the nightmares by dialogue, by practicing back and forth that discursive game of astonishment, questioning, explanations, and other questions that was once called philosophy. There is a didactic emphasis on communication itself in these dialogues, and we realize that this writer imagined himself to be like a mother, or, to say the least, like a teacher. To him, literature is like teaching, and one of the most impressive chapters in the novel deals with the teaching of literature. A young student, almost exactly of Johnson's age, enters a classroom to meet his pupils for the first time. It is the first time that they have been taught how to "read"—in the strict sense of leaving no word of the text unquestioned and unobserved, rethinking and reformulating it in one's own words—and thus think independently. The subject of the lesson is a masterpiece of the Prussian tradition, one of Fontane's novels; and their collective reading shows that old Fontane contains a lot more elements of dissidence and even resistance than the representatives of school and state would expect. Perhaps that is why this reading exercise is recalled in the Grass novel mentioned above.

Meanwhile, Johnson's work of memory became more involved in the disorders of contemporary political struggles than he could ever have expected. In 1968, when the students' rebellion spread over the campuses of the West, another revolution took place in Prague, a slow but deep change toward democracy within a socialist society. Gesine Cresspahl, in her New York bank office, makes plans to go to Czechoslovakia, a decision that can be taken as a deliberate political manifestation, endorsed by her author. As a consequence of its randomly chosen starting point, the last chapter of Johnson's *Anniversaries* is reached with the date of August 20, 1968. This happened to be the day when

Soviet tanks invaded Prague and put an end to its socialist springtime. That, of course, was not accidental.

Although these two German writers seem quite compatible in the biographical parallels of their writing careers, as well as in the historical and political "messages" outlined in their main novels, less similarity is found when the internal aesthetic conditions of their two projects and their different modes of "texture" are considered. While the narrative of Weiss, even in its most emotional moments, shows the manner of its own construction and the concomitant theoretical implications (all of which leads to a remarkable barrier for its reception in the United States), Johnson's novel manages to link the level of historical reflection with the experience of everyday life. Johnson's approach to history offers a kind of narration that passes beyond the writer's former avant-garde techniques toward a new sensibility for the "history of mentalities," or the history of everyday life.

NOTES

1. Peter Weiss, *Die Aesthetik des Widerstands*, 3 vols. (Frankfurt a.M.: Suhrkamp, 1975, 1978, 1981).

2. Some of these encounters between art and literature are analyzed in a new book on Peter Weiss: see Alexander Honold and Ulrich Schreiber, eds., *Die Bilderwelt des Peter Weiss* (Hamburg: Argument, 1995).

3. Uwe Johnson, *Jahrestage: Aus dem Leben von Gesine Cresspahl*, 4 vols. (Frankfurt a.M.: Suhrkamp Verlag, 1970, 1971, 1973, 1983), 1:256.

4. Ibid., vol. 4, 1786.

5. Allegorical elements such as this often result from little manipulations of a biographical subtext: Peter Weiss was born in 1916, but his working-class hero was born one year later, in the very month when the Russian Revolution took place.

23
Anaesthetics: The Shoah in Contemporary Jewish Writing
THOMAS NOLDEN

The emergence of a literature written by Jews who were born toward or after the end of World War II and who spent their formative years growing up and living in Austria, in the German Democratic Republic, and in the Federal Republic is a cultural phenomenon that literary criticism in these countries has not yet acknowledged. From the distanced perspective of German studies practiced in the United States, the writing of these young authors has been greeted as one of the most exciting developments in the postwar culture of German-speaking countries. Within the context of debates concentrating on the aesthetic expression of marginal groups and societal minorities, the writing of Jewish authors has been discussed primarily with respect to its relationship to non-Jewish German literature.

However, this juxtaposition proves to be a rather problematic point of departure for critical analysis because it ignores the fact that in many cases the cultural and societal context of the gentile societies had a stronger impact on the formation of this literature than did the Jewish tradition. From the perspective of literary criticism, the question of how literature written by the Jewish postwar generation differs from the literature written by their non-Jewish peers cannot simply be answered by referring to the Jewish descent of the authors. Such a methodological approach insists in its theoretical supposition on the primacy of ethnicity over cultural influences. This approach faces enormous difficulties with respect to the fact that many of the authors had no or only very limited access to the sources and traditions of Jewish life until they—often rather late in their artistic careers—deliberately turned toward these traditions, which had not been communicated to them during their childhood and adolescence, either because their parents and grandparents had been killed by the Nazis or because the survivors in their families continued to live according to the traditions of assimilation into gentile society. In the countries concerned,

Jewish writing by second- and third-generation authors did not emerge within a cultural and religious context of Jewish traditions, but rather originated in a lack of such tradition. Thus the writer Barbara Honigmann (born in 1949 in East Berlin) has called her generation's attitude a "re-conquest of our Judaism out of nothing" ("Wiederoberung unseres Judentums aus dem Nichts").[1] Honigmann spent the first thirty years of her life without any knowledge about fundamental elements and features of Judaism: "We only knew fragments of the history of our parents, and nothing about Judaism."[2]

Vis-à-vis this biographical pattern that Honigmann shares with such authors as Robert Schindel, Katja Behrens, or Chaim Noll, to name but a few, literary critics must be cautious when reading contemporary Jewish literature in German, according to what one critic has called the "expected line of demarcation between the 'German' (or the 'Austrian') and the 'Jew'."[3] This is not to argue that such a demarcation line would not exist at all. But in most cases, this line does not mark the beginning of the literary productions of the authors, nor does it separate many of their works and literary strategies from those used by their non-Jewish peers. The demarcation line between their Jewishness and the German or Austrian society gains contours only after these authors, from the mid-1980s on, begin to discover their Jewish origins and become Jewish writers in the sense that their works now show a certain awareness of Jewish imagery or themes that up until then were absent in their writing. To render justice to the development in recent literary history, it seems necessary to differentiate heuristically the broad spectrum of contemporary writing by Jews. At one end of this spectrum we find a literary production in which the Jewish descent of the authors for various reasons found no repercussion in the themes, styles, and models of their writing. To be sure, this phenomenon is not at all unprecedented in German literature, but rather is part of a long tradition that Isaac Deutscher called the "Jewish tradition" of the "non-Jewish Jew."[4] However, the reemergence of this phenomenon itself is certainly unique and unprecedented, since it occurred in a historical situation that left most Jews uneasy about the idea of a Jewish diaspora in the country that was responsible for the Shoah.

On the other end of the spectrum of contemporary writing by Jewish authors, we find first signs of what might be called Jewish literature in a more traditional sense, defined as a concept of literary criticism that pays attention not only to the ethnic identity of the authors per se, but also emphasizes the relationship between their works and the cultural traditions of Judaism. Looking at the development of these authors over the course of the last decades, the emergence of a literature by Jewish authors undoubtedly preceded the emergence of a Jewish literature that up until today is still less developed than the former, and less developed than second- and third-generation writing in other national contexts. Careful study of recent literary history helps to avoid the fallacy of a "binary construction of 'Jews in Germany,' " which "in effect contributes to the misplacement of minority discourse in the realm of German studies by hypostatizing both 'Jews' and 'Germans' "[5] and suggests that the line of demarcation between these two molds for identity formation can be so porous that the validity of the metaphor—and with it of the theorem as such—has to be drawn into question.

The poem "On Indirectness II" ("Vom Indirekten II") by the Austrian born writer Robert Schindel (born 1944) can be used as an indicator for the subtle process that evolved in the creation of a Jewish voice, after many years of writing under literary and aesthetic paradigms in which Judaism did not serve as a point of reference at all. Written in the early 1980s, "On Indirectness II" ends Schindel's first volume of poetry, titled *Ohneland: Gedichte* (*Landless: Poems*). Placed so conspicuously, the poem indicates the direction in which Schindel's artistic oeuvre began to develop. The poem commences with the laconic statement: "Your texts are becoming more and more Jewish / People tell me and smile"[6] and goes on to present a dialogue between the poet and an anonymous audience of critics and readers, who seem to reproach the poet for his turn toward a Jewish voice. The poet, on the other hand, presents the development of his work as a response to the fading of literary modes, schools, and fashions that became less and less suitable for the expression of his concerns:

> But instructed: I should rather
> Please in a pleasing manner, well
> What do I say, comprehensible texts, so that you
> Presumably will be able to
> Recognize yourself easily
> in the "Aha."
> But instructed: I should
> Really make a difference
> Send out a message and get involved
> And deliver something together with it
> But instructed: The message
> Would be more important than the messenger
> Even though, although
> Such a messenger is, whereas
> Some message . . . Instructed in this manner[7]

Schindel's "On Indirectness II" reads as an ars poetica that offers a kind of brief survey of the literary styles and periods from the 1960s on—styles and periods that also informed the literary career of the author Schindel himself.

Along with the bleached slogans of political art ("make a difference' [*was wirken*]), the poet rejects the buzzwords of the "New Subjectivity" ("get involved" [*sich einbringen*]), as well as the aesthetic programs that in turn criticize the *Innerlichkeitsliteratur* of the last decade, demanding that the message has to prevail over the artist's persona.

Here is not the space to pursue a detailed reading of the entire poem, which concludes with a rather ironic notion about the abstract language of lyrical poetry. It must suffice to point out that Schindel, whose novel *Gebürtig* (*Born-where*) (1992) has been praised as the renaissance of Jewish storytelling in Austria, consciously reflects on the emergence of his own Jewish voice from within an aesthetic context devoid of any Jewish background. The poem also testifies to the cultural process of mediation between gentile society and culture on the one hand and the Jewish author on the other: Jewish writing occurs not in a direct line or immediate succession to former models of Jewish writing, but as an aesthetic project that—as the poem's title suggests—initially relates to Judaism only indirectly. The development of Schindel's work shows that the author's relationship to Jewish culture and tradition continuously becomes stronger. In this respect, Schindel's own career parallels a general trend that peaked in the late 1980s when a handful of young Jewish authors—most notably Maxim Biller—came out with their first books in which Jewish themes figured prominently (*Wenn ich einmal reich und tot bin* [*When I Am Rich and Dead*], 1990). In a second step in this development, authors whose earlier works had not dealt with or that had hardly addressed issues of Jewish culture and identity in their writing now explicitly turned toward their Jewish heritage (for example, Hans Noll who from then on would publish under the name Chaim Noll). Others began to state publicly that they were of Jewish decent—a fact that their readers up until then would not have been able to learn from reading their works. The erosion of the structure of traditional political thought along the lines of the left and the right undoubtedly led to the rediscovery and positive reevaluation of ethnic, religious, and cultural notions. Anti-Semitic tendencies to be found in some leftist circles would no longer keep Jews among the political left from opening themselves up toward their Jewish background (for example Esther Dischereit). Another factor leading toward the development of a potent cultural discourse of the younger Jewish generation was the growing fragility of the parent generation, whose dominating impact on the official Jewish communities and their cultural organizations would meet with the opposition of their offspring, who demanded representation and reformation. Present young Jewish writing, one could argue, did not so much develop along the demarcation line between "Austrians" or Germans" on the one hand and "Jews" on the other, but rather along what many of the young authors perceived as a demarcation line between the Jewish generations.

Whereas the generational conflict—the critique of the young directed against various forms of assimilation practiced by their parents—is being depicted in more (Seligmann, Biller) or less (Schindel, Behrens) direct form, the representation of the Shoah does not allow for such a choice in the employment of forms. In order to define and describe the literary production of young Jewish authors, literary criticism needs to identify patterns in the literary styles and strategies at work. The following part of this essay will focus on one of the most characteristic of these patterns. It concerns the literary representation of the suffering in the death camps and of the impossibility of communicating this experience that has left the victims in a state of separation not only from gentile postwar society, but also—albeit certainly in a different manner—from their children and grandchildren. For the members of the second and third generations, the central event in modern Jewish life is present as the incommunicable trauma of the previous generations. The protagonist of one of Maxim Biller's stories states laconically: "A trauma isn't really for the living, it is only something for the dead or for those who nearly died."[8]

The hiatus that interrupted modern history separates their literary endeavors from the tradition of Jewish writing before the Shoah, as well as from the writing of the victims and the survivors. Their ways of aesthetically expressing their experience are bound to this very experience. In other words, there is no aesthetic of the Shoah for the younger generation. The phrase "Writing / Poetry After Auschwitz" does not precisely fit the aesthetic dilemma in which the younger generations of writers find themselves. The question that they are confronting could be formulated more accurately as follows: What can Jewish literature look like after the "Writing After 'The Fugue of Death'?" The young authors have developed literary means of mediation that allow them to direct the vector of their writing toward the center of the suffering of the Jewish people without, however, ever trespassing the threshold that separates the victims and survivors from the generations born after the Shoah. The door to the gas chamber marks this threshold that the imagination acknowledges as its boundary.

A passage from a book by Chaim Noll lends insight into the trajectory that the imagination of young Jewish literature takes when it leads to a confrontation with the horrors of the past. Noll was born in 1954 in East Berlin and managed to leave the German Democratic Republic (GDR) for West Berlin in 1984. The following passage is an entry from Noll's diary that records his stay in Rome, where in 1992–1993 he was searching for the traces of Jewish history under the ruins of Rome's imperial architecture. Returning to his apartment in Rome from one of his wanderings through the city, he finds a letter:

> A Letter
>
> Back home I found my mail in the hallway, among it a grey envelope from Hamburg. It contained a photo: in the foreground rubble, behind a brick wall and where you would have the horizon there was a watch tower and the barren trunks of a few freezing, half-dead trees. Immediately the Berlin Wall came to my mind. On the back it said: "Auschwitz-Birkenau, a German Forum Romanum. In the front, beneath the rocks, was the gas chamber. Greetings, Wolf." Thanks. Tomorrow is Friday. I will go to the synagogue. Think of those who are lying beneath the rocks. Whose unborn children could be my friends. Thank the Eternal One that I live.[9]

The photograph brings—and locates—the camp Auschwitz-Birkenau immediately into the present of the receiver of the letter. Involuntarily, he interprets what he first sees on the photograph as an event from the context of his own experience. The political situation of the time (the fall of the Wall) is intimately interwoven with the personal history of the author, who had been thrown into the psychiatric asylums of the GDR before he was allowed to leave the country. The political and personal realms of the present are the point of departure for the receiver's interpretation of the photograph, and they serve as a frame of reference that does not break down until he begins to read the commentary, the caption on the back of the picture. Only now does he become aware of what the photograph signifies—a perception that seems to last only a fraction of a second and which becomes almost immediately transformed into the intention to commemorate the victims in prayer in the synagogue. The text itself does not end with this prayer, it is not itself a Kaddish for the victims, but merely the record of a confrontation with the Shoah to which—and this is a prevalent feature in young Jewish literature—to which the text refers in a mediated manner. In this case, the medium is in the form of a photograph, but it can come in many other forms as well. For example, in the closing passage of Robert Schindel's novel *Gebürtig*, it is a movie made by an American film director who not by chance resembles a figure from a movie by Thomas Brasch. In Maxim Biller's story "Verrat" ("Betrayal"), it is the window-display of a bookstore featuring books on the Shoah. In the stories of Katja Behrens, this role is played by lists found among the files of Auschwitz, and in the autobiography of Richard Chaim Schneider it is an Israeli documentary on Shoah survivors that for the first time enables him to see why his mother—a survivor—acts the ways she acts.

To return to the photograph in Noll's Rome diary: with his commentary, the sender of the postcard put the memory of Auschwitz-Birkenau into the context of his friend's current concerns and their setting. The formulation "Auschwitz-Birkenau: ein deutsches Forum Romanum" equates the center of the genocide with the architectural landscape of Rome's Forum Romanum—an equation that stresses the fact that the former camp, its barracks and buildings, has turned into a site that many visitors cannot but call "romantic," even though they are aware of the fact that beneath the grass there are the remnants of people murdered. The photograph of a camp whose physical appearance has been changed so dramatically by the hands of men, by the politics of remembrance, and by the power of nature—the photograph of this space whose name metonymically stands for the extermination of millions of Jews—suggests that the Shoah for the generations after the victims and the survivors has the status of a trope.

To conceptualize the narrative movement of the passage just analyzed and the course that the attention of the narrator had taken, I would like to turn to Jean-François Lyotard's discussion of Immanuel Kant's *Critique of Judgment*, a treaty in which Kant reconstructed the trajectory of the imagination when it tries to approach the Absolute. Always and necessarily falling back into the state of its departure, imagination, according to Kant, proves unable to confront the Absolute, achieving at most an oscillating movement between the Absolute and itself: "Not only does the imagination, required to present sensibly something that would re-present the Absolute, fail in its task but it falls into an 'abyss' (Kant III, sec. 26, 28)."[10] Transferring this model of the "anaesthetic" to the encounter with the Shoah, Lyotard recognizes that art is unable to provide testimony of the Absolute of the Shoah. According to Lyotard, art after the Shoah "does not say the unsayable, but says that it cannot say it."[11]

I would argue that Lyotard here states more than he actually needs to in order to make his point. The analogy to Kant's analysis of the accessibility of the Absolute seems partly responsible for Lyotard's categorical statement that art cannot reach the insensible of the disaster. There are, after all, books, paintings, and music scores with which victims and survivors attempted to capture the suffering in the camps, and some of them insist that they created viable forms of expressing what they have experienced. Lyotard's idea of anaesthetics, however, adequately describes a pattern prevalent in the representation of the Shoah by those who have not experienced it.

The course of imagination, its return to its point of departure, describes a movement that philosophy calls "re-flection," which is the basic process of the intellect. Lyotard's term "anaesthetics" suggests that the Absolute cannot be perceived by the senses, that an "insensible" (an-aesthetic) perception or "passibility" is at work.[12] The movement of the imagination always results in an "insensible," that is "intellectual" process, that links the imagination back to its starting point, to the present. The comment or, if you will, the title of the photograph of Auschwitz-Birkenau in Noll's diary is an example of this trajectory of the imagination that "re-flects" back to the present of the receiver. Noll's literary rendering of the photograph episode shows the extent to which the Shoah itself has been removed from the author's own imagination. It is present as a photograph, or to be more precise, as a photograph that somebody else had taken and labeled and that nonetheless has the effect of a shock on the receiver. But this shock does not—or at least not at first—originate in the confrontation with the Shoah, but in the acknowledgment that the imagination had missed this confrontation, that it had mistaken it for a representation of something else. The passage in Noll's diary, then, illustrates the failure, the impossibility of an aesthetics of the Shoah and the project of an anaesthetics to which literature after the Shoah has to resign itself.

NOTES

1. Barbara Honigmann, "Damals, dann und danach, " *Literaturmagazin* 34 (1994): 25. Translations are mine unless otherwise noted. They do not strive for an aesthetic rendition of the originals.

2. Ibid., 24.

3. Sander L. Gilman, *Jews in Today's German Culture* (Bloomington: Indiana University Press, 1995), 5.

4. Isaac Deutscher, *The Non-Jewish Jew and Other Essays*, ed. Tamara Deutscher (New York: Oxford University Press, 1968), 26.

5. Leslie A. Adelson, *Making Bodies, Making History. Feminism and German Identity* (Lincoln: University of Nebraska Press, 1993), 93.

6. Robert Schindel, "Vom Indirekten II," in his *Ohneland: Gedichte* (Frankfurt a.M.: Suhrkamp, 1986), 105.

7. Ibid., 105.

8. Maxim Biller, "Roboter," in his *Wenn ich einmal reich und tot bin* (Cologne: Kiepenheuer & Witsch, 1990), 77–78.

9. Chaim Noll, *Taube und Stern. Roma Hebraica. Eine Spurensuche* (Hünefelden-Gnadenthal: Präsenz, 1994), 28.

10. Jean-François Lyotard, *Heidegger and "the jews,"* trans. Andreas Michel and Mark S. Roberts (Minneapolis: University of Minneapolis Press, 1990), 31.

11. Ibid., 47.

12. Ibid., 45.

Bibliography

Aarnes, Sigurd. " 'Det ondes problem'—nazismen i Jens Bjørneboes diktning," in *Nazismen og norsk litteratur*, ed. Bjarte Birkeland and Stein Ugelvik Larsen, pp. 173–194. Oslo: Universitetsforlaget, 1975.
Abrahamsen, Samuel. "The Holocaust in Norway," in *Contemporary Views on the Holocaust*, ed. Randolph L. Braham, pp. 109–142. Boston: Kluwer-Nijhoff, 1983.
Adelson, Leslie A. *Making Bodies, Making History: Feminism and German Identity*. Lincoln: University of Nebraska Press, 1993.
Adler, H. G. *Theresienstadt 1941–1945: Das Antlitz einer Zwangsgemeinschaft*. Tübingen: J.C.B. Mohr, 1960.
Adorno, Theodor W. "Kulturkritik und Gesellschaft," in *Prismen*. Frankfurt a.M.: Suhrkamp, 1955.
———. "Paralipomena," in *Ästhetische Theorie: Gesammelte Schriften*, vol. 7. Frankfurt a.M.: Suhrkamp, 1990.
Allison, David B, ed. *The New Nietzsche: Contemporary Styles of Interpretation*. Cambridge, MA: MIT Press, 1985.
Altbach, Edith Hoshino, Jeanette Clausen, Dagmar Schultz, and Naomi Stephan, eds. *German Feminism: Readings in Politics and Literature*. Albany: State University of New York Press, 1984.
Anz, Thomas, ed. *"Es geht nicht um Christa Wolf:" Der Literaturstreit im vereinten Deutschland*. Munich: Spangenberg, 1991.
Arendt, Hannah. *Eichmann in Jerusalem: A Report on the Banality of Evil*. New York: Viking, 1964
———. *The Human Condition*. Chicago: University of Chicago Press, 1958.
Arlt, Herbert, and Donald G. Daviau, eds. *Geschichte der österreichischen Literatur*, 2 vols. St. Ingbert: Röhrig Universitätsverlag, 1996.
Arnold, Heinz Ludwig, ed. *Die deutsche Literatur von 1945–1960*. Munich: dtv, 1995.
Aschheim, Steven E. "Nietzsche, Anti-Semitism and the Holocaust," in *Nietzsche and Jewish Culture*, ed. Jacob Golomb, pp. 3–20. London: Routledge, 1995.
———. *The Nietzsche Legacy in Germany, 1890–1990*. Berkeley: University of California Press, 1992.

Auckenthaler, Karlheinz. "Anmerkungen zur österriechischen Literatur," in *Lauter Einzelfälle: Beiträge zur modernen östereichischen Literatur*, ed. Karlheinz Auckenthaler, pp. 11–55. Bern: Lang, 1995.

———. "Die Dichtung des Biedermeier—Die erste Geniezeit der österreichischen Literatur? Zum österreichischen Literaturbegriff," *Neohelicon* 14.1 (1992): 71–83.

———. "Überlegungen zum österreichischen Literaturbegriff," *Österreich in Geschichte und Literatur*, 38 (1994): 149–151.

Bachmann, Ingeborg. "Auf das Opfer darf keiner sich berufen," in *Werke*, vol. 4 of 4 volumes, ed. Christine Koschel, p. 335. Munich: Piper, 1978.

Bark, Joachim, Dietrich Steinbach, and Hildegard Wittenberg, eds. *Epochen der deutschen Literatur*. Stuttgart: Klett, 1989.

Barner, Wilfried, ed. *Geschichte der deutschen Literatur von 1945 bis zur Gegenwart*. vol. 18. Munich: Beck, 1994.

Barthelemy, Francoise, and Lutz Winckler, eds. *Mein Deutschland findet sich auf keinem Atlas—Schriftsteller aus beiden deutschen Staaten über ihr nationales Selbstverständnis*. Frankfurt a.M.: Suhrkamp, 1990.

Bathrick, David. "Anti-Neonazism as Cinematic Practice: Bonengel's *Beruf Neonazi*," *New German Critique* 67 (1996): 133–146.

Batts, Michael. *A Brief History of Germanic Studies at Canadian Universities From the Beginnings to 1995*. New York: Peter Lang, 1998.

Baudrillard, Jean. *Cool Memories*, trans. Chris Turner. New York: Verso, 1990.

———. *Simulacra and Simulation*, trans. Sheila Faria Glaser. Ann Arbor: University of Michigan Press, 1994.

———. *The Transparency of Evil*. New York: Verso, 1993.

Baumann, Gerhart. *Erinnerungen an Paul Celan*. Frankfurt a.M.: Suhrkamp, 1992.

Becker, Peter von. "Der lebende Mythos," *Der Tagesspiegel* (May 5, 2000), 27.

Behler, Diana. "Nietzsche and Postfeminism," *Nietzsche-Studien* 22 (1993): 354–370.

Behler, Ernst. "Nietzsche jenseits der Dekonstruktion," in *Nietzsche und Hegel*, ed. Josef Seimon, pp. 88–107. "Nietzsche in der Diskussion" series. Würzburg: Königshausen & Neumann, 1985.

Benda, Ernst. "Ab ins Grundbuchamt? Richter Orlet sollte vor dem Bundesverfassungsgericht angeklagt werden," *Die Zeit* 12 (March 17, 1995), 10.

Benjamin, Walter, and Gershom Scholem. *Briefwechsel 1933–1940*, ed. Gershom Scholem. Frankfurt a.M.: Suhrkamp, 1980.

Benn, Gottfried. "Nietzsche: Nach Fünfzig Jahren," in *Essays. Reden. Vorträge*, vol. 1 of 4 volumes, ed. Dieter Wellershoff, pp. 488–493. Wiesbaden: Limes, 1965.

———. "Rede auf Else Lasker-Schüler," in *Gesammelte Werke*, vol. 4, *Reden und Vorträge*. 8 volumes, ed. Deiter Wellershoff, pp. 1101–1104. Wiesbaden: Limes Verlag, 1968.

Benseler, David P., Walter F.W. Lohnes, and Valters Nollendorfs, eds. *Teaching German in America: Prolegomena to a History*. Madison: University of Wisconsin Press, 1988.

Bergmann, Werner. "Antisemitismus in öffentlichen Konflikten 1949–1994," in *Antisemitismus in Deutschland. Zur Aktualität eines Vorurteils*, ed. Wolfgang Benz, pp. 64–88. Munich: Deutscher Taschenbuch Verlag, 1995.

Bernhardt, Elizabeth B., and Russel A. Berman. "From German 1 to German Studies 001: A Chronicle of Circular Reform," *Die Unterrichtspraxis* 32 (1999): 22–31.
Bertram, Ernst. *Nietzsche: Versuch einer Mythologie*. Berlin: G. Bondi, 1918.
Bhabha, Homi K. "Culture's in Between," *Artforum* (September 1993): 167–168, 211–214.
———. *The Location of Culture*. New York: Routledge, 1994.
Biller, Maxim. "Roboter," in Biller, *Wenn ich einmal reich und tot bin*, pp. 77–78. Cologne: Kiepenheuer & Witsch, 1990.
Bjørneboe, Jens. "Det utrolige," *Spektrum* (1949): 103.
———. *Før hanen galer*. Oslo: Aschehoug, 1952.
———. *Om teater*, ed. Tone Bjørneboe. Oslo: Pax, 1978.
———. *Stillheten*. Oslo: Gyldendal, 1969.
Bloom, Harold. *The Anxiety of Influence: A Theory of Poetry*. New York: Oxford University Press, 1973.
Boeschenstein, Hermann. *A History of Modern German Literature*, ed. Rodney Symington. Bern: Lang, 1990.
Bohrer, Karl Heinz. "Why We Are Not a Nation—And Why We Should Become One," *New German Critique* 52 (1991): 72–83.
Bradley, Marion Zimmer. *The Firebrand*. New York: Simon & Schuster, 1987.
Braham, Randolph L., ed. *Contemporary Views on the Holocaust*. Boston: Kluwer-Nijhoff, 1983.
Briegleb, Klaus, and Ingrid Wiegel, eds. *Gegenwartsliteratur seit 1968*, vol. 12. Munich: dtv, 1992.
Brinker-Gabler, Gisela, "Alterity—Marginality—Difference: On Inventing Places for Women," *Women in German Yearbook* 8 (1993): 235–245.
Brinkmann, Rolf Dieter. *Westwärts 1 & 2*. Reinbek: Rowohlt, 1975.
Broch, Hermann. "Hofmannsthal und seine Zeit," in *Schriften zur Literatur/Kritik 1*, ed. Paul Michael Lützeler, vol. 9:1. Frankfurt a.M.: Suhrkamp, 1975.
Brunotte, Ulrike. "Wissen über Glauben," *Die Zeit* (April 21, 1995), 18.
Bubis, Ignatz, "No Double Loyalty," in *Thirty Years of Diplomatic Relations Between the Federal Republic of Germany and Israel*, ed. Otto Romberg and Heiner Lichtenstein, pp. 75–81. Frankfurt a.M.: Tribüne Verlag, 1995.
Bubner, Rüdiger. "Philosophen und die deutsche Einheit," *Merkur* 44.10/11 (Oct./Nov. 1990): 1018–1025.
Budde, Enno. "Das Land Hadeln," *Alt-Hannoverscher Volkskalender* 37 (1934): 55–57.
———. "Langenrehm," *Deutsch-Hannoverscher Volkskalender* 36 (1933): 49–50.
———. "Ostfriesland unter preußischer Herrschaft," *Alt-Hannoverscher Volkskalender* 39 (1936): 67–68.
———. "Wie aus einer Verteidigung eine Anklage wurde," *Deutsch-Hannoverscher Volkskalender* 35 (1932): 49–50.
Burgard, Peter, ed. *Nietzsche and the Feminine*. Charlottesville: University of Virginia Press, 1994.
Burleigh, Michael, and Wolfgang Wipperman. *The Racial State: Germany 1933–1945*. New York: Cambridge University Press, 1991.

Byrnes, Heidi. "The Future of German in American Education." *Newsletter of the American Association of Teachers of German* 32.1, 1996.
Carmichael, Joel. *The Satanizing of the Jews: Origin and Development of Mystical Anti-Semitism.* New York: Fromm, 1993.
Celan, Paul. "Ansprache anläßlich der Entgegennahme des Literaturpreises der Freien Hansestadt Bremen," in *Paul Celan: Gesammelte Werke in fünf Bänden*, vol. 3, ed. Beda Alleman and Stefan Reichert, pp. 185–186. Frankfurt a.M.: Suhrkamp, 1983.
———. *Gedichte I* in *Gesammelte Werke in fünf Bänden*, ed. Beda Alleman and Stefan Reichert. Frankfurt a.M.: Suhrkamp, 1983.
Chadash, Udi. "Der 20. Juli und die Juden," *Tribüne* 33.130 (1994): 62–64.
Cixous, Hélène, and Catherine Clément. *The Newly Born Woman*, trans. Betsy Wing. Minneapolis: University of Minnesota Press, 1986.
Clark, Maudemarie. "Language and Deconstruction: Nietzsche, de Man, and Postmodernism," in *Nietzsche as Postmodernist*, ed. Clayton Koelb, pp. 75–90. Albany: State University of New York Press, 1990.
Colin, Amy. *Paul Celan: Holograms of Darkness*. Bloomington: Indiana University Press, 1991.
———. "Paul Celan's Poetics of Destruction," in *Argumentum e Silentio: International Paul Celan Symposium*, ed. Amy Colin, pp. 157–182. New York: Walter de Gruyter, 1987.
Craig, Gordon A. "German Intellectuals and Politics, 1789–1815: The Case of Heinrich von Kleist," *Central European History* 2 (1969): 3–21.
Craig, William. *Enemy at the Gates: The Battle for Stalingrad*. Toronto/New York: Bantam Books, 1982.
Daviau, Donald G., and Herbert Arlt, eds. *Geschichte der österreichischen Literatur*, 2 vols. St. Ingbert: Röhrig Universitätsverlag, 1996.
Dean, Martin. *Die gefiederte Frau: Erzählungen*. Munich: Carl Hanser Verlag, 1982.
———. *Der Guayanaknoten: Roman*. Munich: Carl Hanser Verlag, 1994.
———. *Die Verborgenen Gärten*. Munich: Carl Hanser Verlag, 1995.
Debrunner, Hans Werner. *Presence and Prestige: Africans in Europe*. Basel: Basler Afrika Bibliographien, 1979.
Del Caro, Adrian. *The Early Poetry of Paul Celan: In the beginning was the word* [*sic*]. Baton Rouge and London: Louisiana State University Press, 1997.
Derrida, Jacques. "La loi du genre," *Glyph* 7 (1980): 176–201.
———. "Otobiographies: the Teaching of Nietzsche and the Politics of the Proper Name," in *The Ear of the Other: Otobiography, Transference, Translation*, ed. Christie V. McDonald, trans. Peggy Kamuf and Avital Ronnell, pp. 1–38. New York: Schocken, 1985.
———. *Specters of Marx: Mourning, The New International and the State of the Debt*. New York: Routledge, 1994.
———. *Spurs. The Styles of Nietzsche*, trans. Barbara Harlow. Chicago: University of Chicago Press, 1979.
———. *The Ear of the Other*. Lincoln: University of Nebraska Press, 1985.
———. *Writing and Difference*. London: Routledge, 1981.

Deutscher, Isaac. *The Non-Jewish Jew and Other Essays*, ed. Tamara Deutscher. New York: Oxford University Press, 1968.

Di Donato, Robert. "Undergraduate Programs: Strategies for Success," *ADFL Bulletin* 30.1 (1998): 12–14.

Diner, Dan. "Negative Symbiose," *Babylon* I (1986): 9–20.

Dische, Irene. *Fromme Lügen: Sieben Erzählungen*, trans. Otto Bayer and Monika Elwenspoek. Frankfurt a.M.: Eichborn Verlag, 1989.

———."Eine Jüdin für Charles Allen," in *Fromme Lügen: Sieben Erzählungen*, trans. Otto Bayer and Monika Elwenspoek (Frankfurt a.M.: Eichborn Verlag, 1989).

Dischereit, Esther. "Es gibt Menschen—und es gibt Juden," *Allgemeine jüdische Wochenzeitung* (Sept. 8, 1989).

———. *Joëmis Tisch*. Frankfurt a.M.: Suhrkamp, 1988.

———. *Merryn*. Frankfurt a.M.: Suhrkamp, 1992.

———. "No Exit From This Jewry," trans. Michael Roloff, in *Reemerging Jewish Culture in Germany*, ed. Sander L. Gilman and Karen Remmler, pp. 266–281. New York: New York University Press, 1994.

Doerry, Martin, and Volker Hage. "Tausendfacher Tod im Hirn," *Der Spiegel* 41 (Oct. 9, 1995), 228.

Dönhoff, Marion, Meinhard Miegel, et al. *Weil das Land sich ändern muß: Ein Manifest*. Reinbeck bei Hamburg: Rowohlt, 1992.

Draper, Jamie B., and June H Hicks,. "Foreign Language Enrollments in the Public Secondary Schools, Summary Report of the American Council on the Teaching of Foreign Languages," *ACTFL Annals* 29.3 (1995): 303–306.

Drews, Jörg, ed. *Dichter beschimpfen Dichter*. Leipzig: Reclam, 1994.

Eagleton, Terry. "Awakening From Modernity," *Time Literary Supplement*, Feb. 20, 1987, 194.

———. *Against the Grain: Essays 1975–1985*. London: Verso, 1986.

Ecker, Gisela, ed. *Feminist Aesthetics*, trans. Harriet Anderson. Boston: Beacon Press, 1985.

Ecker, Hans-Peter. "Blick über den Rhein: Das alte und neue Interesse an Schweizer Literatur," *Passauer Pegasus* 11.21–22 (1993): 25–45.

Elsaesser, Thomas. "Filming Fascism: Is History Just an Old Movie?" *Sight and Sound* 2.5 (1992): 18–21.

———. "Subject Positions: From *Holocaust, Our Hitler,* and *Heimat* to *Shoah* and *Schindler's List*," in *The Persistence of History: Cinema, Television, and the Modern Event*, ed. Vivian Sobchack, pp. 145–183. New York: Routledge, 1996.

Engelmann, Bernt. *Deutschland ohne Juden: Eine Bilanz*. Munich: dtv, 1974.

Enzensberger, Hans Magnus. "Steine der Freiheit," *Merkur* 13 (1959): 770–775.

Eshel, Amir. "Auschwitz als Metapher. Zu Jakob Hessing's 'Gedichte nach Auschwitz'," *Merkur* 530 (1993): 462–464.

Eyferth, Klaus, Ursula Brandt, and Wolfgang Hawer. *Farbige Kinder in Deutschland: Die Situation der Mischlingskinder und die Aufgaben ihrer Eingliederung*. Munich: Juventa Verlag, 1960.

Eysel, Karin. "Christa Wolf's *Kassandra*: Refashioning National Imagination Beyond the Nation," *Women in German Yearbook* 9 (1994): 163–181.

Fanon, Frantz. *Black Skin White Masks*, trans. Charles Markmann. New York: Grove Press, 1967.
Faschinger, Lilian. *Magdalena Sünderin*. Cologne: Kiepenhauer, 1995.
Ferry, Luc, and Alain Renaut. *Heidegger and Modernity*, trans. Franklin Philip. Chicago: University of Chicago Press, 1992.
Fessmann, Meike. *Spielfiguren: Die Ich-Figurationen Else Lasker-Schülers als Spiel mit der Autorrolle: Ein Beitrag zur Poetologie des modernene Autors*. Stuttgart: M&P Verlag, 1992.
Fichte, J. G. *Die Anweisung zum seligen Leben*, vol. 5 of 8 volumes, *Johann Gottlieb Fichte's Sämmtliche Werke*, ed. J. H. Fichte. Berlin: Veit und Comp., 1848.
———. *Reden an die deutsche Nation*, vol. 7, *Johann Gottlieb Fichte's Sämmtliche Werke*, ed. J. H. Fichte. Berlin: Veit und Comp., 1848.
Finkielkraut, Alain. *The Defeat of the Mind*, trans. Judith Friedlander. New York: Columbia University Press, 1995.
Fischer, Eugen. *Die Rehobother Bastards und das Bastardsproblem beim Menschen*. Jena: Verlag von Gustav Fischer, 1913.
Fisher, Mark. "The Rewriting on the Wall," *Washington Post*. July 24, 1994.
Forster, Leonard, ed. *German Tales of Our Time*. Toronto: Harrap, 1953.
Foucault, Michel. *The History of Sexuality*, vol. 1 of 3 volumes, trans. Robert Hurley. New York: Vintage, 1980.
Fremegen, Gisela. *Und wenn du dazu schwarz bist: Berichte schwarzer Frauen in der Bundesrepublik*. Bremen: Edition CON, 1984.
Friedländer, Saul. *Reflections of Nazism: An Essay on Kitsch and Death*. New York: Harper & Row, 1984.
Friedrich, Jörg. "Verbrechen, die sich auszahlen: Nazi-Opfer und Nazi-Täter vor dem Entschädigungsamt," *Die Zeit* (June 30, 1989), 15–16.
Frye, Northrop. *Anatomy of Criticism: Four Essays*. Princeton, NJ: Princeton University Press, 1957.
Gallati, Ernst. *Hermann Boeschenstein: Eine Biographie*. Bern: Lang, 1995.
Garton, Janet, trans. *Jens Bjørneboe: Prophet Without Honor: Contributions to the Study of World Literature IX*. Westport, CT: Greenwood Press, 1986.
Gary, Romain. *The Dance of Genghis Cohn*. New York: World Publishing, 1968.
Gebhardt, Jürgen. *Die Revolution des Geistes: Politisches Denken in Deutschland 1770–1830: Goethe—Kant—Fichte—Hegel—Humboldt*. Munich: List Verlag, 1968.
Geisner, Christoph. *Das Gefängnis der Wünsche: Roman*. Zurich: Nagel & Kimche, 1992.
Gemes, Ken. "Nietzsche's Critique of Truth," *Philosophy and Phenomenological Research* 52.1 (1992): 47–65.
Gestrein, Norbert. *Der Kommerzialrat*. Frankfurt a.M.: Suhrkamp, 1995.
Geyer, Michael, and Miriam Hansen,. "German-Jewish Memory and National Consciousness," in *Holocaust Remembrance: The Shapes of Memory*, ed. Geoffrey Hartman, pp. 175–190. Cambridge, MA: Basil Blackwell, 1994.
Gilman, Sander L. *Jews in Today's German Culture*. Bloomington: Indiana University Press, 1995.

———. *On Blackness Without Blacks: Essays on the Image of the Black in Germany.* Boston: G.K. Hall & Co., 1982.

———. *The Case of Sigmund Freud: Medicine and Identity in the Fin de Siècle.* Baltimore: The Johns Hopkins University Press, 1993.

———. *The Jews' Body.* New York: Routledge, 1991.

Gilman, Sander L., and Rosemarie K. Lester. "Blacks in Germany and German Blacks: A Little Known Aspect of Black History," in *Blacks and German Culture,* ed. Reinhold Grimm and Jost Hermand, pp. 113–134. Madison: University of Wisconsin Press, 1986.

Glenn, Jerry. *Paul Celan,* New York: Twayne, 1973.

Giordano, Ralph. *Die zweite Schuld oder Von der Last Deutscher zu sein.* Hamburg: Rasch & Röring Verlag, 1987.

Grass, Günther. *Deutscher Lastenausgleich: Wider das dumpfe Einheitsgebot. Reden und Gespräche.* Frankfurt a.M.: Suhrkamp, 1990.

———. *Ein weites Feld.* Göttingen: Steidl, 1995.

———. *Two States—One Nation?* trans. Krishna Winston with A. S. Wensinger. San Diego: Harcourt, Brace, Jovanovich, 1990.

Grieg, Nordahl. "The Sprinters," in *Modern Scandinavian Poetry: The Panorama of Poetry 1900–1975,* ed. Martin Allwood. Mullsjö, Sweden: Anglo-American Center, 1982.

Grillparzer, Franz. *Sämmtliche Werke,* ed. August Sauer. Vienna: Schroll, 1925.

Grünbein, Durs. *Falten und Fallen.* Frankfurt a.M.: Suhrkamp, 1994.

———. *Schädelbasislektion.* Frankfurt a.M.: Suhrkamp, 1993.

Heer, Friedrich. *Der Glaube des Adolf Hitler: Anatomie einer persönlichen Religiosität.* Munich: Bechtle, 1968.

Haar, Michel. "The Play of Nietzsche in Derrida," in *Derrida: A Critical Reader,* ed. David C. Wood, pp. 52–71. Oxford: Blackwell, 1992.

Habermas, Jürgen. *Die Normalität einer Berliner Republik.* Frankfurt a.M.: Suhrkamp, 1995.

———. *Die nachholende Revolution: Kleine politische Schriften VII.* Frankfurt a.M.: Suhrkamp, 1990.

———. *The Philosophical Discourse of Modernity: Twelve Lectures,* trans. Frederick G. Lawrence. Cambridge, MA: MIT Press, 1987.

———. "Yet Again: German Identity—A Unified Nation of Angry DM-Burghers," *New German Critique* 52 (1991): 84–101.

Hahnl, Hans Heinz. *Hexeneinmaleins.* Vienna: Österreichische Staatsbücherei, 1993.

Hamburger, Michael, ed. and trans. *Poems of Paul Celan.* London: Persea, 1988.

Hartung, Harald. "Drei Lyriker aus Israel," *Merkur* 537 (1993): 1091–1096.

Harvey, Paul. *The Oxford Companion to Classical Literature.* Oxford: Oxford University Press, 1984.

Haslinger, Josef. "Die Vernichtung des Österreichischen," *Standard Album: Buchmesse Spezial.* Oct. 6, 1995, 1f.

Hauptmann, Gerhart. *Gesammelte Werke,* ed. Hans Egon Hass. Berlin/Hamburg: Fischer, 1966.

Heger, Wanda. *Jeden Freitag vor dem Tor.* Munich: Schneekluth Verlag, 1989.

Heidegger, Martin. *Grundbegriffe. Freiburger Vorlesung Sommersemester 1941*, ed. Petra Jaeger. Frankfurt a. M.: Klostermann, 1981.

———. *Introduction to Metaphysics*, trans. Ralph Mannheim. Garden City, NJ: Anchor Books, 1959.

———. "The Rectorate 1933/4: Facts and Thoughts," trans. Karsten Harries *Review of Metaphysics* 38 (1985): 467–502.

Heine, Heinrich. *Deutschland: A Winter's Tale*, trans. T. J. Reed. London: Angel Books, 1986.

———. *Deutschland. Ein Wintermärchen*. Stuttgart: Reclam, 1977.

Helwerth, Ulrike, and Gislinde Schwarz, eds. *Von Muttis und Emanzen: Feministinnen in Ost- und Westdeutschland*. Frankfurt a.M.: Fischer, 1995.

Hendrich, Dietrich. *Eine Republik Deutschland: Reflexionen auf dem Weg aus der deutschen Teilung*. Frankfurt a.M.: Suhrkamp, 1990

Henningsen, Manfred. "Der deutsche Sondwerweg—am Ende?" *Merkur* 49.5 (May 1995): 379–389.

Hering, Rainer. "Der 'Fall Nieland' und sein Richter. Zur Kontinuität in der Hamburger Justiz zwischen 'Drittem Reich' und Bundesrepublik," *Zeitschrift des Vereins für Hamburgische Geschichte* 81 (1995): 207–222.

Hessing, Jakob. *Die Heimkehr einer jüdischen Emigrantin: Else Lasker-Schülers mythisierende Rezeption 1945–1971*. Tübingen: Niemeyer, 1993.

———. "Gedichte nach Auschwitz," *Merkur* 524 (1992): 980–992.

Hilbert, Gerhard. *Moderne Willensziele*. Leipzig: Deichert, 1911.

Hillgruber, Andreas. *Zweierlei Untergang: Die Zerschlagung des Deutschen Reiches und das Ende des europäischen Judentums*. Berlin: Siedler, 1986.

Hirschmann, C., and O. Lehmann. "Die österreichische Literatur ist mutiger und vitaler. John Irving, Siegfried Unseld, Hellmuth Karasek, und Dacia Maraini über ihre Präferenzen," *News* 42 (Oct. 19, 1995), 176.

Hitler, Adolf. *Mein Kampf*, trans. Ralph Mannheim. Boston: Houghton Miflin, 1943.

———. *Hitler's Secret Conversations: 1941–1944*, ed. H. R. Trevor-Roper, trans. Norman Cameron and R. H. Stevens. New York: Farrar, Straus and Young, 1953.

Hoel, Sigurd. *Sigurd Hoel: Litteraere Essays*, ed. Helge Nordahl. Oslo: Dreyer, 1990.

Hofmannsthal, Hugo von. *Reden und Aufsätze II: 1914–1924* in *Gesammelte Werke*, vol. 9 of 10 volumes, ed. Bernd Schoeller and Rudolf Hirsh. Frankfurt a.M.: Fischer, 1979.

Holub, Robert C. "Nietzsche and the Women's Question," *The German Quarterly* 68.1 (1995): 67–71.

Homer. *The Iliad*, trans. Robert Fagles. New York: Penguin, 1990.

Honigmann, Barbara. "Damals, dann und danach," *Literaturmagazin* 34 (1994): 24–25.

———. *Eine Liebe aus nichts*. Berlin: Rowohlt, 1991.

Honold, Alexander, and Ulrich Schreiber, eds. *Die Bilderwelt des Peter Weiss*. Hamburg: Argument, 1995.

hooks, bell. "The Feminazi Mystique," *Transition* 7.1/73 (1998): 156–162.

Huyssen, Andreas. *Twilight Memories: Marking Time in a Culture of Amnesia*. New York: Routledge, 1995.

Jaspers, Karl. *Die Schuldfrage: Ein Beitrag zur deutschen Frage.* Zurich: Artemis-Verlag, 1946.

———. *Wohin treibt die Bundesrepublik? Tatsachen—Gefahren—Chancen.* Munich: Piper, 1988.

Jedan, Dieter. "Shifting Enrollment Patterns: Departmental Perspectives," *ADFL Bulletin* 30.1 (1998): 15–17.

Jelinek, Elfriede. *Die Kinder der Toten.* Reinbek: Rowohlt, 1995.

Jenks, Chris. *Visual Culture.* New York: Routledge, 1993.

Joeres, Ruth-Ellen B. "Sisterhood? Jede für sich? Gedanken über die heutige feministische Diskussion in den USA," *Feministische Studien* 12.1 (May 1994): 6–16.

———. "Von Frauenstudien zur Frauenforschung: Neuere Trends im akademischen Feminismus in den USA," *Feministische Studien* 6.1 (Nov. 1988): 129–135.

———. " 'Language Is Also a Place of Struggle': The Language of Feminism and the Language of American *Germanistik*," *Women in German Yearbook 8: Feminist Studies in German Literature and Culture* (1993), 247–257.

Johnson, Uwe. *Anniversaries: From the Life of Gesine Cresspahl*, 2 vols. New York: Harcourt Brace Jovanovich, 1975 and 1987.

Jones, Nigel H. *Hitler's Heralds: The Story of the Freikorps, 1918–1923.* New York: Dorset Press, 1992.

Jünger, Ernst. *Das Wäldchen 125,* in *Ernst Jünger Werke*, vol. 1 of 10 volumes,*Tagebücher* 1. Stuttgart: Ernst Klett Verlag, 1960.

———. *Der Kampf als inneres Erlebnis* in, *Ernst Jünger Werke* vol. 5, Essays 1. Stuttgart: Ernst Klett Verlag, 1960.

Kaes, Anton. *From Hitler to Heimat: The Return of History as Film.* Cambridge, MA: Harvard University Press, 1989.

Kaufmann, Walter. *Nietzsche: Philosopher, Psychologist, Antichrist.* Princeton, NJ: Princeton University Press, 1950.

———. ed. and trans., *The Portable Nietzsche.* New York: Viking, 1961.

Kinzer, Steven. "Germans Reflect on Meaning of Auschwitz," *New York Times*, Jan. 28, 1995.

Klee, Ernst, Will Dressen, and Volker Riess, eds. *'The Good Old Days': The Holocaust as Seen by Its Perpetrators and Bystanders*, trans. Deborah Brunstone. New York: The Free Press, 1991.

Kleist, Heinrich von. *Penthesilea*, trans. Humphry Trevelyan, in *Heinrich von Kleist: Five Plays*, ed. Walter Hinderer, pp. 159–258. New York: Continuum, 1982.

———. *Sämtliche Werke und Briefe in vier Bänden*, ed. Helmut Sembdner. Munich: Hanser, 1982.

Kling, Thomas. *erprobung herzstärkender mittel. geschmacksverstärker. brennstabm. nacht. sicht. gerät. Ausgewählte Gedichte 1981–1993.* Frankfurt a.M.: Suhrkamp, 1994.

Klüsener, Erika. *Else Lasker-Schüler.* Hamburg: Reinbeck/Rororo, 1980.

Knapp, Fritz Peter, ed. *Die Literatur des Früh- und Hochmittelalters in den Bistümern Passau, Salzburg, Brixen und Trient von den Anfängen bis zum Jahre 1273.*

Geschichte der Literatur in Österreich von den Anfängen bis zur Gegenwart, ed. Herbert Zeman, vol. 1. Graz: Bundesverlag, 1994.

Koebner, Thomas. "Triumph des Wollens," *Kölner Stadt-Anzeiger*, Feb. 26, 1994.

Koch, Gertrud. *Die Einstellung ist Die Einstellung: Visuelle Konstruktion des Judentums*. Frankfurt a.M.: Suhrkamp, 1992.

Koelb, Clayton, ed. *Nietzsche as Postmodernist: Essays Pro and Contra*. Albany: State University of New York Press, 1990.

Koepnick, Lutz. "Fascist Aesthetics Revisited," *Modernism/Modernity* 6.1 (1999): 51–73.

Kolakowski, Leszek. *Modernity on Endless Trial*. Chicago: University of Chicago Press, 1990.

Komar, Kathleen L. "The Communal Self: Re-Membering Female Identity in the Works of Christa Wolf and Monique Wittig," *Comparative Literature* 44.1 (1992): 42–58.

Kramer, Jane. "The Politics of Memory," *New Yorker* (Aug. 14, 1995): 48–65.

Krondorfer, Björn. *Remembrance and Reconciliation*. New Haven, CT: Yale University Press, 1995.

Kuhn, Anna. K. *Christa Wolf's Utopian Vision: From Marxism to Feminism*. Cambridge: Cambridge University Press, 1988.

Labanyi, Peter. "Images of Fascism: Visualization and Aestheticization in the Third Reich," in *The Burden of German History 1919–45*, ed. Michael Laffan. London: Methuen, 1988.

Laqueur, Walter. "Fin-de-siècle; Once More With Feeling," *Journal of Contemporary History* 31 (1996): 5–47.

Lasker-Schüler, Else. *Gesammelte Werke*, vol. 2, *Prosa und Schauspiele*. 3 volumes, ed. Friedrich Kempf. Munich: Kösel Verlag, 1962.

———. *Wo ist unser buntes Theben: Briefe von Else Lasker-Schüler*, ed. Margarete Kupper. Vol. 2 of 2 volumes. Munich: Kösel Verlag, 1969.

———. *Ichundich*, ed. Margarete Kupper. Munich: Kosel Verlag, 1980.

Lebzelter, Gisela. "Die 'schwarze Schmach': Vorurteile, Propaganda, Mythos," *Geschichte und Gesellschaft* 11 (1985): 37–58.

Lederer, Zdenek. *Ghetto Theresienstadt*, trans. K. Weisskopf. London: Edward Goldston & Son, Ltd., 1953.

Le Gloannec, Anne-Marie. "On German Identity," *Daedalus* 123.1 (Winter 1994): 129–148.

Leiter, Brian. "Perspectivism in Nietzsche's Genealogy of Morals," in *Nietzsche, Genealogy, Morality: Essays on Nietzsche's "Genealogy of Morals,"* ed. Richard Schacht, pp. 334–357. Berkeley: University of California Press, 1994.

Lester, Rosemarie. *Trivialneger: Das Bild des Schwarzen im westdeutschen Illustriertenroman*. Stuttgart: Akademischer Verlag Hans Dieter Heinz, 1982.

Leonhardt, Rudolf Walter. *X-mal Deutschland*. Munich: Piper, 1962.

Levkov, Ilya. *Bitburg and Beyond*. New York: Shapolsky, 1987.

Lilla, Mark. "A Taste for Pain: Michel Foucault and the Outer Reaches of Human Experience," *Times Literary Supplement*, March 26, 1993.

Lipstadt, Deborah. *Denying the Holocaust: The Growing Assault on Truth and Memory*. New York: Plume, 1994.

Longum, Leif. *Drama-analyser fra Holberg til Hoem*. Bergen: Bergen University Press, 1977.
Lorentzen, Justin J. "Reich Dreams: Ritual Horror and Armoured Bodies," in *Visual Culture*, ed. Chris Jenks, pp. 161–169. New York: Routledge, 1995.
Love, Myra. "Christa Wolf and Feminism: Breaking the Patriarchal Connection," *New German Critique* 16 (1979): 31–53.
Lugones, Maria. "Purity, Impurity, and Separation," *Signs* 19.2 (Winter 1994): 458–479.
Lyotard, Jean-Francois. *The Postmodern Condition: A Report on Knowledge*, trans. Geoff Bennington and Brian Massumi. Minneapolis: University of Minnesota Press, 1984.
———. *Heidegger and "the jews,"* trans. Andreas Michel and Mark. S. Roberts. Minneapolis: University of Minnesota Press, 1990.
Mann, Thomas. "Kultur und Sozialismus," in *Werke: Das essayistische Werk*, vol. 2 of 8 volumes, ed. Hans Bürgin, pp. 165–173. Frankfurt a.M.: Fischer, 1968.
———. "Nietzsche's Philosophy in the Light of Contemporary Events," in *Thomas Mann's Address: Delivered at the Library of Congress 1942–1949*. Washington: Library of Congress, 1963.
———. *Reflections of a Nonpolitical Man*, trans. Walter D. Morris. New York: Frederick Ungar, 1983.
———. "Warum ich nicht nach Deutschland zurückgehe." *Gesammelte Werke in zwölf Bänden*, vol. 12, ed. Hans Bürgin, pp. 953–962. Frankfurt a.M.: S. Fischer, 1960.
Marc, Franz. *Letters From the War*, ed. Klaus Lankheit and Uwe Steffen, trans. Lieselotte Dieckmann. New York: Peter Lang, 1992.
Markovits, Andrei S. "The Politics of Memory: The Predicament of German-Jewish Relations in the Former Bundesrepublik and in Post-Wall Deutschland," in *Brücken über dem Abgrund: Auseinandersetzungen mit jüdischer Leidenserfahrung, Antisemitismus und Exil. Festschrift für Harry Zohn*, ed. Amy Colin and Elisabeth Strenger, pp. 63–78. Munich: Fink, 1994.
Marks, Elise. "The Alienation of 'I': Christa Wolf and Militarism," *Mosaic* 23.3 (1990): 73–85.
Marks, Sally. "Black Watch on the Rhine: A Study in Propaganda, Prejudice and Prurience," *European Studies Review* 13 (1983): 297–334.
Marx, Karl. "Manifesto of the Communist Party," in *The Marx-Engels Reader*, ed. Robert C. Tucker, pp. 469–500. New York: Norton: 1972.
Mattenklott, Gert. "Zur Darstellung der Shoa in deutscher Nachkriegsliteratur," *Jüdischer Almanach 1993*. Frankfurt a.M.: Jüdischer Verlag, 1993.
McCarthy, John A., and Katrin Schneider, eds. *The Future of 'Germanistik' in the USA: Changing Our Prospects*. Nashville, TN: Vanderbilt University Press, 1996.
McDonald, Christie V., ed. *The Ear of the Other: Otobiography, Transference, Translation*, trans. Peggy Kamuf and Avital Ronell (New York: Schocken, 1985).
Meinecke, Friedrich. *The German Catastrophe*. Boston: Beacon Press, 1963.
Menasse, Robert. *Schubumkehr*. Salzburg: Residenz, 1995.
Mertes, Michael. "The Germans and Historical Inhibitions," *German Comments* 37 (1995): 15–18.

Miller, Jim. *The Passion of Michel Foucault.* New York: Anchor Books, 1993.
Mosse, George. *Fallen Soldiers: Reshaping the Memory of the World Wars.* New York: Oxford University Press, 1990.
———. *The Nationalization of the Masses: Political Symbolism and Mass Movements in Germany from the Napoleonic Wars Through the Third Reich.* New York: Howard Fertig, 1975.
———. *Toward the Final Solution: A History of European Racism.* New York: Howard Fertig, 1978.
Mulvey, Laura. *Visual and Other Pleasures.* Bloomington: Indiana University Press, 1989.
Mundimbe, V.Y. *The Invention of Africa.* Bloomington: Indiana University Press, 1988.
Nachbaur, Petra, and Sigurd Paul, eds. *Literatur über Literatur: Eine österreichische Anthologie.* Graz: Scheichl, 1995.
Nagl, Johann Willibald, Jakob Zeidler, and Eduard Castle, eds. *Deutsch-Österreichische Literaturgeschichte: Ein Handbuch zur Geschichte der deutschen Dichtung in Österreich in vier Bänden.* Vienna: Verlagsbuchhandlung Carl Fromme, 1899–1938.
Nehamas, Alexander. "Subject and Abject: The Life of Michel Foucault," *The New Republic*, Feb. 15, 1993.
Nieland, Friedrich. *Wieviel Welt [Geld]-Kriege müssen die Völker noch verlieren? Offener Brief an alle Bundesminister und Parlamentarier der Bundesrepublik.* Stade: Heimberg, 1957.
Nietzsche, Friedrich. *The Antichrist,* in *The Portable Nietzsche,* ed. and trans. Walter Kaufmann, pp. 592–593. New York: Viking, 1961.
Nizon, Paul. "Ich bin ein Hund meiner Zeit: Im Gespräch mit Peter Henning und Horst Sumerauer," *Akzente* 41.2 (April 1994): 203–214.
Noll, Chaim. *Taube und Stern. Roma Hebraica. Eine Spurensuche.* Hünefelden-Gnadenthal: Präsenz, 1994.
Nolte, Ernst. "Between Myth and Revisionism," in *Aspects of the Third Reich,* ed. H. W. Koch, pp. 17–38. London: Macmillan, 1985.
———. *Der europäische Bürgerkrieg 1917–1945: Nationalsozialismus und Bolschewismus.* Frankfurt: Ullstein, 1987.
———. *Nietzsche und der Nietzscheanismus.* Frankfurt a.M.: Propyläen, 1990.
Ochse, Katharina. " 'What Could Be More Fruitful, More Healing, More Purifying?' Representations of Jews in the German Media After 1989," in *Reemerging Jewish Culture in Germany*, ed. Sander L. Gilman and Karen Remmler, pp. 113–129. New York: New York University Press, 1994.
Odenwald, Theodor. *Friedrich Nietzsche und das heutige Christentum.* Giessen: Alfred Töpelmann, 1926.
Oliver, Kelly. *Womanizing Nietzsche: Philosophy's Relation to the "Feminine."* New York: Routledge, 1995.
Paeffgen, Manfred. *Das Bild Schwarz-Afrikas in der öffentlichen Meinung der Bundesrepublik Deutschlands 1949–1972.* Arnold-Bergstraeser Institut Materialen zu Entwicklung und Politik. Munich: Weltforum, 1976.

Page, Clarence. "What Color Are You?" *Chicago Tribune*, Sept. 9, 1995.
Pagis, Dan. *Erdichteter Mensch*, trans. Tuvia Rübner. Frankfurt a.M.: Jüdischer Verlag, 1993.
Parker, Andrew, Mary Russon, Doris Sommer, and Patricia Yaeger, eds. *Nationalisms and Sexualities*. New York: Routledge, 1992.
Parry, Adam. "The Language of Achilles," *Transactions of the American Philological Association* 87 (1956): 1–7.
Patton, Paul, ed. *Nietzsche, Feminism and Political Theory*. New York: Routledge, 1993.
Pauls, Rolf, interview. In *Thirty Years of Diplomatic Relations Between the Federal Republic of Germany and Israel*, ed. Otto Romberg and Heiner Lichtenstein, pp. 50–54. Frankfurt a.M.: Tribüne Verlag, 1995.
Pickle, Linda Schelbitzki. "Christa Wolf's *Cassandra*: Parallels to Feminism in the West," *Critique* 28.3 (1987): 149–157.
Pinthus, Kurt, ed. *Menschheitsdämmerung: Ein Document des Expressionismus*. Hamburg: Rowohlt Verlag, 1959.
Pois, Robert. *National Socialism and the Religion of Nature*. London: Croom Helm, 1986.
Pomerin, Reiner. *Sterilisierung der Rheinlandsbastarde: Das Schicksal einer farbigen deutschen Minderheit 1918–1937*. Düsseldorf: Droste Verlag, 1979.
Quack, Sibylle. "Das Bewahren des Grauens: Mahnwachen, Denkmäle und KZ-Gedenkstätten," *Vorgänge* 125 (1995): 35–47.
Ransmayr, Christoph. *Die Schrecken des Eises und der Finsternis*. Frankfurt a.M.: Fischer, 1987.
———. *Morbus Kithara*. Frankfurt a.M.: Fischer, 1995.
Rauschning, Hermann. *Hitler Speaks: A Series of Political Conversations With Adolf Hitler on His Real Aims*. London: Heinemann, 1939.
Reich, Asher. *Arbeiten auf Papier. Gedichte*, trans. Efrat Gal-Ed et al. Reinbek: Rowohlt, 1992.
Remarque, Erich Maria. *All Quiet on the Western Front*, trans. A. W. Wheen. New York: Ballantine Books, 1984.
Rentschler, Eric. *The Ministry of Illusion: Nazi Cinema and Its Afterlife*. Cambridge, MA: Harvard University Press, 1996.
Rheinz, Hanna. "Bitterkraut," *Freitag*, July 10, 1992.
Rhodes, James M. *The Hitler Movement: A Modern Millenarian Movement*. Stanford: Stanford University Press, 1980.
Rich, Adrienne. "When We Dead Awaken: Writing as Re-Vision (1971)," in Adrienne Rich, *On Lies, Secrets, and Silence: Selected Prose 1966–1978*. New York: Norton, 1979.
Richardson, John. *Nietzsche's System*. New York: Oxford University Press, 1996.
Riefensathl, Leni. *Leni Riefenstahl: A Memoir*. New York: St. Martin's Press, 1992.
Roche, Jörg, and Thomas Salumets, eds. *Germanics Under Construction*. Munich: Luicium, 1996.
Rockmore, Tom. *Heidegger's Nazism and Philosophy*. Berkeley: University of California Press, 1992.

Rohnstock, Katrin, ed. *Stiefschwestern: Was Ost-Frauen und West-Frauen voneinander denken*. Frankfurt a.M.: Fischer, 1994.
Ronnell, Avital. *Finitudes's Score: Essays for the End of the Millennium*. Lincoln: University of Nebraska Press, 1994.
Rosen, Klaus-Henning. "Vorurteile im Verborgenen. Zum Antisemitismus in der Bundesrepublik Deutschland," in *Antisemitismus. Von der Judenfeindschaft zum Holocaust*, ed. Herbert A. Strauss and Norbert Kampe, pp. 256–279. Bonn: Bundeszentrale, 1984.
Roth, Gerhard. *Das doppelköpfige Österreich*. Frankfurt a.M.: Fischer, 1995.
Ryan, Judith. "Twilight Zones: Myth, Fairy Tale, and Utopia in *No Place on Earth* and *Cassandra*," in *Responses to Christa Wolf: Critical Essays*, ed. Marilyn Sibley Fries, pp. 312–325. Detroit: Wayne State University Press, 1989.
Sachs, Nelly. *Fahrt ins Staublose*. Frankfurt a.M.: Suhrkamp, 1988.
———. *Suche nach Lebenden*. Frankfurt a.M.: Suhrkamp, 1971.
Sadler, Ted. "The Postmodernist Politicization of Nietzsche," in *Nietzsche, Feminism and Political Theory*, ed. Paul Patton, pp. 225–243. New York: Routledge, 1993.
Saint Point, Valentine de. "Futurist Manifesto of Lust 1913," in *Futurist Manifestos*, ed. Umbro Apollonio, pp. 70–74. New York: Viking 1973.
———. "Manifesto of the Futurist Woman," in *Futurism and Futurisms*, ed. Karl Hulten, pp. 602–603. New York: Abbeville Press, 1986.
Santner, Eric L. "The Trouble With Hitler: Postwar German Aesthetics and the Legacy of Fascism," *New German Critique* 57 (1992): 5–24.
Sax, Benjamin, and Dieter Kuntz, eds. *Inside Hitler's Germany: A Documentary History of Life in the Third Reich*. Lexington: D.C. Heath & Co., 1994.
Schacht, Richard, ed. *Nietzsche, Genealogy, Morality: Essays on Nietzsche's "Genealogy of Morals."* Berkeley: University of California Press, 1994.
Schenk, Ralf. "Die Nazis, Das Kino, die Hilflosigkeit," *Neues Deutschland*, Feb. 17, 1994.
Scheider, Theodor. *Hermann Rauschnings "Gespräche mit Hitler" als Geschichtsquelle*. Opladen: Westdeutscher Verlag, 1972.
Schindel, Robert. "Vom Indirekten II," in his *Ohneland: Gedichte vom Holz der Paradeiserbäume. 1979–1984*, p. 105. Frankfurt a.M.: Suhrkamp, 1986.
Schlösser, Manfred, ed. *An den Wind geschrieben: Lyrik der Freiheit 1933–1945*. Darmstadt: Agora, 1960.
Schmidt-Dengler, Wendelin. "Haltbar bis zur nächsten Ernte?" *Die Presse: Spectrum* 7.8 (Oct. 1995): 1f.
Schödel, Helmut. "Bruder Eichmann, Bruder Sharon," *Die Zeit* (Feb. 4, 1983), 12.
Schulz, Dagmar, ed. *Farbe Bekennen*. Berlin: Orlanda, 1986.
Schulz, Gerhard. "Die Steppenwölfin schnuppert," *Frankfurter Allgemeine Zeitung*, May 23, 1992.
Schütt, Peter. *Der Mohr hat seine Schuldigkeit getan . . . Gibt es Rassismus in der Bundesrepublik? Eine Streitschrift*. Dortmund: Weltkreis, 1981.
Seibt, Gustav. "Historien der Deutschen: Ein Literaturbericht," *Merkur* 47.1 (1993): 46–58.
Seligmann, Raphael. *Rubinsteins Versteigerung*. Munich: dtv, 1989.

Shapiro, Gary. "Translating, Repeating, Naming: Foucault, Derrida and *The Genealogy of Morals*," in *Nietzsche as Postmodernist: Essays Pro and Contra*. Albany: State University of New York Press, 1990. pp. 39–55.
Sichrovsky, Peter. *Born Guilty: Children of Nazi Families*. New York: Basic Books, 1988.
Silbermann, Edith. *Begegnung mit Paul Celan: Erninnerung und Interpretation*. Aachen: Rimbaud, 1993.
Sironneau, Jean-Pierre. *Sécularisation et religions politiques*. New York: Mouton, 1982.
Smith, Gregory Bruce. *Nietzsche, Heidegger and the Transition to Postmodernity*. Chicago: University of Chicago Press, 1996.
Sokel, Walter H. "Political Uses and Abuses of Nietzsche in Walter Kaufmann's Image of Nietzsche," *Nietzsche-Studien* 12 (1983): 436–442.
Solomon, Robert C. "Nietzsche, Postmodernism and Resentment: A Genealogical Hypothesis," in *Nietzsche as Postmodernist: Essays Pro and Contra*. Albany: State University of New York Press, 1990: 267–293.
Sombart, Werner. *Die Zukunft der Juden*. Leipzig: Duncker und Humblot, 1912.
Sontag, Susan. "Fascinating Fascism," in Susan Sontag, *Under the Sign of Saturn*, pp. 73–105. New York: Farrrar, Straus, Giroux, 1972.
Speer, Albert. *Inside the Third Reich: Memoirs*, trans. Richard and Clara Winston. New York: Macmillan, 1970.
Starkman, Ruth. "Mother of All Spectacles: Ray Müller's *The Wonderful, Horrible Life of Leni Riefenstahl*," *Film Quarterly* 51.2 (1997-1998): 21–31.
Steinbach, Peter. "Der Historikerstreit," *Tribune* 34.135 (1995): 120–133.
Steiner, George. "Das lange Leben der Metaphorik: Ein Versuch über die *Shoah*," trans. Jörg Trobitius, *Akzente* 3 (1987): 194–212.
———. "The Long Life of Metaphor," in *Writing and the Holocaust*, ed. Berel Lang, pp. 154–171. New York: Holmes & Meier, 1988.
Stern, Frank. *Im Anfang war Auschwitz: Antisemitismus und Philosemitismus im deutschen Nachkrieg*. Gerlingen: Blecher Verlag, 1991.
Syberberg, Hans-Jürgen. *Vom Unglück und Glück der Kunst in Deutschland nach dem letzten Kriege*. Munich: Matthes & Seitz, 1990.
———. *Hitler: A Film From Germany*. WDR (Germany): Academy Video VHS, 420 mins., 1977.
Szyszkowitz, Gerald. *Die Badenweiler oder Nichts wird bleiben von Österreich*. Vienna: Boesskraut & Bernardi, 1995.
Tabucchi, Antonio. *Erklärt Pereira*. Munich: Carl Hanser, 1995.
Thamer, Hans-Ulrich. "Hitler, ein Film: Bilanz der ZDF-Reihe," *Frankfurter Allgemeine Zeitung*, Dec. 13, 1995.
Thielicke, Helmut. "Der Antisemitismus in Hamburg," *Die Kirche in Hamburg* 6.5 (1959): 3–4.
Thim, Karin, and DuRell Echols. *Schwarze in Deutschland*. Munich: Piper, 1973.
Thurnher, Eugen. "Das Problem der Periodenbildung in der österreichischen Literaturgeschichtsschreibung," in *Studien zur Literatur des 19. Und 20. Jahrhunderts in Österreich: Festschrift für Alfred Doppler zum 60. Geburtstag*,

ed. Johann Holzner, Michael Klein, Wolfgang Wisemüller, pp. 271–274. Innsbruck: Universität Innsbruck, 1981.
Toew, John. Review of *The Nietzsche Legacy* by Steven E. Aschheim, in *Central European History* 26.3 (1993): 353–355.
Tucker, Robert C., ed., *The Marx-Engels Reader*. New York: Norton, 1972.
Turneaure, Brigitte M. *Im Spiegel der Literatur: Kurzprosa aus dem 20. Jahrhundert*. New York: Norton, 1992.
Václavek, Ludvík. "Deutsche Lyrik im Ghetto Theresienstadt 1941–1945," *Weimarer Beiträge* 5 (1982): 14–34.
Van Cleve, John, and A. Leslie Willson, eds. *Remarks on the Needed Reform of German Studies in the United States*. Columbia, SC: Camden House, 1993.
Vaughn, Edwin Campion. *Some Desperate Glory: The World War I Diary of a British Officer*. New York: Henry Holt & Co., 1981.
Virilio, Paul. *The Vision Machine*. Bloomington: Indiana University Press, 1994.
Volmert, Johannes. *Ernst Jünger: "In Stahlgewittern."* Munich: Wilhelm Fink Verlag, 1985.
Von Krockow, Christian Graf. *Die Deutschen in ihrem Jahrhundert: 1890–1990*. Reinbeck bei Hamburg: Rowohlt, 1990.
Waite, Robert G. L. *Vanguard of Nazism: The Free Corps Movement in Postwar Germany, 1918–1923*. New York: W. W. Norton, 1969.
Waldstein, Edith. "Christa Wolf's *Kein Ort. Nirgends*: A Dialogic Re-Vision," in *The Enlightenment and Its legacy: Studies in German Literature in Honor of Helga Slessarev*, ed. Sara Friedrichsmeyer and Barbara Becker-Cantarino, pp. 181–193. Bonn: Bouvier, 1991.
Warren, Mark. *Nietzsche and Political Thought*. Cambridge, MA: MIT Press, 1988.
Washburn, Katharine, and Margret Guillemin, trans. *Paul Celan: Last Poems*. San Francisco: North Point Press, 1986.
Wassermann, Jakob. *My Life as a German and Jew*. London: George Allen & Unwin, 1933.
Weber, Ilse. *Theresienstadt*. Tel Aviv: Mafil, 1964.
Welch, John. "Twelve Years Under Hitler," *Pittsburgh Courier*, May 6, 1944.
Weiss, Peter. *Die Aesthetik des Widerstands,* 3 vols. Frankfurt a.M.: Suhrkamp, 1975, 1978, 1981.
Weiss, Walter. "Das Salzburger Projekt einer österreichischen Literaturgeschichte: Konzept und Probleme," *Sprachkunst* 14.2 (1983): 56–66.
Whalen, Robert Weldon. *Bitter Wounds: German Victims of the Great War, 1914–1939*. Ithaca: Cornell University Press, 1984.
Wilson, Jean. *The Challenge of Belatedness: Goethe, Kleist, Hofmannsthal*. Lanham, MD: University Press of America, 1991.
Windmöller, Eva. "Mein Schwiegersohn, der Neger," *Stern* 39 (1972): 80–87.
Winkler, Heinrich August. "Rebuilding A Nation: The Germans Before and After Reunification," *Daedalus* 123.1 (1994): 107–127.
Winter, Gabriele. "Suche nach Identifikation," *Auftritt: Rhein-Main-Illustrierte*, March 1989.
Winterson, Jeanette. *Sexing the Cherry*. London: Vintage, 1989.

Wolf, Christa. *Cassandra: A Novel and Four Essays*, trans. Jan van Heurck. New York: Farrar, Straus & Giroux, 1984.

———. "Documentation: Christa Wolf," *The German Quarterly* 57.1 (1984): 91–115.

———. "In Touch," trans. Jeanette Clausen, in *German Feminism: Readings in Politics and Literature*, ed. Edith Hoshino Altbach, Jeanette Clausen, Dagmar Schultz, and Naomi Stephan, pp. 161–169. Albany: State University of New York Press, 1984.

———. *The Author's Dimension: Selected Essays*, ed. Alexander Stephan, trans. Jan van Heurck. New York: Farrar, Straus, & Giroux, 1993.

———. *The Fourth Dimension: Interviews With Christa Wolf*, trans. Hilary Pilkington. London: Verso, 1988.

Wolffsohn, Michael. *Eternal Guilt? Forty Years of German-Jewish-Israeli Relations*. New York: Columbia University Press, 1993.

———. *Ewige Schuld? 40 Jahre deutsch-judisch-israelische Beziehungen*. Munich: Piper, 1988.

———. *Keine Angst vor Deutschland*. Erlangen: Straube, 1990.

———. *Verwirrtes Deutschland? Provokative Zwischenrufe eines deutsch-jüdischen Patrioten*. Munich: Ferenczy bei Bruckmann, 1993.

Wolin, Richard. *Labyrinths: Explorations in the Critical History of Ideas*. Amherst: University of Massachusetts Press, 1995.

———. *The Politics of Being: The Political Thought of Martin Heidegger*. New York: Columbia University Press, 1990.

Young, Robert J. C. *Colonial Desire: Hybridity in Theory, Culture and Race*. New York: Routledge, 1995.

Zeman, Herbert, ed. *Geschichte der Literatur in Österreich von den Anfängen bis zur Gegenwart*. Vol. 1. Graz: Bundesverlag, 1994.

Zeyringer, Klaus. *Innerlichkeit und Öffentlichkeit: Österreichische Literatur der achtziger Jahre*. Tübingen: Francke, 1992.

Zimmerman, Michael E. *Heidegger's Confrontation With Modernity, Technology, Politics and Art*. Bloomington: Indiana University Press, 1990.

Zipes, Jack, "The Negative German-Jewish Symbiosis," in *Insiders and Outsiders: Jewish and Gentile Culture in Germany and Austria*, ed. Dagmar C. G. Lorenz and Gabriele Weinberger, pp. 144–154. Detroit: Wayne State University Press, 1994.

Zizek, Slavoj. "Eastern Europe's Republics of Gilead," *New Left Review* 183 (1990): 50–62.

Zmegac, Viktor, ed. *Geschichte der deutschen Literatur vom 18. Jahrhundert bis zur Gegenwart*, vol. 3.2. Weinheim: Betz, 1994.

Contributors

Steven E. Aschheim holds the Vigevani Chair of European Studies at the Hebrew University, Jerusalem, where he teaches German and cultural history. He is the author of *Brothers and Strangers: The East European Jew in German and German Jewish Consciousness, 1800–1923* (1982), *The Nietzsche Legacy in Germany, 1890–1990* (1992), and *Culture and Catastrophe: German and Jewish Confrontations with National Socialism and Other Crises* (1996). He is the editor of the forthcoming conference volume *Hannah Arendt in Jerusalem*. Two other works will appear in 2001: "In Times of Crisis: European Culture, Germans and Jews" and "Scholem, Arendt and Klemperer: Intimate Chronicles in Turbulent Times."

Karlheinz F. Auckenthaler is Professor of Austrian Literature and Culture at the József Attila University in Szeged, Hungary, where he teaches literature and religion of the German-speaking countries. His research is mainly concerned with Franz Werfel, the literature of Prague, the concept of Austrian literature, and literary theory. His publications include *Die Verweigerung und Beziehungslosigkeit in der modernen österreichischen Literatur* (1989); *Franz Werfel: Neue Aspekte seines Werkes* (ed., 1992); *Numinoses und Heiliges in der österreichischen Literatur nach 1945* (ed., 1995). He is president of the International Franz Werfel Gesellschaft and a member of the International PEN Club.

Kathrin M. Bower is Assistant Professor of German at the University of Richmond, where she teaches German Studies and German language. Her areas of research and publication include contemporary German women writers, Holocaust representation and remembrance, German-Jewish identity, and German film. Her book *Ethics and Remembrance in the Poetry of Nelly Sachs and Rose Ausländer* is scheduled to appear in 2000.

Martin R. Dean is a writer, journalist, and essayist, and lives in Basel. His novels are *Monsieur Fume oder das Glück der Vergesslichkeit* (1998), *Die Ballade von Billie und Joe* (1997), *Der Guayanaknoten* (1994), *Ausser Mir* (1990), *Der Mann ohne Licht* (1988), *Die gefiederte Frau* (1984), and *Die verborgenen Gärten* (1982). He has also written a play, *Gilberts letztes Gericht,* which was performed in Basel in 1992. In 1989 he was the recipient of a scholarship at the Swiss Institute of Rome.

Adrian Del Caro, Professor of German Studies and former Chair of Germanic and Slavic Languages and Literatures at the University of Colorado at Boulder and organizer of the " 1945–1995" symposium, teaches courses on humanities and German literature and thought. Special interests are philosophy and literature from the Enlightenment to the present, including Austrian literature, with emphasis on poetics, intellectual history, and existentialism. He has published books on Hölderlin, Nietzsche, Hofmannsthal, and Paul Celan. His literary translations include the novel *Puntigam* by Gerald Szyszkowitz. He has published extensively since 1980 in Germanic, philosophy, and humanities journals.

Erk Grimm is Assistant Professor of German at Barnard College, Columbia University. He has published articles on nineteenth-century novelists, East German literature, and contemporary German poetry. An essay, "Mediamania? Contemporary German Poetry in the Age of New Information Technologies: Thomas Kling and Durs Grünbein" appeared in the special issue on contemporary German poetry in *Studies in 20th Century Literature,* ed. James Rolleston, 21.1 (Winter 1997). His book *Semiopolis: Texturen der Moderne und Nachmoderne im Zeichen der Städte* is scheduled to appear in 2000 in the C. Winter Verlag. He is currently working on the theme of visuality in the German avant-garde, focusing on the writings and photographs of Raoul Hausmann.

Kari Grimstad, Associate Professor of German in the Department of Languages and Literatures at the University of Guelph in Canada, researches nineteenth- and twentieth-century Austrian literature. She has written a book on Karl Kraus *(Masks of the Prophet,* 1982) and articles on Schnitzler, Nestroy, Dor, Kraus, the Viennese Burgtheater, and the Austrian *Volksstück.* Currently she is working on a select edition of the correspondence of Arthur and Olga Schnitzler and an English biography of Schnitzler.

Silvia Henke is Assistant Professor of German literature at the University of Basel. She has published a book titled *Wie es ihr gefällt—Wissenschaft, Künste und alles andere* (1991), and her thesis has been published as *Fehl am Platz: Studien zu einem kleinen Drama im Werk von Alfred Jarry, Else Lasker-Schüler, Marieluise Fleisser und Djuna Barnes* (Würzburg, Königshausen und Neumann, 1997). She has published articles on Friederike Mayröcker, Marguerite Duras, Alfred Jarry, Djuna Barnes, Birgit Kempker, and Georg Büchner, and on theories of myth, feminist theory, and forms of the love story. In 1992 she organized a symposium in Basel on the relationship of feminism and postmodernism. Her current research is on the epistolography (the relationship between correspondence and literary work) of Rahel Varnhagen Levin, Rainer Maria Rilke and Robert Walser.

Rainer Hering is a senior archivist at the Hamburg State Archives and teaches German history, church history, and archival science at Hamburg University. He has co-written *Wilhelm Heydorn—Nur Mensch sein!* (1999) and has written *Die Theologinnen Sophie Kunert, Margarete Braun, Margarete Schuster* (1997); *Vom Seminar zur Universität: Die Religionslehrerausbildung in Hamburg zwischen Kaiserreich und Bundesrepublik* (1997); *Die Bischöfe Simon Schöttel, Franz Tügel* (1995), *Theologie im Spannungsfeld von Kirche und Staat* (1992), and *Theologische Wissenschaft und "Drittes Reich"* (1990), as well as over 100 articles on the history of science, university history, archival science, church history, the history of antisemitism, political history, and the history of urban planning.

Todd Herzog is assistant professor of Germanic Languages and Literatures at the University of Cincinnati. He recently completed his Ph.D. in German Studies at the University of Chicago, with a dissertation on criminality and crime fiction during the Weimar Republic. He is co-editor (along with Sander L. Gilman) of *A New Germany in a New Europe* (Routledge, 2000).

Thomas A. Hollweck, Associate Professor of German and Chair of Germanic and Slavic Languages and Literatures at the University of Colorado at Boulder, teaches nineteenth- and twentieth-century German literature and culture. His research interests include political philosophy, twentieth-century German and Austrian intellectual history, and contemporary German and Austrian literature. He is a member of the editorial board for the *Collected Works of Eric Voegelin*. Among his publications are a book on Thomas Mann as well as articles on Voegelin's political philosophy. He is coeditor of Voegelin's *What is History and Other Late Unpublished Writings,* and the forthcoming volume VII of his *History of Political Ideas*.

Alexander Honold, Assistant Professor of German at the Freie Universität Berlin, is coordinator of the DFG-research program *Literatur- und Kulturgeschichte des Fremden.* He is the author of recent books on Robert Musil (*Die Stadt und der Krieg,* Munich 1995), Peter Weiss (*Die Bildervelt des Peter Weiss,* Hamburg 1995), and Thomas Bernhard (*Thomas Bernhard—Eine Einschärfung,* Berlin 1998), and a forthcoming book titled *Hölderlin: Exzentrische Revolution.*

Ruth-Ellen B. Joeres is Professor of German and Women's Studies at the University of Minnesota, and from 1990–1995 she was editor of *Signs: Journal of Women in Culture and Society.* Her research interests are feminist, interdisciplinary, and comparative. She has written and edited twelve books on topics ranging from the social and literary history of German women to the interpretation of personal narratives by women to the politics of the essay. Her most recent book *is Respectability and Deviance: Nineteenth-Century German Women Writers and the Ambiguity of Representation* (University of Chicago Press, 1998). Other areas of scholarly interest include feminist theorizing, women and madness, women's autobiographies, and revelations and codings of sexuality in pre-twentieth-century texts.

Andreas Michel is Assistant Professor of German and European Studies at Rose-Hulman Institute of Technology. His main teaching interests are theory, cultural studies, intellectual history, and philosophical aesthetics. He just completed a study on the German writer and art critic Carl Einstein, and has published articles on Victor Segalen, Carl Einstein, German Romanticism, theory in German Studies, Lyotard, Rorty, and Luhmann. He is a co-editor and co-translator of selected texts by A.W. Schlegel, F. Schlegel, and Novalis, as well as of Lyotard's *Heidegger and "the jews."*

Thomas Nolden, Associate Professor of German at Wellesley College, has published articles on cultural literacy, fin-de-siècle, Rilke, and contemporary literature. He is the author *of "An einen jungen Dichter": Studien zur epistolaren Poetik* and *Junge jüdische Literatur: Konzentrisches Schreiben in der Gegenwart* (both 1995), and is currently working on a comparative study of Jewish literature in post-war Europe.

Robert A. Pois, Professor of History at the University of Colorado at Boulder, teaches and researches modern German history, with particular emphasis on German philosophy of history, Expressionism in the plastic arts, historicism and psychohistory, Nazism, and European history between 1870 and 1920 (particularly World War I). His books are *The Great War* (1994), *National Socialism and the Religion of Nature* (1986), *Emil Nolde* (1982), *The Bourgeois Democrats of Weimar Germany* (1976), *Friedrich Meinecke and German Politics in the Twentieth Century* (1972), and *Alfred Rosenberg: Selected Writings* (editor, 1970).

William Safran is Professor of Political Science at the University of Colorado at Boulder. He has written *The French Polity* (5th. ed. 1998), *Ideology and Politics: The Socialist Party of France* (1983), and *Veto-Group Politics* (1967), and has co-authored *Politics in Western Europe* (1993, 1998) and *Comparative Politics* (1983). He has coedited *Identity and Territorial Autonomy in Plural Societies* (2000) and *Ethnicity and Citizenship* (1996). He has contributed thirty book chapters and numerous articles on French, German, comparative, and ethnic politics. He is editor-in-chief of *Nationalism and Ethnic Politics,* editor of a book series on nationalism, and is currently serving as president of the Research Committee on Politics and Ethnicity, International Political Science Association.

Susann Samples is Morisson Professor of International Studies at Mount Saint Mary's College, where she teaches medieval and contemporary (especially ex-GDR) German society. She has published on medieval German Arthurian romances, medieval German literature, and Afro-Germans. A book, *The Nibelungs and Dietrich of Bern: The Historical Legends of Medieval Germany and Scandinavia,* co-authored with Edward R. Haymes, was published in 1996.

Ann Schmiesing is Assistant Professor of German and Scandinavian at the University of Colorado at Boulder. Her research interests include Lessing and the German Enlightenment, eighteenth-century European drama and dramatic criticism, narratology, and modern Scandinavian narrative fiction. She has published articles on Norwegian novelist Johan Falkberget and on Lessing, and is currently completing a study of Lessing's theory and practice of dramatic characterization.

Robert Shandley is Assistant Professor of German at Texas A&M University. He has recently completed a manuscript titled *Rubble Films: Cinema in the Shadow of the Third Reich.* He has published an edited volume titled *Unwilling Germans? The Goldhagen Debate* (University of Minnesota Press, 1998), as well as articles on German-Jewish filmmakers, collective memory in the New Germany, fairy tales, and political economy.

Walter H. Sokel is Professor Emeritus of the University of Virginia, where he taught as Commonwealth Professor of German and English. He is the author of numerous articles on modern German literature, world literature, and intellectual history, as well as the books *Franz Kafka: Tragik und Ironie, Franz Kafka* and *The Writer in Extremis*. He has served on the Executive Committee of the MLA and on the Advisory Board of the Leo Baeck Society. He was a founding member and first President of the Kafka Society of America, and has been its honorary President since that time. He is a member of the American Academy of Arts and Sciences.

Janet Ward is Associate Professor of German at the University of Colorado at Boulder. She is the co-editor of *Agonistics: Arenas of Creative Contest* (1997) and the author of *Weimar Surfaces: Urban Visual Culture in 1920s Germany* (2001). She is currently working on a book on the post-Wall architectural identity of Berlin titled *Berlin Borders: Architectural Reformations of a Millennium Metropolis*.

Jean Wilson is Associate Professor of German and Comparative Literature at McMaster University, Canada. She is also affiliated with Peace Studies, Women's Studies, and the Institute on Globalization and the Human Condition. Her publications include *The Challenge of Belatedness: Goethe, Kleist, Hofmannsthal* (1991) and articles on dramatic theory, women and Romanticism, Kleist, and various contemporary women writers.

OHIO UNIVERSITY LIBRARY

Please return this book as soon as you have finished with it. In order to avoid a fine it must be returned by the latest date stamped below. All books are subject to recall after two weeks or immediately if needed for reserve.

DEC 16 2002
MAR 27 2003

CF